Michael + Fat

God Bless you —
So happy to be a part
of your life — you
have my prayer
Jesus is Lord!

Fred H Wolfe

JESUS IS LORD

JESUS IS LORD

THE LIFE AND LEGACY OF
FRED H. WOLFE

BY MARK WYATT

WHP
Wyatt House Publishing
www.wyattpublishing.com
Mobile, Alabama

Wyatt House books may be ordered through booksellers or by contacting:

WYATT HOUSE PUBLISHING
399 Lakeview Dr. W.
Mobile, Alabama 36695
www.wyattpublishing.com
editor@wyattpublishing.com

Because of the dynamic nature of the Internet, any web address or links contained in this book may have changed since publication and may no longer be valid.

Cover design by: Sam Noerr/Arrow Identity
samnoerr@gmail.com
Author photo courtesy of Bill Starling

ISBN 13 HC: 978-0-9896119-3-0
Library of Congress Control Number: 2013917846

Printed in the United States of America

First Edition

DEDICATION

Dr. Mark Wyatt and Dr. Fred Wolfe
would like to dedicate this book to the memory of

Dr. Richard M. (Ricky) Cagle,

who went to meet Jesus face to face while this book was being written.
We know why Ricky went to Heaven ahead of us —
so that he can meet us when we get there and say,
"Tell you what you ought to do…"

What Others Are Saying About
JESUS IS LORD:
THE LIFE AND LEGACY OF FRED H. WOLFE

"Dr. Fred Wolfe has been a mentor and friend to me for over thirty years. God has given him a powerful insight into the Word of God resulting from his daily practice of prayer, as he bows down to the Lordship of Jesus Christ. He is a true Servant of the Savior!"

Dr. Don Boone
First Baptist Church
Vancleave, Mississippi

"It is hard to believe that it has been forty-four years since I first met Fred Wolfe. During that time, he has been my closest confidant, pastor, mentor, advisor, and God's greatest influence on my life and ministry. Fred Wolfe is a man whose walk with God, impeccable character, outstanding people skills, and remarkable motivational as well as communication skills have blessed thousands. Every day of my life, I realize and value more and more all that I have learned from this fine man of God. Indeed, his legacy lies in the fact that Jesus is Lord of his life!"

Len Turner
Evangelist
Woodstock, Georgia

"In my work over the past 40 plus years, I have been blessed to meet and know many of God's most gifted and dedicated servants and I have been enriched by them all. But no one has impacted my life more beneficially than Dr. Fred Wolfe. Fred more lives what he preaches than any man I have ever known. His messages always flowed out of his life, and and over time, his life became his greatest message. How grateful I am to have been called 'friend' by Fred Wolfe."

Rick Scarborough
Vision America

"I became close friends with Dr. Fred Wolfe when he was not Dr. Fred Wolfe. We played football together in high school. I played tackle, and he played end, and he was just Fred. We went to college together, and we were both young married students who lived next door to each other. For 18 years, our families took vacations together, and he was still just Fred. I have watched him down through the years while serving the Lord in ministry, and he was still just Brother Fred.

I highly recommend the reading of *Jesus Is Lord*, about the ministry of a man who has been mightily used of the Lord. This book is humorous. It will change you and challenge you. This fulfills the scripture Philippians 4:13 – 'I can do all things through Christ who strengthens me.'"

Ron Long, D.Min.
Assistant to the President for Missions and Church Relations
Luther Rice University and Seminary

"Like many of my peers, I applaud the writing of Pastor Fred Wolfe's biography. As with so many others, I have been profoundly encouraged by this magnificent man of God. He was instrumental in my call to ministry and served as a role model for how to pastor. It is to his credit and God's glory that some two hundred young men have been called to preach through his ministry. His life is well worth studying and emulating! I am blessed to call him friend and in a biblical sense my father in the ministry."

Dr. Jerry Sutton
Dean of Faculty, Midwestern Baptist Theological Seminary
Kansas City, Missouri

"Fred Wolfe has been a pastor, mentor, and friend to more people than can be counted. To me, however, he has been a model of the Spirit-filled life. His joy-filled walk in the Spirit has kept his heart focused on souls, his eyes fixed on Jesus, and his life formed for purpose. As you read the pages of this book, listen for the heartbeat of heaven in one man's life and then ask the Lord to emulate the same in yours."

David Jett
Senior Pastor, Crossgates Baptist Church
Brandon, Mississippi

"Dr. Fred Wolfe understands the importance of the Lordship of Christ in the life of the church corporately and the Christian individually. Read his life story and learn from his own experience. You will be blessed and helped."

Jerry Vines,
Pastor-Emeritus, First Baptist Church
Jacksonville, Florida
Two time President, Southern Baptist Convention.

CONTENTS

Dr. Mark Wyatt's Acknowledgments

The 19th century British politician Benjamin Disraeli said, "The best way to become acquainted with a subject is to write a book about it." That quote encourages me to take risks and write new things, but it also lets me know that I had better be ready to research.

I was more than just acquainted with Fred Wolfe before I began this project, but I had no idea how much research and fact-finding would be required to put muscle and skin onto the skeleton of his life's story. However, what I also didn't know at the outset was how much of that work had already been done for me. For that, I owe an incalculable debt of thanks and gratitude to the late Dr. Carl E. Todd.

In the course of the writing, I discovered that Dr. Todd had written and published the definitive, detailed, encyclopedic history of Cottage Hill Baptist Church, *Remembering Whose We Are...* Three meticulously researched volumes of that book were published, with Volume III being in two parts, covering everything from the beginning of the church to the end of the 1980s. A fourth volume was in process when Dr. Todd moved to Heaven in 2008.

I relied heavily on Dr. Todd's work for much of the detailed timeline in this book, especially from 1972-1989. I did not footnote everything that I applied from his volumes, because if I had, this book would have looked like a college textbook and it would not be nearly as fun or easy to read. So, herein is my deep and grateful bow to Dr. Carl E. Todd, for his posthumous contribution to the book that you now hold in your hands.

I would also like to recognize a few other people who made this book possible. My sincere thanks go to:

- Bob Johnson and Martin Dorsett for making the aforementioned works by Dr. Todd available to me.

- The people of Deeper Life Fellowship for once again affording me the time, freedom, and encouragement to write.

- As always, my wife, Mary Ann, and my children-- Samuel, Sarah, Nathaniel, and Autumn. Thank you for always being interested (or at least acting like it) when I would tell you how many words I had written on any given day. You cheered me across the finish line.

- And, of course, Dr. Fred Wolfe, without whom there would be no story.

But most of all, "thanks be to God, who gives us the victory through our Lord Jesus Christ!"

-- 1 Corinthians 15:57

DR. FRED WOLFE'S
ACKNOWLEDGMENTS

This book is about my life of 76 years. There are thousands of people who have been a part of my life, Anne's, and our family's. We have been greatly encouraged and blessed by many people. It is impossible to recognize all the people who have blessed us.

I thank God for my parents, Fred and Margaret Wolfe, who provided a wonderful home life. I am thankful for my brother, Bill, and my sisters, Betty, Margaret, Freida, Nancy, and Jane, and their spouses, who have been a real encouragement to Anne and me.

Of course this journey would not have been possible without Anne, my wife of fifty-seven years, who was faithful and steadfast all along the way. I love her deeply and am so thankful for her.

I am thankful for my two sons, Mark and Jeff, and their wives and children, who are truly a joy to our lives.

I am thankful for every staff member of the churches I have pastored. The journey would not have been possible or complete without them.

I am greatly blessed by all the churches I have pastored and the thousands of people who have blessed, prayed for, and encouraged Anne and me.

I am thankful for all the godly people who God put in my life to teach me the great truths of God's Word.

Above all, I am thankful to and for our Lord Jesus Christ for His abundant love, mercy, grace, forgiveness, and strength that He has so faithfully poured in to my life. To God be the glory. Truly, Jesus is Lord!

My prayer as you read this book and take the journey through my life with me, is that Jesus will be real to you and speak to you, and that you will give God all the praise.

I am thankful for Mark Wyatt, who listened to God and made the call that was really an answer to the desire of my heart. This biography is God's will, and would not have happened without the giftedness, encouragement, and many hours of labor — a labor of love — put into this book by Mark Wyatt.

Now it is time to read of the faithfulness of God, and the reality of the Lordship of Christ in my life and in the lives of many touched by God. The message is powerful yet simple: Jesus Christ is Lord!

Fred H. Wolfe
II Corinthians 4:5

FOREWORD

"That at the name of Jesus every knee should bow, of those who are in heaven, and on earth, and under the earth, and that every tongue should confess that Jesus Christ is Lord, to the glory of God the Father"

Philippians 2:10-11

Serving as a pastor of a local church is both a privilege and a challenge. Ministering to the needs of a congregation can wear on one's soul. The constant demands of sermon preparation and leadership cause many pastors to grow weary. Some even quit the ministry. They are not tired *of* the ministry, but they are tired *in* the ministry.

In the late 1960s, that taxing weariness had engulfed a young pastor named Fred Wolfe. Fred knew there had to be more to the Christian life than he was experiencing. Each Sunday, he felt emptier within. He decided to make a two hundred-mile trip from his church in Greenville, South Carolina to a Bible conference in Greensboro, North Carolina to hear several renowned preachers. As he drove, he asked the Lord to give his heart and soul a fresh touch from heaven.

That evening, Dr. Stephen Olford preached on the Lordship of Christ and the filling of the Holy Spirit. As he listened, Fred's hungry heart began to burn within. He left that place a renewed man. Jesus was not only His Savior, but also His Lord. The Holy Spirit had filled Fred with fresh power. All the power he needed was in Christ. He began to daily surrender to the Lordship of Christ and to daily ask the Holy Spirit to fill him. His life, and the lives of thousands of others would never be the same!

A few years later, Fred began his pastorate at Cottage Hill Baptist Church in Mobile. The winds of revival began to blow. Multitudes were converted to Christ. Answers to prayers became common. People were healed physically. Christians were set free from besetting sins. Many began walking in the fullness of the Holy Spirit. Cottage Hill became known across the Southern Baptist Convention and the nation as a church on fire that walked in spiritual awakening. Many young people were called into full-time Christian service and became pastors, missionaries, evangelists, and Bible teachers. Jesus proved that He is alive and that He is still Lord!

I met Fred Wolfe on a rainy night at a Bible Conference in Tennessee where he was preaching. I too was a young pastor who was "tired in the ministry." God knit our hearts together. We became close friends. His heart for revival and the Spirit-filled life has indelibly marked my ministry. God has used Fred in my life in countless ways for which I will be forever grateful.

You hold in your hand more than a biography. This book is a blueprint for revival. The Lord said to Zerubbabel, "(It is) is not by (your) might, not by (your) power, but by My Spirit" (Zechariah 4:6)! That is how God's work must be done. The sooner you learn that, the better off you will be.

I invite you to get to know the one and only, Fred Wolfe. Like Elijah, He is a man of God and the word in his mouth is truth. As you read these pages, may the Holy Spirit stir within you. Our nation, the Southern Baptist Convention, and all the other denominations need revival. You and I need revival. I'm convinced God wants to send revival. But first, we must surrender to Christ's Lordship and allow Him to fill us with His Spirit!

My prayer is that your search for "more" be satisfied in these blessed pages. O taste and see that our Lord is good.

Steve Gaines, Ph.D.
Senior Pastor
Bellevue Baptist Church
Memphis, TN

INTRODUCTION

Not long after my wife and I arrived in Fort Worth, Texas, and I began classes at Southwestern Seminary, I became aware at a new level of what pastors sometimes have to endure. I was serving as the Associate Pastor of a small church, and one Sunday morning, I walked by the Pastor's office to witness him being screamed at, (with the Pastor's six-year-old son looking on) by a man who was very upset that the teacher for the 4-year-olds' Sunday School class had not shown up yet.

I decided that I might not want to be a pastor.

Southwestern had just started a new degree in Communications, focused on using media in the church, and I figured that I could use that route in order to stay faithful to my commitment to ministry, without having to get yelled at on a Sunday morning. I went on to earn that degree and began serving as Media and Singles Minister in a large church in east Fort Worth.

About three years later, the yearning to pastor was back. I had to preach. It was like "a fire shut up in my bones," and I was ready. One problem, though. My degree from seminary was in radio and television production, not theology. I had all the same core courses as the theology students, just not as many courses on Daniel, or Hermeneutics.

Right about that time, I heard that Brother Fred was coming to the Dallas area to speak, so I arranged to be the one to pick him up at the airport and take him to his hotel. It was precious time with my pastor, just the two of us in a car, so I took that opportunity to ask his advice.

"Brother Fred," I said, "I believe God is calling me back to my original vision of being a pastor. But, I didn't get the Master of Divinity from Southwestern. Do you think that's going to hurt me as I look for a church?

He thought for a moment. "What do they call your degree?" he asked. "Master of Arts in Communications," I said.

He shrugged and waved his hand like he was shooing a fly. "Hey," he said, "people are just going to think that means you can talk good."

And that is the kind of homespun, humble, and accessible wisdom that has endeared Fred Wolfe to thousands and thousands of people over the last 50 plus years. Time and time again, as I talked with and interviewed people from Brother Fred's life for this book, it was not uncommon to hear grown men choke back tears as they said, "Fred Wolfe is the finest man I have ever known. He is my pastor, and he will always be my pastor. I don't make any major decisions in my life or ministry without talking to him first."

As I wrote this book, I went back in time. I was ten years old when Brother Fred came to Cottage Hill Baptist Church, and my very first thought on hearing him preach his trial sermon was, "Wow. That's this first time I have ever stayed awake for a whole sermon."

The 1970s were my "wonder years," and I spent them immersed in the excitement of the Jesus movement and under the care and teaching of men like Fred Wolfe and Ed Keyes. I am grateful every day for what was poured into me then, and I hope that the people under my care can recognize the DNA of those days in me. Almost every good thing I know about pastoring, I learned from Fred Wolfe. He has been open and teachable, humble in success and honest in shortcomings.

Like many of you reading this, I could go on all day describing the legacy of Fred Wolfe. But I have a better idea. Let's allow the story of his life to unfold it for us. And in the telling of it, you will see, as I have, the unmistakable impact of a man who walks with God. And I think, if you listen very closely, you will hear four powerful words repeated a thousand different ways:

Jesus Christ is Lord.

Dr. Mark A. Wyatt
Mobile, Alabama
October, 2013

"For we preach not ourselves, but Christ Jesus the Lord; and ourselves your servants for Jesus' sake."

II Corinthians 4:5

PART I

Summer, 1957- Asheville, North Carolina

The young man's brain felt full. It had been a long ride to the Ben Lippen campgrounds in Asheville, but he wished it had been longer so that he could have more time to process all that he had heard in the Bible conference. The mountain retreat had been designed to host cool summer meetings to promote the Keswick Movement, or Deeper Life Movement, and the young man didn't think it could have been any deeper. Fred Hartwell Wolfe was only in his sophomore year at the University of South Carolina, but he had recently been changed forever by an encounter with God. As a result, he had surrendered his life to the work of the Gospel ministry, and he was desperately hungry to know more of the Lord. And now here he was, riding back to Columbia in a car with a few other young men, drowning in the deluge of theology of the last few days. L.E. Maxwell, the renowned author of *Born Crucified*, had been impassioned and correct in his teaching, but Fred knew, that as a young believer, it was all a good bit over his head.

Something else was happening on this car ride, though, something that Fred found much more intriguing at the moment than the recent sermons. Fred was thinking about how he had just seen the life of God displayed in a way that he had never heard in a sermon. One of the men at the conference was a member of a prominent family of tobacco company fame, but when he became a Christian and was filled with the Holy Spirit, his family thought he was crazy and they committed him to a mental institution. Now he was out, and he had shown Fred that he had not only memorized Psalm 119, the longest of the psalms, but he could also quote almost the whole New Testament. He was so completely different from anyone Fred had ever met, so beyond his experience, that he commanded Fred's attention. *There is no other explanation for him but God,* Fred thought. And that was intriguing. *Is this what life with Jesus could be?*

Fred Wolfe had just had his first exposure to someone who was filled with the Holy Spirit and was unashamed to live it. He had encountered someone who had demonstrated what it was to know, in a new and radical way, that Jesus Christ is Lord.

CHAPTER 1

FIRST CALL

Rock Hill, South Carolina, 1937

Margaret Wolfe and her husband had four wonderful daughters already, and they loved them deeply, but their father was desperate for a son this time. Margaret placed her hand gently on the round swell of her abdomen, the sure promise of another blessing on the way. She, too, had special hopes for this child. She felt like Hannah of old, the prophet Samuel's mother, and she gained the courage from that ancient woman to pray what was constantly on her heart throughout the fall of 1937. "Lord," she prayed, "you know how bad Fred wants a boy. If you will give me a son, I will give him back to you to be a preacher of the gospel."

And on December 5th of that year, it became evident that God had heard the cry of Margaret's heart. On that day, Margaret and Fred welcomed their first baby boy, and Fred Hartwell Wolfe drew his first breath of South Carolina air. Older sisters Betty, Margaret, Freida, and Nancy marveled at their new little brother, and they began to wonder right away how this new baby boy was going to fit into this household of girls.

Another boy, Bill, and another girl, Jane, would soon complete the Wolfe family, and Fred and Margaret would make a picturesque southern life for their seven children. Fred, Sr. worked hard on the Rock Hill police force, a respected Detective, as Margaret formed the hearts and minds of their house full of children.

Rock Hill lay nestled in the Piedmont section of South Carolina, just 15 miles south of the North Carolina border. The town was named for a large flint rock that stuck up out of the ground and stood in the way of the Charlotte and South Carolina Railroad. After blasting a path through the flint, the railroad built a depot at its base and it eventually became known as the Rock Hill station. One of the town's favorite sons was the artist Vernon Grant, the creator of Snap, Crackle, and Pop®.

Rock Hill had a warm but tolerable summer average of ninety degrees, winter days hovering in the low thirties, average rainfall, a little snow, and about 212 sunny days each year. It was Mayberry and Norman Rockwell, innocence and family, school, church, ball fields, and first loves. It was the aroma of fried chicken and butterbeans that called all of Rock Hill's children home in the deep pink and purple of a summer day's last light. It was a place to learn about God, fishing, football, and how grass stains on the knees of your pants never quite come out. It was a good place to be a boy.

The Wolfe family attended First Baptist Church of Rock Hill for some years, where young Fred H. Wolfe heard many wonderful messages from wonderful preachers about how to be saved. There was never much teaching on anything deeper, but it was Biblical and effective all the same. At nine years of age, Fred gave his heart to Christ at Vacation Bible School. Many times of rededication followed as he would continue to realize the importance of a right relationship with God.

From time to time, Fred would attend services across the street from his house, at Park Baptist Church, where the solid Biblical preaching continued. On one Sunday night, though, Fred saw something that he had never seen before. As a young boy of ten, Fred sat transfixed as the pastor, B.F. Hawkins, concluded his sermon, leaned into the pulpit, and wept over the congregation. *This man has a broken heart for these people*, Fred thought. It fascinated the young boy, and he never forgot the sight.

Camp Cox sat like a hidden gem just seventeen miles north of Rock Hill, and hundreds of children and teenagers connected with God under its canopy of pines each summer during church camps and retreats. It was during one of those summers, when Fred Wolfe was eleven years old, that he sat in a circle of other boys and girls just outside the chapel, listening to Ruth Epps talk about God. Ruth, the popular youth leader at Fred's home church, sat with these children under the shade of a cedar tree and taught them from her heart, hoping to help them understand how much God loved them. As he listened to Miss Epps teach, Fred began to feel a stirring in his soul, and he knew that one day, he wanted to do the same thing that she was doing. "Miss Epps?" said Fred, quietly raising his hand.

"Yes, Fred?" she said.

"I think God wants me to be a preacher when I grow up," he said.

Ruth Epps smiled at him, and Fred could tell that she felt a pleasant sense of fulfillment in her role in this exchange between him and God. And Fred knew that he wanted to feel that someday, too.

Having been taught well in the disciplines of the Christian life, young Fred Wolfe consistently read his Bible and said his prayers every night. As he entered high school, though, the passion for the gospel that had marked the past couple of years faded into the background of football and popularity. His love for the Lord cooled, even though he never stopped reading the Bible and praying. But, as he grew, sports called his name along with the crowds and lifestyle of a high school athlete, and Fred put his spiritual life into a closet and quietly closed the door.

Still, though, God continued to present himself to Fred. One of the girls in school, Birgitta Wright, served as a reminder that a relationship with Jesus could still be relevant, even in high school. Birgitta carried her Bible and lived her convictions, and Fred didn't quite know what to do with her. He didn't really join his friends in making fun of Birgitta, but he didn't understand her, either. Birgitta was an anomaly in Fred's world. She was a teenager who walked with God.

Early in his senior year at Rock Hill High School, Fred was lightning-struck by a dark-haired beauty with deep brown eyes, and in only a moment, he belonged forever to Anne Heath. A few months later they began dating, the football player and the cheerleader, and by the time Fred was a senior and Anne was in her junior year, they were making plans with an eye toward forever.

By the time he graduated in 1956, Fred's career as an end for the Rock Hill Bearcats had earned him a full scholarship to the University of South Carolina to play football for the Gamecocks under head coach Warren Giese. Fred was anxious to make the seventy mile trip south to Columbia to live his dream of playing college ball.

As his high school senior year drew to a close, though, Fred and Anne became less and less willing to be apart. Anne still had a year left in high school, and they knew that the next school year with

Fred off in Columbia would be difficult. And so, on June 28, 1956, Bobby Thompson and his girlfriend drove them twenty miles to nearby Chester, the seat of the neighboring county. Anne lied about her age, and they paid Hattie Y. Hardin five dollars to marry them. Bobby and his girlfriend stood as witnesses as they made their vows in secret.

Fred and Anne fully intended to keep their marriage hidden. They would each live at home this summer, and in the fall, Fred would move to Columbia, coming home every weekend to see Anne. At least that was their plan.

Three weeks after the secret ceremony, as Fred was walking to church on a Sunday morning, he saw his sister, Nancy, coming toward him on the sidewalk.

"Fred!" she said, hands on her hips as she blocked his path.

"What?"

"Is it true that you're married?"

"Well... yes," he said.

"Well, you just got to tell Mama and Daddy," she said. "That's all there is to it. You've got to tell Mama and Daddy."

Fred did tell his mother, who took the news in her usual calm demeanor, but he left it to her to prepare his father. Upon hearing the news that his oldest son had gotten himself married three weeks earlier, the elder Wolfe only had one question. It wasn't "How are you going to support her?" It wasn't "Where are you going to live?" It was really a simple question, but still it left Fred speechless. It was: "What'd you wanna go do that for?"

CHAPTER 2

COMING BACK

Fred Wolfe began his college career at the University of South Carolina in the fall of 1956 as a football player, student, and newlywed. He lived in the athletic dorm, traveling the 150-mile round trip from Columbia to Rock Hill and back every weekend— except during football season—to be with his young wife. They would normally stay with Fred's family on those weekends, though occasionally at Anne's parents, while she finished her senior year at Rock Hill High.

Anne's father was initially angry with the secret marriage, afraid that Anne would drop out of school, but Fred and Anne's commitment to her diploma seemed to calm the boiling waters enough for them to get along decently until she was officially done.

Fred lived his freshman year at USC in the athletic dorm. Surrounded by single friends on the weekdays, he would transition back into the life of a married man on the weekends. Fred didn't participate in a lot of the things that his friends were doing, but neither was he swimming against the current. He still had not regained a sense of the importance of a walk with God that had marked his earlier years. But that would change for good in the coming March.

At least once each week, Fred would get a knock on his dorm room door. A group from Campus Crusade for Christ held regular meetings in the assembly room of the athletic dorm, and before the meetings started, they would go through the building, inviting the athletes to the meeting. Usually, Fred wouldn't even answer the door. He knew very well how he was living his life, and he knew how it should be, and he generally was not interested in hearing it from someone else.

One night, though, whether out of curiosity or boredom he didn't know, Fred wandered down the hall to see what the meeting was like. And even though he wasn't expecting it, as the meeting progressed, Fred became more and more aware that the Holy Spirit was speaking to his heart. Conviction over the life he was leading, or more to the point, the life that he wasn't leading, settled into him with a weighty certainty. Eventually, the speaker for the night offered the opportunity that was always given at the end of the meeting, but this time it seemed to be aimed directly at Fred.

"If you believe that the Lord has spoken to your heart tonight, raise your hand." Fred raised his hand. When the meeting was over, a short, small student by the last name of Shull took Fred to a corner of the room and said, "Let's talk."

For the next few minutes, Shull took Fred through the Scriptures that spoke of how to have a relationship with God, and although Fred knew that he had given his heart to Christ as a boy, he took that opportunity to rededicate his life to a relationship with Jesus. That evening, in that meeting room, Fred knew that a new commitment to the Lord would require a new lifestyle. It was customary for all of the athletes to go to the bars together, and he was well aware that it would be tough to break away from those expectations. But, whatever it took, Fred was going to take this seriously. God, he felt, had backed him into a corner and had shone a spotlight into his soul from which he could not hide.

Fred returned to his room, determined to follow through. He began to find his spiritual footing again, and he took his first few steps in this renewed walk with God.

About two weeks later, though, as he stood in his room, he was overwhelmed by paralyzing fear. He found it difficult to move or even breathe. He felt it move from the top of his head down through his whole body, to the bottoms of his feet. A cold, unbelievably pervasive fear. *What is this?* he thought. *Am I having a nervous breakdown?*

Fred struggled to get himself in bed, but as he closed his eyes and did his best to force himself to sleep, the darkness only intensified the terror. Finally, out of desperation, he opened his Bible and laid it on his chest. And the only way he could sleep, that night and for many nights after, was with the pages of the open Bible pressed against his fast-beating heart.

The days turned slowly to weeks, but no lasting relief came. The only time that the fear seemed to loosen its grip on Fred was when he was reading the Bible, or praying, or attending worship. In every other moment of the day, he battled the fear. In class. At football practice. Studying.

Fred was convinced that he must be going crazy.

Fred made an appointment with a doctor, hoping for an answer. "Doctor," he said, "I don't know what this is. I am having horrible thoughts, just awful thoughts, and I don't know what to do."

"Well," said the doctor, "just don't think about it."

Fred was incredulous. Don't think about it? "But doctor," Fred said, "I don't know how to stop being so afraid! What can I do?"

The doctor shook his head and shrugged his shoulders. "I don't really know, son," he admitted. "I just don't understand it. Maybe you need to talk to a pastor."

So Fred sat down with his pastor and told him what was happening to him, thinking that maybe this time, a man of God would know how to help him.

"I'm sorry," said the pastor. "I don't know what to tell you. I don't understand what's going on with you, and I don't know how to help."

So Fred kept battling. It was the only thing he knew to do. He kept reading the Bible, kept praying, kept going to worship. He became involved with Campus Crusade as a participant now, a doer and not a hearer only. He went out with them regularly, witnessing on campus. And still, the oppressive fear was always waiting for him in the shadows. Only many years later would Fred be able to identify what had come on him so heavily that night.

After a year, the black cloud lifted. Fred figured he just wore it out with the Word of God. In fact, as Fred looked back on that year, he became aware that what was trying to kill his newfound relationship with Jesus had been a vital part of his growth. He had sought God more in the past year than any time before. It was the only way he could stay alive.

During this time of recommitment, Fred once again heard the call to ministry that had been so simple and so clear as a boy under a cedar tree at Camp Cox. One night, while at home in Rock Hill on a weekend night, Fred figured he had better tell his mother. He sat her down in the kitchen to deliver the news that he now knew what he was going to do with the rest of his life.

"Mama, you know that this year I rededicated my life to the Lord."

"Yes, I do. I've seen it in you."

"Well... I think that God is calling me into full time ministry. I'm going to be a preacher, Mama."

"I know," she said.

Fred was more than a little confused. He had given no hints to this new direction in any of his previous trips home. He hadn't told anyone else, one of his sisters, for instance, who would have told his mother. "You know? How could you know?"

"Fred, when I was expecting you, I knew your father wanted a son so badly. I told the Lord then that if I had a boy, I would give him back to Him as a preacher."

Fred felt a little bit behind, like he was just now hearing a long-time family secret. "Why didn't you ever tell me?" he said.

"Because," said his mother, "I wanted the Lord to tell you."

In the years since, Fred would recall that conversation many times and gain great strength from it. He would find that in a life of ministry, there are some things so hard, it is only the certainty that God has called you that gets you through. And only God's call is strong enough to do that. Mama's call would not have been enough.

CHAPTER 3

INTO THE PULPIT

After Anne graduated from Rock Hill High School in June, Fred and Anne finally moved to Columbia as a couple, into apartment R5 at a public housing complex, Gonzales (pronounced *gonza-leez*) Gardens. Even in 1957, public housing was not the environment where a young husband wanted to install his new wife, but they had other friends in the same situation and the same apartment complex, so they all shared in both the humor and the adventure of it all.

For an athlete on a full football scholarship, an outside job was out of the question. Between practices, games, and class work, there just wasn't time for employment. For just that reason, full ride players received a stipend from the school of $95 per month. Rent on the apartment in Gonzales Gardens was $25/month, and Anne worked at a local bakery at the rate of fifty cents an hour. All in all, they could make it alright in a college town.

That next summer, as Fred's desire to preach intensified, he served as the director of Camp Cox, the same setting where he had first sensed the call to preach as a boy. He spent the pleasantly hot South Carolina months teaching children, loving them and sharing the gospel, just as he had experienced others doing for him a decade earlier. As the summer ended and Fred and Anne headed back to Columbia, he began to pray for a church at which to begin his pastoral ministry.

During that Fall of 1957 and Spring of 1958, Fred prayed almost daily for God to provide a place for him to preach in the coming summer. Before the spring had ended, he and Anne were invited to be the Park Superintendent at Edisto Island State Park for the summer months.

Soon, he found himself preaching weekly at Hopewell Baptist in Adams Run, South Carolina. Fred and Anne were living and working at Edisto State Park in Edisto Island, and each Sunday, they would drive twenty miles to Adams Run so that Fred could preach in their worship service, which was held at two o'clock in the afternoon. Years later, Fred would consider this to be one of the greatest ministry opportunities of his life. To him, it was clearly a testimony to the faithfulness of God.

At the beginning of his junior year, after a wonderful summer at Edisto Island, a friend named Wilbur Johnson recommended Fred as pastor to what would become his first church, Pine Grove Baptist Church in Salters, South Carolina, about nine miles from Greelyville and a full ninety miles from where they were living in Columbia. Admittedly quite a trek every weekend, Fred and Anne faithfully made the drive so that they could serve together.

Having now received his first real call to serve as pastor, the following announcement appeared in the local Rock Hill, South Carolina newspaper in November of 1958:

"Fred H. Wolfe, former outstanding athlete at Rock Hill High School, will be ordained to the ministry at 4 p.m. Sunday at the First

Baptist Church of Rock Hill. The Rev. C. Michael Warr, pastor, will have charge of the ordination service."

Fred pastored Pine Grove for a year, and it was a good year. The people of Pine Grove were kind and gentle, and they loved their young preacher and his wife. Fred enjoyed the freshness and the challenge of preparing a new sermon every week, but he couldn't help feel that his messages were about as shallow as a teacup. He had never had a Bible class of any kind, and he was becoming painfully aware that if he was going to be serious about his call, he was going to need some serious training. Still, it was a good ministry at Pine Grove, and the church grew some under Fred's fledgling leadership. After a year at Pine Grove, Fred was recommended to a church back in Leesville, Providence Baptist Church. Providence hosted about 125 faithful members, and Fred and Anne were happy and blessed.

One of the strong families at Providence was the Quattlebaums. It was, in fact, a Quattlebaum who led the worship each Sunday morning, holding an open hymnbook in both hands and keeping time with the music by moving it dramatically up and down, like an elevator above the pulpit.

Fred's tenure as a pastor, both at Piney Grove and now at Providence, had been fairly uneventful. One day, though, about two months after he arrived at Providence, Fred stood to preach, looked into the crowd, and saw C.R. Quattlebaum with a shotgun. He didn't really know C.R., just that he was sweet but kind of "slow." Fred was understandably unnerved, but he kept his composure, kept one eye on C.R., and successfully finished his message. When the service was over, C.R. Quattlebaum and his shotgun quietly left.

The next Sunday, Fred stepped into the pulpit, and there, once again, sat C.R. Quattlebaum cradling his shotgun. Fred didn't know what to do with this yet, so, like the week before, he kept a wary watch and preached the Word.

This went on for a few weeks, and as each week passed, Fred became less concerned and more curious. Finally, he approached C.R. before he could leave. "Hey, C.R.," he said, "I've been trying to figure this out for weeks, now, but I just have to know why you keep bringing your shotgun to church. It's got me a little on the nervous side."

"Oh, that," said C.R. "Don't you worry none about that, Preacher, it ain't for you. See, I have to walk about a mile to church every Sunday, and this is to keep the dogs off me."

In the Spring of 1959, Fred was fully enjoying his new position at Providence, but the realization kept growing that he was out of his depth. He had already come to the end of everything he thought he knew about the Bible, and he was becoming more and more convinced that he needed seminary, but he was still a year away from graduating college. By April, he knew that his life was about to change in every way. Anne was very pregnant. She was staying with her family back in Rock Hill, and when she delivered their first son, Mark, on April 30, Fred received a message that he was now a father, and he immediately drove the 80 miles home to meet his newborn son.

In August of 1960, Fred graduated from the University of South Carolina, and the next month, he began coaching football and teaching at Lexington High School, along with pastoring Providence Baptist Church, while Anne stayed at home with Mark. Fred faithfully preached and gave it his all every week, and the people were kind, but he knew that there was more to the Bible than what he was finding and delivering to them. So, in the summer of

1961, Fred resigned his positions at Lexington High, packed up his little family and whatever they owned, and moved 250 miles away to Wake Forest, North Carolina, where he enrolled at Southeastern Baptist Theological Seminary. Fred and his little family still made the trip back to Providence to preach and pastor the church.

In 1961, the evangelical world was still in the throes of debating philosophical theology, especially as made popular by scholars like Rudolf Karl Bultmann. Bultmann advocated the "demythologizing" of the New Testament, believing that the historical accuracy of the Gospel accounts were not only unreliable, but were basically irrelevant to a society that had already become steeped in science and technology. Bultmannian theology, then, also questioned the veracity and the reality of the New Testament stories of miracles. This new kind of liberal Christianity as voiced by Bultmann had found its way into the halls and classrooms of seminaries around the world, including Southeastern.

Fred knew that he didn't know much, but immediately he knew that believing that the Bible was mostly myth was wrong. Southeastern had its share of wonderful men of God who taught orthodox Christianity faithfully and fervently, but it also had three theology professors who took away most of the Bible by declaring it sadly out of date with modern thinking. The undermining of Scripture ate at Fred constantly, as it did other students. A friend would tell Fred some years later that he would study with a loaded gun on his desk, ready to take his own life, so hopeless were the things that he had to read.

Fred carried on with his studies, even as he struggled with what was being taught. After about two months in town, Fred was called to be the pastor of Piney Green Baptist, a church of about 150 people in Salemburg, North Carolina, seventy miles south of Wake Forest. Fred resigned as pastor of Providence Baptist Church, and he and Anne moved to Salemburg with Mark, now about one and a half years old. Fred drove the seventy miles each way to seminary and back every Tuesday through Friday.

In Spring of 1962, Fred was beginning his second semester at Southeastern Seminary and had been pastoring Piney Green Baptist for six months. Soon, the Wolfe family would add another little mouth to the table. On April 20, 1962, their second son joined them, and Jeff made them a family of four. This time, though, something was different. In fact, it was very wrong.

Fred knew that often, after giving birth, new mothers experience what has been called the "baby blues"-- mood swings, irritability, trouble sleeping. Fred realized, though, after a few weeks, that what Anne was experiencing went beyond the "baby blues." It would be years before Anne's illness would be recognized by the medical field as postpartum depression. It is not at all uncommon for new mothers, but Anne's case was severe. Fred knew right away that they both needed help.

After two months, with Anne no better, Fred resigned his pastorate at Piney Green. He had only completed one year in seminary, but he and Anne took their two boys and moved back home to Rock Hill. There are just some times in life, he knew, when only family would do. And Fred needed family right now as much as anyone.

For the next year, Anne was in and out of hospitals, and Fred took a job teaching history in seventh and eighth grades at Sylvia Circle Elementary School, where he also coached football. The Wolfe and Heath families both stepped in and took great care of Anne and the boys, and Fred knew that until Anne got better, his seminary training would have to wait. Still, he had no intention of going back to Southeastern. Although the postpartum depression was difficult, he thanked God for using it to get him out of the atmosphere of theological liberalism.

Fred continued to teach at Sylvia Circle, raise his sons, love Anne, and pray and wait for her healing. During this waiting, he was asked to preach at Eastview Baptist Church, eight miles outside of Rock Hill. It was a small church, with only one building, but right away, God began to move. People were giving their lives to Jesus, families were coming to visit, and the sense of expectancy among the people began to grow. After only a year of teaching at Sylvia Circle, Fred was able to move into pastoring full time at Eastview.

In the next three years, Fred loved this little church and led them in a building program as they added a 300-seat auditorium to their campus. The church grew to 250 people, baptized more than 50 people, and Eastview became a wonderful place to be. The people there were welcoming and loving to Fred, and they took Anne in and cared for her as if they were her own family. Eastview Baptist Church became a refuge for Fred Wolfe, a place where Anne could heal from depression and where Fred could heal from the wounds of exposure to theology that denied the Word of God. He preached with all of his heart every week, loved the people through their births, weddings, and funerals, and found his feet again as a preacher of the Gospel.

By 1964, Anne was much better. The depression had subsided and she was once again able to make it day to day and resume her role as mother and wife. Fred began to consider finishing his seminary education, and his attention turned toward Southwestern

Baptist Theological Seminary in Fort Worth, Texas. Southwestern had a reputation for being Biblically sound and conservative, thanks to the influence of men like Professor of Evangelism Roy Fish, and New Testament professor Curtis Vaughn. So, as with everything else in his life, Fred made this a matter of prayer. "God," he prayed, "I am willing to move to Southwestern, but you're going to have to make a way. If you open a door, I'll go, but I'm not going with a wife and two kids with no job and nowhere to preach!" He knew that the answer to that prayer would be supernatural, because there were already two thousand students at Southwestern looking for somewhere to preach.

Fred had a friend from Camden, South Carolina who was now the pastor of 8th Avenue Baptist Church in Fort Worth. Fred called him to tell him that he would be coming to Dallas to attend the Southern Baptist Convention Annual Meeting from June 1st through the 4th. "Tell you what," the pastor told Fred, "If you will preach for me on the Sunday that you're out here, I'll get some pulpit search committees to come hear you."

Fred preached at 8th Avenue Baptist Church on June 6, 1964, and at least one committee came to hear him. That week, Fred received a call from Forest Park Baptist Church, and he knew that this had to be God. He had asked for a church, and now one that was located only two miles from the school was asking him to come and was offering to pay all of the expenses to move him out there.

It was difficult to resign from Eastview. The people had loved Fred and his family, and had seen them through dark times. Fred had enjoyed a close relationship with the people there, had seen God do great things, and he was grateful for who they had been to him. Still, he could not deny that God had opened the door that he was looking for.

Fred Wolfe had not lived more than 190 miles from his hometown of Rock Hill in his entire life. Now he was about to take his wife and his two young sons more than a thousand miles to the west.

This had better be worth it.

CHAPTER 4

OUT WEST AND BACK EAST

The years in Fort Worth were good ones for Fred and Anne and their boys. The people of Forest Park Baptist, about a hundred in all, had paid the moving expenses, and the young family moved into the parsonage on Sandage Avenue. It had uneven floors and humidifiers instead of air conditioning, but even in the hot Texas summers, they were grateful for a place to live, so close to the school.

Fred's salary at Forest Park was going to be a hundred dollars less a month than what he left behind at Eastview. There was no way to make it up, but Fred and Anne were convinced that they were exactly where God wanted them, so they trusted him for the difference.

Soon after Fred began his pastorate at Forest Park, a man began showing up and sitting in the back row. His name was Paul Watson, and he was a businessman who owned a local equipment company. Without saying why, he began to send Fred one hundred dollars each month. Fred became good friends with the man, and he knew that Mr. Watson had been sent by God to make sure that his family lacked nothing from the move. That one hundred dollars a month continued until Fred took another pastorate at Golden Gate Baptist

Church, a larger church in the Fort Worth suburbs that was in a transitional neighborhood and wasn't sure how to move forward.

One evening, Fred was visiting his brother, Bill, who was a student at Southwestern. Bill and Fred sat in his apartment and discussed school, church, and what their family was up to back home. Bill looked up as he heard footsteps on the stairs. As his upstairs neighbor began to pass by, Bill called out to him. "Hey, Ed!" he said. "Come here and meet my brother."

The neighbor stuck his head in the partially open door of the apartment. He had wavy black hair, black-framed glasses, and an easy smile. "Ed Keyes," said Bill, "this is my brother, Fred Wolfe."

"Hello," said Ed, "it's very nice to meet you."

"Glad to meet you, too," said Fred. "What are you studying here, Ed?"

"I'm in the Music program," he said.

"Well, Amen," said Fred, "that's good. I just may call on you some time to lead music for me, if that's alright."

"Happy to help if I can," said Ed. "I'm sorry, but I have to get going to an appointment. Good to see you, Bill. And Fred, nice to meet you. Maybe we can serve together some time."

Fred graduated from Southwestern Baptist Theological Seminary in December of 1967, two and a half years after moving to Texas. His time at Golden Gate was going well, and the Lord was blessing his ministry there, but after graduation, Fred began to feel an inexorable pull back to the Carolinas.

"Lord," he prayed, "I am grateful for your faithfulness to me here at Southwestern and the churches I've pastored in Fort Worth. But this is not where I belong. I have no roots here. If you will open a door for me to go back to South Carolina, I'd love to go home."

That summer, Fred and Anne took the boys home for vacation, and while he was there, Fred mentioned his heart's desire to a friend, Ron Long. Much like the Lord had done to get him to Texas, he was now orchestrating a move back. Ron told Fred that if he would preach at his church while he was on vacation, Ron would send his name to some churches and invite them to come and hear him preach. One of those churches did send a committee, and Monaghan Baptist Church, in Greenville, South Carolina, jumped at the chance to call this newly minted seminary graduate back to his stomping grounds as their new pastor.

Monaghan Baptist Church was a "Mill Hill," what the locals called a textile mill village. At that time, Greenville was the "Textile Center of the South," and the Monaghan Mill was a vital part of that operation. Started before the turn of the century, the Monaghan Mill would go on to operate continuously for 100 years. Fred began to preach in this village, and the attendance at Monaghan Baptist jumped from 250 to 400 in a very short time. God was moving.

In February of 1969, a few months into his time at Monaghan, Fred felt an irresistible draw to attend an Evangelism Conference in Greensboro, North Carolina. He knew very little, if anything, about the men who would be preaching, but he was confident that whatever Stephen Olford and Vance Havner had to say, it was going to be important.

Born in Zambia and raised in Angola as the son of missionaries, Dr. Stephen Olford had become widely known as the pastor of Calvary Baptist Church in New York, where he pioneered the role of ministry on television with his show, "Encounter." He was now traveling and speaking in many different places, and was about to publish a soon-to-be classic book, *Heart-Cry For Revival*.

As Dr. Olford preached that cold February night, Fred Wolfe

was captured in a way that he had never been before. "I've come to see," said Dr. Olford in his regal British accent, "that there is one thing that matters, and really, only one thing that matters-- and that is that I become more, and more, and more like Jesus Christ. There is so much unlikeness to Christ Jesus in my life, so much imperfection and failure, in my life... It is when the corporate image of Jesus Christ is clearly seen, that the impact that we long for, for revival, will be felt across our land."

Fred became unaware of the dropping temperatures as, much like John Wesley, his heart was "strangely warmed" by the message he was hearing. Dr. Olford was preaching on the Lordship of Jesus Christ in the life of a believer. "Jesus is either Lord of all, or He is not Lord at all!" *Lord of all... not Lord at all...* The words echoed in Fred's heart as a heaviness fell on him. But this wasn't like the heaviness he felt that first year of college, no, this was the weight of God's glory, pulling him up, driving him deeper into a dimension of knowing Christ that he had never thought possible.

Of course Fred had heard people speak of the fact that Jesus is Lord, but this... this was something altogether different. This was a new way of living. This was the total and absolute surrender of everything we are and everything we ever hope to be, surrendered gladly and put voluntarily under the control of Jesus Christ. Jesus as Lord. *Yes*, Fred thought. *Jesus Christ is Lord.*

The power of God accompanied the message that night. Before the night was finished, many of the hundreds of pastors at the conference were on their faces before God. When it was over, Fred drove the three hours home, weeping as every one of the 200 miles passed beneath his feet. But the weeping didn't stop there. Downstairs, in his study at his home, Fred wept for two more weeks.

Over the next month, this change affected everything in Fred's life. The way he loved Anne and Mark and Jeff. The way he saw life.

The way he loved the people of Monaghan Baptist Church. And it most definitely affected his preaching. It was as if Fred had a new Bible, one that spoke of the Lordship of Jesus on every page. It was like reading the Bible through a new and exciting set of lenses, lenses that colored everything he thought he knew with the one commanding phrase, "Jesus is Lord!"

After about a month, as the Lord was gently but firmly breaking Fred, molding him as the potter does the clay, one of the men in his church approached him on a Sunday morning. "You know," the man said, "I don't quite get all of this that you're preaching right now, but there is one thing I can say for sure. You're not the man you used to be. Something has definitely happened to you."

Fred had been pastoring Monaghan Baptist Church for a year and a half when a woman in the church, who had relatives in Decatur, Georgia, brought her family to hear him preach. Their home church, Woodlawn Baptist, was in the search for a new pastor, and they were impressed with Fred Wolfe.

Woodlawn had a weekly attendance of about 400, and after a series of interviews, they issued a call for Fred to come and be their pastor. But the people of Monaghan didn't want him to leave. Fred resigned one Sunday, and the next week, a man in the choir made a formal motion to rescind Fred's resignation. Fred was grateful and flattered, but he shook his head, smiled, and said, "I'm sorry, but that's just not the way it works. God has called me to Decatur. I have to go."

The year was 1970, and the city of Decatur, Georgia was home to some 18,000 residents, but it was just beginning a population decline that would continue for the next twenty years. In spite of the decline, though, Woodlawn Baptist Church almost immediately doubled in size under Fred's leadership. Soon after arriving in Decatur, Fred had a life-changing conversation with Bill Powell from the North American Mission Board, the Southern Baptist Convention's agency in charge of overseeing mission work within the United States.

"Fred," Bill told him, "there is a very interesting move going on in independent churches that we need to consider. A lot of churches are growing like crazy by using buses to bring children to church whose parents won't or can't bring them. I think we need to study that. A bus ministry might work here, too."

That was just about all the discussion Fred needed. He thought it was a simple and brilliant idea. The church procured a number of used buses, recruited volunteers, and in short order they were going into the different neighborhoods in their Atlanta suburb and bringing in 150 to 200 children each Sunday for Sunday School and worship services. Woodlawn Baptist became the first Southern Baptist Church to have a bus ministry.

The volunteers would canvas the neighborhoods every Saturday, inviting everyone they met to come to church the next day at Woodlawn. "If you don't have a way to get there," they said, "we'll be right here at the corner tomorrow morning to pick you up, and we'll bring you back after church."

At first, they just picked up children whose parents wanted them out of the house for a few hours. Eventually, though, they would get to meet these parents and start building a relationship with them. In short order, these bus ministry volunteers were bringing whole families into a relationship with Christ. Woodlawn Baptist soared from 400 in weekly attendance to 800. They went from one worship service and one Sunday School to two services, two Sunday Schools, and a Children's Church. As the attendance doubled, they baptized over 100 people that year, making them one of the top ten Southern

Baptist churches in Georgia.

There was another, less predictable but just as powerful, effect of Woodlawn's bus ministry. As they went out into the surrounding neighborhoods and brought in children and parents, it became evident that many of them were African American. At the turn of the decade from the 1960s to the 1970s, civil rights in the South had not yet led to racial blending in the congregations of most Southern Baptist churches. The people of Woodlawn could not deny, though, that God was at work. As Fred began to see the color line change, he could only admit that this was the easiest way to integrate a church that he had ever heard of, and could never have foreseen. But it was good. It was God.

One of the women who had been on the pastor search committee for Woodlawn approached Brother Fred one day and suggested they bring in a guest speaker, a woman with whom she was familiar. And so it was that Fred Wolfe first heard of "Miss Bertha."

Olive Bertha Smith was born on November 16, 1888, near Cowpens, South Carolina, and in July of 1917 had been appointed as a Southern Baptist missionary to China. While serving, she saw the roots of the historic Shantung Revival, and stayed on the mission field until retiring in 1958 at the age of 70. After her retirement, she became a sought after speaker in churches around the United States and the world. Fred was primed for her message.

Bertha Smith arrived at Woodlawn for a special conference, and her teaching took the message of Lordship that had so captured Fred's heart, and drove it deeper. Miss Bertha spoke firmly and convincingly of the holiness of God, and on our responsibility to walk in that same holiness. This was the first time that Fred had ever heard someone speak of being filled with the Holy Spirit with such clarity and passion. Here is how she expressed it in her life's story, *How The Holy Spirit Filled My Life*:

"One day I said, 'Lord, since you count me dead in your Son, I will count myself dead in him, no matter how much alive I may be appearing.'

"When I began to praise the Lord for having taken me to death, I was 'faithing' myself dead. This gave the Holy Spirit a chance to so control the old self that it was ineffective over me. No more 'death struggles.'

"It is the business of the Holy Spirit to take care of the old self and to magnify Christ through our personalities. When he is ungrieved in us and can fill up all the space that is left when the 'Big I' moves out, he is free to do his work. Life becomes glorious!"[1]

Miss Bertha began teaching the people of Woodlawn how to keep their sins confessed up-to-date. She also encouraged them to experience the cleansing of forgiveness by making a sin list, then confessing each one, and burning the list, knowing that they were clean before the Lord. As she taught, the sense of urgency in the congregation grew, but she refused to pray with anyone for the first two days. "Make the sin list," she said, "then when you're ready, I'll pray with you."

By the end of the first two days, the people were in agony because of conviction. They were ready to forsake their sin and ask God to fill them with the Holy Spirit. Scores of people were changed forever in that conference as they received the gift of forgiveness and acceptance from the Lord.

One such man was the Minister of Music. By nature a dry and fairly joyless man, he was a very nice person, but he never smiled, never laughed. After praying with Miss Bertha, he was filled with the Holy Spirit, and his personality was totally transformed. He received the joy of the Lord, and he never lost it. He was changed by the radical power of the Holy Spirit.

Miss Bertha's visit at Woodlawn also marked Fred's first exposure to spiritual warfare. One evening, Fred and a couple of the men went to the hotel where Bertha was staying to bring her to church. She told them, "You men come into my room here. Leave the door open, but gather around the bed. We are going to pray."

The five or six men present did as they were told, which was common around Miss Bertha, and they all knelt around the bed and began praying. After a time, Bertha addressed them again. "Stand to your feet," she commanded, "we're going to resist the enemy," she told them.

Resist the enemy?!? Fred thought. He looked around quickly. *What's happened? Has someone broken into the room?* And Miss Bertha began to speak. She spoke directly to satan and his demons, bound them in the name of Jesus, and resisted them and their influence, banning them from the meetings that were to come that night at the church.

And for Fred Wolfe, the message of the lordship of Jesus became bigger. No longer would he be distracted by battling against people, against flesh and blood. He now knew who his enemy was. It was 1971, and no one was talking about this kind of thing in most Baptist churches, bur Fred recognized the truth and the power of it. And he would practice it for the rest of his life.

After the conference with Bertha Smith, Fred was energized. It was as if his eyes were open for the first time, and he saw what was going on around him, both in the natural and in the spirit. Not long after, another man came through town and told Fred that if they were going to go on with God, they would need to start praying. Really praying. "Get a group of faithful men," he said, "and start praying together for the power of God. A praying church will be a powerful church." So Fred gathered some men to join him, and they began to meet two mornings each week, at six in the morning, to pray.

And the church grew.

One day, late in 1971, Fred was sitting in his study at the church and was reading a copy of *The Alabama Baptist*, the state newspaper of the Alabama Baptist Convention. He didn't know how he came by this copy. He didn't subscribe to it and had never read it before. But on the front page, an article not only caught his eye, it caused something to leap in his spirit. He read that Don Watterson, the pastor of Cottage Hill Baptist Church in Mobile, Alabama, had resigned in order to take a position at the Sunday School Board in Montgomery. The Holy Spirit spoke to Fred, as clearly as any time before, and said, "I want you to be recommended to that church."

Fred immediately called his friend and former professor at Southwestern Seminary, Dr. Roy Fish, and asked him to recommend him to Cottage Hill. Dr. Fish wrote them a letter, and within a few weeks, a search committee from Mobile was coming to Decatur after deciding whether they wanted to go hear Fred preach and observe the church.

They took it as a positive sign that they had chosen correctly to hear Fred, because so much went wrong with their trip to Atlanta. They considered it opposition from the enemy, indicating that they were on the right track. They heard Fred preach at Woodlawn on a Sunday morning, and it was obvious that the Lord was moving powerfully in the service. After, Fred went to lunch at Stone Mountain with Harlan Taylor and two other men.

They were very positive, but they didn't ask him many questions until the rest of the committee could come hear him. Fred understood completely, but he was undaunted. He immediately went home and told Anne, "We are going to Cottage Hill Baptist Church in Mobile, Anne. We are going to go there, and Ed Keyes will be our Minister of Music, Len Turner will be our Youth Minister, and Bob Rowell will be our Minister of Education. That is what we are going to do."

Anne had never heard of Cottage Hill Baptist Church, and wasn't quite sure she had even heard of Mobile, Alabama. But she knew Fred. When he said that he had heard from the Lord, he was probably right. There was no sense arguing, lest you find yourself fighting against God Himself.

a Sermon

The Lordship of Christ

The Lordship of Christ

by
Fred H. Wolfe

Up to this point we have established that walking in the Spirit on a consistent basis involves keeping all sins confessed up to date and choosing against self, the flesh, and sin. This brings us to the third principle. If you are going to walk in the Spirit, you must understand and apply what the Bible teaches about submission to the Lordship of Jesus Christ. You will not walk in the Spirit unless Jesus is your Lord, unless you are totally yielded to Him and trusting Him in every area of your life.

Just as the Holy Spirit makes certain confessions about who you are in Christ, He also makes certain confessions about who Christ is in you. And it is just as important to respond to what He says about Jesus as it is to respond to what He says about you. Notice carefully what the Bible says about Jesus in Philippians 2:9-11:

Therefore God also has highly exalted Him and given Him a name which is above every name, that at the name of Jesus every knee should bow, of those in heaven, and of those on earth, and of those under the earth, and that every tongue should confess that Jesus Christ is Lord, to the glory of God the Father.

If you are going to walk in the Spirit, you will have to bow your knee and make Jesus Lord. If you haven't made Jesus Lord, you have made provision for the flesh. Walking in the Spirit means responding to the Holy Spirit's confessions - you believe what He says about you, but you believe what He says about Jesus. And what He says is that Jesus Christ is Lord!

In my opinion, the classic passage in all the Bible about the Lordship of Christ is Romans 14:7-9. Notice how many times the word "Lord" is used here:

For none of us lives to himself, and no one dies to himself. For if we live, we live to the Lord; and if we die, we die to the Lord. Therefore, whether we live or die, we are the Lord's. For to this end Christ died and rose and lived again, that He might be Lord of both the dead and the living.

Why did Jesus die? Why did He rise from the dead? Why does Christ live today? That He might be Lord of the dead and of the living. He died to purchase you as Lord. He rose to pardon you as Lord. He lives to possess you as Lord. And you are to submit to His Lordship.

Lordship Applied

What does it mean for Jesus to be Lord of your life? It means that He is not only resident in your heart, He is ruler in your heart. It means that Jesus is not only present in your life, He is president of your life. It means that Jesus is not only Savior in your heart, He is sovereign in your heart. For Jesus to be Lord means that He is not only mediator in your life, He is master in your life. In other words, you bring every aspect of your life under His control. Romans 6:13

says, "And do not present your members," (the members of your body: your brain, your eyes, your tongue, your hands, your feet, your heart), "as instruments of unrighteousness to sin, but present yourselves to God as being alive from the dead, and your members," (your mind, your emotions, your will, your body, your soul, your spirit) "as instruments of righteousness to God." Submission to the Lordship of Christ, therefore, means yielding ourselves totally to Jesus as Lord and trusting Him with our lives.

Let me suggest one reason you may be powerless and defeated. Perhaps there is one area of your life you have never really given to Jesus. You're holding back on Him. You have bowed your knee and said, "Jesus, be Lord of my life here," and "Jesus, be Lord of my life there." But you have taken a little corner of your life and reserved that for yourself. You've hung a "Keep Out Jesus" sign over that area of your life, yet you don't understand why you can't walk in the Spirit. It is because you have made provision for the flesh. If Jesus is not Lord, the flesh is free to exercise tyranny over you in that area of your life where He is not Lord!

Submitting to Jesus as Lord begins in your home life. As a husband, or as a wife, you are to bring your life at home under His control. "Jesus, be Lord of my life. I yield my life to you as a husband. I yield my life to you as a wife." Submission also means yielding your life in the church. "Jesus, be Lord of my life in the church. I want everything I do in the body of Christ to be under your control." It also means you bring your life in the world under His control. "Jesus, be Lord of my job. I want you to control what I do in my job. Be Lord of my social life, and my recreational life."

The Lordship of Christ means there is no area of your life that you do not bring under His control. Have you ever made Jesus Lord of your money? Do you know why that is so hard? Because the Bible says that the love of money is the root of all evil (1 Timothy 6:10).

The Bible says, "You shall not covet" (Exodus 20:17). If you haven't made Jesus Lord over your money, it is no wonder the flesh rises up to oppose you.

Have you ever made Jesus Lord of your mouth? Boy, that's hard. Have you ever told Him, that you don't want to say anything but what He says - nothing but what is pleasing to Him? If you have an area of your life that you have not brought before Jesus and submitted to His Lordship, you have a pocket of resistance in your life that the enemy can exploit. He will use that pocket of resistance to defeat you in your Christian life.

In Romans 13:14, Paul says, "But put on the Lord Jesus Christ." What a picture! Get up in the morning and put on Jesus! He is Lord of your marriage, Lord of your family, Lord of your job, Lord of your life at school, Lord of your money, Lord of your mouth, your mind. But Paul goes on. "But put on the Lord Jesus Christ, and make no provision for the flesh, to fulfill its lusts." Now when you don't put Jesus on, guess what you do? You make a little provision for the flesh, and it takes over. You then start walking in the flesh. You must clothe yourself totally with Jesus Christ, and make no provision for the desires of the flesh.

Satan's Little Acre

Why is it so important that every part of your life be under the Lordship of Christ? Well, suppose you have clear title to 39 acres of a 40-acre piece of land, and one acre right in the middle belongs to someone else. It is not yours - you don't have title to it. What would happen if the owner of that one acre came roaring up one day on his Harley Davidson, rode right through your property, and put up a tent and began to live on his one acre? You might go to him and say, "What are you doing on my property? You have no right there!"

"Wait a minute, he would reply, "you don't understand. I know that you own 39 acres of this land, but I want you to know there is one acre you don't own, and it belongs to me." And he would reach into his pocket and pull out a deed. Sure enough, of that 40-acre tract, one acre belongs to him. It has his name on it. You could argue that you own the 39 acres around it. You could demand that he get off. You could even hire a lawyer, but because he owns that acre he is entitled to be on it any time he wants and to stay on it as long as he wants.

This is the problem with many Christians. You come to Jesus and say, "Now Jesus, I want you to be Lord of 39 acres of my life." You take those 39 acres of our life and you sign it over to Him. He has clear title to that deed, but for some reason there is one acre you hold back. You just won't let Him be Lord of that acre of your life. Well, for a while you grow spiritually. You get revived, and you begin to experience new life and power. Then one day the devil comes roaring up on his motorcycle, rides his way right into the middle of your life, and pitches a tent there. You say to him, "Satan, get off that acre of my life. It doesn't belong to you! It belongs to Jesus."

The devil replies, "Oh, no. You never gave that acre to Him. You never put His name on it. He doesn't have clear title to it. And if it doesn't belong to Jesus, I can have access to it any time I want to get on it." And guess what? He does. You have the right to tell the devil and every demon of hell to get off any part of your life that is under the authority of Christ. In the name of Jesus, he has to leave you alone. But if it is not under Christ's Lordship, it is wide open to the world, the flesh, and the devil.

The reason many Christians are defeated is because they have not yielded all the acres of their life to Jesus. They are holding something back on God, and just won't let God have it. But has it ever occurred to you why a Christian would not let God have everything? What reason would any child of God have to hold back from God some acre of his life? One reason could be that there may be some sin involved in that area of their life. Because they love that sin, they are unwilling to release it to the Lord.

I believe, however, that the basic reason many Christians will not let God have all the acres is that they don't really believe they can trust God with that acre. The best illustration I have ever read of that was in Hannah Whitehall Smith's, *The Christian's Secret of a Happy Life*. This unforgettable story described me completely. A little boy went to his daddy one day and said, "Daddy, I am six now, and I have been watching you the last few years. I want you to know I believe you are the greatest daddy in all the world. I have decided to absolutely yield all of my life to you. My life is yours, and whatever you want to do with it, that's what I want, too."

The father looked at him and said, "Boy, I've been waiting since the day you were born for you to give me all of your life. Come with me to your room." In the boy's room, the father said, "Now, son, get out all of your toys." The boy got out all his toys, including his new video game and his little train and laid them on the floor. Then his daddy stomped on every one of them. He completely destroyed all the toys, leaving them in a shambles there in the six-year-old's room.

The little boy looked at his father and said, "Well, daddy, you know I love you, and I have given you my life, and that includes my toys. If you want to stomp my toys, that is your privilege."

The father said, "Well, that's fine, son. Now there is just one other thing. Since you have given me your life, I want you to come every morning at eight o'clock and get into the closet. And I want you to stay there until six at night. But don't worry. Your mother is going to be by at eight to give you a steaming bowl of spinach. She'll be back again at twelve with another bowl of spinach, and at six with another."

By now you are probably thinking, "That's ridiculous. If a little boy went to his father who loved him and said, 'I love you, and I want to give you my life,' that father wouldn't take that boy and destroy all of his toys. If he told his daddy, 'You can do anything you want with my life,' he wouldn't put him in a closet and feed him spinach three times a day. He would take him up in his arms and say, 'Boy, if you are giving me your life, I want you to know you can trust me with it. Come on, son, let's get in the car.' He would take him down to Baskin Robbins and get him a double dip of rocky road ice cream. He would do everything he could to bless and to minister to that boy!"

Now, here is the problem. Some Christians have believed a lie. Perhaps you have allowed yourself to be deceived into thinking that if you go to God in an attitude of love and trust and give Him all your life, the Lord is going to take all your toys away and make you miserable. Maybe you are afraid He is going to put you in a closet somewhere. You refuse to make Him Lord of your marriage for fear that He will mess the whole thing up. After all, it took you fifteen years to get your wife straightened out, and you really don't want Jesus to foul it up. Your attitude is, "After fifteen years, I know how to handle her."

You may be afraid of trusting God with your children. Your attitude is, "Lord, it is good to know you love my children, but I am not going to really give them into your hands and let you do what is best for them. Lord, you need my help!" He does need for you to pray for them, but if you don't learn to trust God with your children, you will soon get ulcers, and need a doctor's care! You must learn to be able to give them to God and to trust God to give you wisdom as a parent.

A lot of people have the idea that just as sure as they make an absolute surrender to God and allow Jesus to be Lord, it won't be three weeks until He has them living in Africa with the heathen, hanging in the trees with the monkeys. They really believe that God will put them somewhere that is not best for them. The Lord settled that for me when I heard a fellow say once, "If you give your life to God completely and He wants you to be a missionary, He will give you such a desire to go that if you can't catch a boat, you'll swim to get there, to be where God wants you to be." You see, God never puts a burden on us. His will is good. It is acceptable. It is delightful and it is very, very desirous.

If you have somehow believed that God won't do what is best for you, then you have believed a lie from the devil. God will do what is best for you. If you can't trust God, you may as well forget it, throw your Bible away, and become an agnostic. God can be trusted, and there is no reason for you not to give Him all of your life.

The Fullness of the Holy Spirit

We are now ready to examine the fourth principle for walking in the Spirit. When a person has all of his sins confessed, when he has chosen against the flesh, sin and self, when as far as he knows he has yielded and submitted himself to the Lordship of Christ, then he is free for the Holy Spirit to fill his life. Ephesians 5:18 says, "And do not be drunk with wine, in which is dissipation; but be filled with the Spirit." This refers not to a once-and-for-all filling (there is no such thing), but to a daily filling of the Holy Spirit. Did you know that being filled with the Spirit is just as much a command from God as not being drunk with wine? The fullness of the Holy Spirit is not an option for super-saints, but a command for every child of God.

What does it mean to be filled with the Holy Spirit? It simply means to be controlled by the Spirit in the same way that alcohol controls a drunk person. Have you ever noticed how a person behaves when he is intoxicated? It affects his mind - the way he thinks. It affects his speech - the way he talks. It affects his emotions -the way he feels. It affects his hands - the way he handles. It affects his feet - the way he walks. When a person is intoxicated, every area of his life is affected.

"Be not drunk with wine. . . but be filled with the Spirit." So let the Holy Spirit fill you and control your mind, your eyes, your tongue, your heart, and your hands. You see, if you respond to the Holy Spirit's conviction, and you respond to His confessions, then you will respond to His commands. You can be filled with the Holy Spirit!

Let me ask you a question. Why is it that so many Christians are not living in the power of the Holy Spirit? Why do we just go along defeated day after day after day with no real power to be Christlike, and no real power to serve God? I believe part of the problem is ignorance. I believe part of it is refusing to meet the conditions of letting this power of God be released. Many Christians are willing to do whatever God says to live in the power of the Holy Spirit. But others are content to go on as they have been - winning a few, losing a few; up one day, down the next. Well, God help you if that describes you, my friend! Life is too short to live without the dynamic, enabling power of the Spirit of the Living God. You must live in His power or you will be defeated.

The Gift of the Spirit

At conversion, you received the gift of the Holy Spirit. Now there is a difference between receiving the gift of the Holy Spirit and being filled with the Holy Spirit. There is a difference between the gift of the Spirit and walking in the Spirit. There is a difference between the gift of the Spirit and the power of the Spirit. But understand very clearly that at conversion you received the gift of the Spirit.

When Peter preached at Pentecost, and they asked him what they needed to do to be saved, notice what he said: "Repent, and let every one of you be baptized in the name of Jesus Christ for the remission of sins; and you shall receive the gift of the Holy Spirit" (Acts 2:39). When you repented of your sins, and personally, willfully invited Jesus Christ to be your Savior and your Lord, you received the gift of the Holy Spirit.

Now what is involved in this gift of the Holy Spirit you receive at conversion? It involves Jesus, coming to live in you in the person of the Holy Spirit. Visibly and bodily, Jesus is at the right hand of the Father. Hebrews 10:12 says, "But this Man, after He had offered one sacrifice for sins forever, sat down at on the right hand of God." But wait a minute. While Jesus is visibly and bodily at the right hand of the Father, He is also in us. How does Christ come to live in you and me? Not bodily! Jesus comes to live in us in the person of the Holy Spirit.

Let me show you what Jesus Himself said about the indwelling Holy Spirit. In John 14:16, He said, "And I will pray the Father, and He will give you another Helper, that he may abide with you for ever;" That word "another" means another of the same kind. That word Helper is with a capital "h." Jesus said the Comforter (KJV) will abide with you forever.

Who is the Comforter? Look at verse 17: "even the Spirit of truth; whom the world cannot receive, because it neither sees Him nor knows Him; but you know him, for He dwells with you, and will be in you." The Holy Spirit is the Spirit of Jesus who comes to live in us! How do I know? Look at the remainder of that passage:

A little while longer and the world will see Me no more, but you will see Me. Because I live, you will live also. At that day you will know that I am in the Father, and you in Me, and I in you. He who has My commandments and keeps them, it is he who loves Me. And he who loves Me will be loved by My Father, and I will love him and manifest Myself to him. . . . If anyone loves Me, he will keep My word; and My Father will love him, and We will come to him and make Our home with him.

How do the Father and the Son come and make their home with us? In the person of the Holy Spirit. Let me show you one other verse - one we have looked at previously. When I was in college someone said to me, "First you get Jesus, and then later on you get the Holy Spirit." That had me greatly disturbed for some time. I read some passages in Acts, and I was confused until I read this verse: "But you are not in the flesh, but in the Spirit, if indeed the Spirit of God dwells in you. Now if anyone does not have not the Spirit of Christ, he is not His."

Friend, when you receive Jesus, you receive the Holy Spirit, too, for the Holy Spirit is the very Spirit of Jesus.

Let me mention a couple of other things about the gift of the Spirit. In 1 Corinthians 12:13 Paul says, "For by one Spirit we were all baptized into one body - whether Jews or Greeks, whether slaves or free - and have all been made to drink into one Spirit." That's a beautiful picture. By one spirit every Christian was baptized into one body, the body of Christ. And we have all been made to drink of one Spirit. That's the gift of the Spirit!

Also, 1 Corinthians 6:19 tells us that we are indwelt by the Holy Spirit. "Or do you not know that your body is the temple of the Holy Spirit who is in you, whom you have from God, and you are not your own?" The gift of the Spirit means that Jesus comes to live in us through the person of the Holy Spirit. We drink of the Holy Spirit, we are indwelt by the Holy Spirit, and John 7:38 tells us that the Spirit will flow out of us. There Jesus says, "He who believes in Me, as the Scripture has said, out of his heart will flow rivers of living water." Then John adds this comment: "But this He spoke concerning the Spirit, whom those believing in Him should receive; for the Holy Spirit was not yet given; because Jesus was not yet glorified" (v. 39).

All Christians have received the gift of the Spirit. But here is where the confusion is: You can receive the gift of the Spirit and not walk in the Spirit. You can have the gift of the Spirit and not be filled with the Spirit. You can receive the gift of the Spirit and not live in the power of the Holy Spirit. Now if you are saved, you have received the gift of the Spirit. But are you walking in the Spirit? Are you controlled by the Spirit? Are you living in the power of the Holy Spirit?

The Bible commands us to be filled with the Spirit. I give a certain questionnaire to people from time to time, and one of the questions it asks is, "Have you ever been filled with the Holy Spirit?" Ninety-nine percent of the time, the response is, "I was filled with the Spirit when I was saved." But that is not accurate. When you were saved, you received the gift of the Spirit, but not the fullness of the Spirit. Otherwise, why does Galatians 5:25 say, "If we live in the Spirit, let us walk in the Spirit?" You can live in the Spirit and not walk in the Spirit, and that is the problem with the church today. There are scores of people who are alive in the Spirit, but who are not walking in the Spirit, not controlled by the Spirit, not living in the power of the Spirit. That is why God commands us in Ephesians 5:18 to be filled with the Spirit!

The Power of the Spirit

There are several passages in which the Bible gives special emphasis to walking in the power of the Holy Spirit. For example, notice what Paul prayed for the Ephesian Christians: "that He would grant you, according to the riches of His glory, to be strengthened with might by His Spirit in the inner man."

Again in Colossians 1:11, Paul talks about our need to be strengthened by the Spirit: "strengthened with all might, according to His glorious power, for all patience and longsuffering with joy."

The need of the church today - your need and mine - is to be controlled and empowered by the Spirit. Let me give you two reasons why. First, the power to have Christian character comes from walking in the Spirit. You say you want to live a Christian life - let me show you where the power is. "But the fruit of the Spirit is love, joy, peace, longsuffering, kindness, goodness, faithfulness, gentleness, self-control." It is the Holy Spirit that produces love! It is the Holy Spirit that produces peace! It is the Holy Spirit that produces any and every resemblance of Christian character. If you are having difficulty walking in love, in patience, or in self control, the truth is, you are alive in the Spirit, but you are not being filled by the Spirit. When you are walking, living, and being controlled by the Spirit, the Spirit bears His fruit

- Christian character. This is the very life of Jesus revealed in you.
- The power to do Christian work comes from the Holy Spirit.

No question about it! Acts 1:8 says, "But you shall receive power when the Holy Spirit has come upon you; and you shall be witnesses to me in Jerusalem, and in all Judaea and Samaria, and to the end of the earth." The power to witness comes from being filled with the Holy Spirit.

- The power to pray comes from the Spirit. "Praying always with all prayer and supplication in the Spirit, being watchful to this end with all perseverance and supplication for all the saints" (Ephesians 6:18).

- The power to teach or preach comes from the Spirit. Corinthians 2:4 says, "And my speech and my preaching were not with persuasive words of human wisdom, but in demonstration of the Spirit and of power."

The power to witness, the power to pray, the power to teach and preach all comes from the enabling, controlling, energizing power of the Holy Spirit. I see today many churches that are orthodox - in other words, they believe the Bible. In fact, they will fight you over the fact that they believe the Bible. But you can believe the Bible and have no power. You can have it all in your head, but you will never live it out until you are walking, and controlled, and living under the power of the Spirit of God. The word of God without the power of the Spirit kills. The word of God in the power of the Holy Spirit brings life.

Receiving the Fullness

How are you filled with the Spirit? How does a person walk, live, move in the power of the Spirit? By a definite act of faith, you receive the fullness of the Holy Spirit. You say to God, "God, I put every known sin out of my life. I'm trusting the blood of Jesus and the power of the cross to take away sin and its power from my life. God, as far as I know, I am surrendered to your will. I'll do anything you tell me to do. I'll obey the light I have. And now, God, as a definite act of faith, I receive the fullness of the Holy Spirit to live the Christian life, and to do the Christian work. Many people believe that to be filled with the Spirit, you must speak with other tongues. Let me say this: I believe in all the gifts of the Holy Spirit. I believe that all of the gifts are present and operative today, and should be done scripturally. But if anybody says to you that in order to be filled with the Spirit, or that the evidence you have been filled with the Spirit is you have to speak in tongues, they are not telling you the truth. If they have the gift of tongues, that is between them and God. The Holy Spirit gives gifts severally as He wills, and I am in no way putting down any spiritual gift.

Every spiritual gift is good! But I'm saying that you can be filled with the Spirit, walk in the Spirit, be energized by the Spirit, and never speak in tongues.

What is the evidence that we are filled with the Holy Spirit? Is it that we feel spiritual? Frankly, I don't know what it means to feel spiritual. I wish I did. Does it mean that your spine tingles, or that you have goose bumps? I know there are times when I sense the presence of God in a special way - is that is what it means to feel spiritual? The point is that the evidence that you are filled with the Spirit is not the way you feel. If you live by your feelings, you are in deep, deep trouble.

The evidence that you are filled with the Spirit is the fruit of the Spirit. The evidence that you are filled with the Spirit is the manifestation of the Spirit in Christian character and Christian service. How do I know that an apple tree is an apple tree? By the fruit on it. It has apples. How do I know a person is filled with the Holy Spirit? Because there is the evidence of the fruit of the Spirit in their life, and the fruit of the Spirit is the life of Jesus.

Now this fruit of the Spirit is manifested in four areas. It is manifested first in worship. After the word of God commands us to be filled with the Spirit, it goes on to say, "speaking to one another in psalms and hymns and spiritual songs...." (Ephesians 5:19).

It is also manifested in marriage. Verse 21-25 of that same fifth chapter says, "submitting to one another in the fear of God. Wives, submit to your own husbands as to the Lord...Husbands, love your wives, just as Christ also loved the church and gave Himself for it."

The fruit of the Spirit is manifested in your relationship to your children. In Ephesians 6:4, Paul says, "And, you, fathers, do not provoke your children to wrath, but bring them up in the training and admonition of the Lord." This is still seen in the context of being filled with the Spirit.

The fruit of the Spirit will also be seen in your work life. "Servants, be obedient to those who are your masters according to the flesh, with fear and trembling, in sincerity of heart, as to Christ" (Ephesians 6:5).

Being filled with the Spirit is very practical. It is not otherworldly. The evidence that you are filled with the Spirit will be the fruit of the Spirit in your worship life, in your husband-wife relationship, in your parent-child relationship, and in your relationships at work.

God will let you know whether you are walking in the Spirit or not. Let me illustrate how He does that. In my hand is a lemon. If I squeeze that lemon hard enough, what is going to come out? Whatever is inside it. How does that apply to walking in the Spirit? Many times when we genuinely believe we are filled with the Spirit, the Lord sends someone to "squeeze" us. And whatever is inside of us is what will come out. If you are walking in the Spirit, the fruit of the Spirit will come out when you are squeezed. The fruit of the Spirit is patience. Sometimes God will let somebody drag their feet when you are in a hurry, just to see if the patience comes out when you are squeezed.

If you are not in the Spirit, guess what will come out? The flesh. The Lord sure knows how to squeeze me! I'll be thinking, "Man, I'm just doing real good spiritually." I'm sailing right along, and then somebody will come along and squeeze me, and the flesh comes out. I say, "Lord, I'm not in the Spirit. I need to check myself out here. Lord, is there some sin I haven't confessed? Lord, am I really not choosing against them? Have I not yielded this area of my life?"

Praise God, sometimes when I get squeezed, the fruit of the Spirit comes out. I praise the Lord for that. I would be discouraged if it didn't! I believe if you keep your sins confessed, self, flesh and sin in the place of death, Jesus as Lord, and the Holy Spirit filling your life daily, you will consistently walk in the Spirit. You will demonstrate the fruit of the Spirit, and when you are squeezed, the fruit of the Spirit will come out of your life.

There is power to live now! You have that power in the person of the Holy Spirit. You just need to release it.

You won't overcome the flesh unless you are walking in the Spirit. Some people think that they have to overcome the flesh to walk in the Spirit, but that is backwards. You walk in the Spirit in order to overcome the flesh. And the way you walk in the Spirit is to say, "Yes," when the Holy Spirit says, "Yes." Say, "No," when He says, "No." Believe what He says about you in Jesus, and let Jesus have all of your life. Put on Jesus, and don't leave any area for the flesh. And then you just say, "God, You fill me with the Spirit. Holy Spirit, control me today." Stop trying to overcome the flesh with the flesh! Be filled with the Spirit, and by the Spirit you will overcome.

PART II

CHAPTER 5

GULF COAST CALLING

February, 1972

Fred Wolfe had been driving for almost five hours when he and Anne and his two young sons crested the hill on Highway 90 in Spanish Fort, Alabama, and were greeted with their first breathtaking view of Mobile Bay. Interstate 65 did not yet connect directly with Mobile, but a project was underway, and even now a long bridge was being built just north of the city, across the swampy delta over the five rivers that came together in the brackish headwaters of the bay. As it was, Fred had to get off at Bay Minette, the last stop before the swamp, and wind his way through a few small south Alabama towns to arrive at this view.

The expanse of water that lay before them glinted in the setting sun, and as they descended the hill and drove across the water-level causeway, their eyes were drawn to the USS Alabama, a hulking WWII battleship moored on the opposite shore. Since it was the dead of winter, most of the water was out of the bay, but even the marshy mud and tall weeds in the shallower parts looked like a miniature version of the forbidding everglades. It would have barely surprised them to see a twelve-foot alligator charge their car from out of the mire, snapping, swinging its fierce head after them as they passed by.

The early Spanish settlers had named this the "Bay of the Holy Spirit," and even now, Fred felt a growing sense of certainty that he was arriving at a pivotal moment in his life, a moment that would change the course of everything. He had, indeed, heard the voice of the Holy Spirit in accepting the call to come to Mobile. He was, he knew, right where God wanted him to be.

Just a few weeks earlier, Fred Wolfe had preached his trial sermon in the chapel, so it did not shake his sense of destiny that he would begin his new pastorate in the same 500-seat building, not the modern, space-age looking main auditorium that could accommodate more than 1,600. It had been explained to them that the building had a leak in the roof, but not to worry, they had guarantees from the contractor that it would soon be fixed. After all, the building was only a few years old, and surely they wouldn't have to pay for such a repair.

Not only did the temporary venue fail to dampen Fred's optimism, it actually made the transition easier. Preaching in the chapel felt more like the room he was used to in Decatur, and he felt a quicker connection with the people by being closer to them. He could not deny, though, that he was itching to stand behind the enormous, white aggregate-rock podium that waited for him in the next building over and proclaim the gospel with boldness.

Before his first two sermons were preached at Cottage Hill in the morning and evening services of February 27, 1972, Fred wrote the first of what would be well over a thousand articles to the church family in his weekly column, "It's On My Heart," in a newsletter that was then called *The Cottage Hill Baptist*. In this first one, Fred anticipated the upcoming Sunday: "God, through the working of the Holy Spirit, has brought us together. We praise Him for what He has done and is going to do at Cottage Hill. I am glad to serve as your Pastor. Do not hesitate to call on me if I can minister to you in any way-- I am here to serve the Lord, and I serve the Lord by ministering to you and your family. The verse that I have chosen for my life verse (II Corinthians 4:5) expresses my feeling as we begin our ministry together: 'For we preach not ourselves, but Christ Jesus the Lord; and ourselves your servants for Jesus' sake.'"

The next week's issue of *The Cottage Hill Baptist*, for March 5, gave Fred a chance to evaluate his first Sunday's experience: "Last Sunday the spirit in our services was exciting and tremendous. There was a friendliness that blessed my heart. The response to the messages preached was tremendous. It is a real joy to be serving as Pastor of Cottage Hill Baptist Church. We praise the Lord for the ten new members He added to our Church Sunday."

The next Sunday, March 12, the congregation returned to what was still being called the New Auditorium. After only about three weeks at Cottage Hill, excitement was spreading and people were coming to hear this young, 34-year old preacher from South Carolina. Before Fred started, Cottage Hill was averaging about 800 people in worship. On that day, 1,178 people attended Sunday School, and about 1,400 attended the morning worship service, including 78 visitors. Sixteen people became new members that morning. This afforded Brother Fred, as he was now being called, another chance to express his joy in the next newsletter: "The wonderful spirit, attitude of friendliness, and willingness to work among our people are inspiring and encouraging to me as Pastor.

Great things are in store for us because of the way we are working together for the glory of Christ. In a Church with this potential and size, we need a competent Staff. Pray for the leadership of the Holy Spirit as we seek Staff members to serve with us here. We want God's will to be done."

What Brother Fred did not feel the need to share with the people at that time was that he already had a pretty good idea what God's will was for the upcoming staff hires. Of course, he would never presume to railroad anything past the people under his care, but he was at least going to pursue Len Turner, Ed Keyes, and Bob Rowell. If he had missed God, and if the Lord had other plans, so be it. But he didn't think so.

Within a week or so after Fred assumed the helm of Cottage Hill Baptist Church, he began to get more acquainted with the theological makeup of the congregation. The previous pastor, Don Watterson, had been a good man and a good preacher, but in the interim period, a professor from Mobile College who at least had leanings toward theological liberalism had occupied the pulpit. Fred wasn't sure just how much had permeated the people, but he was not afraid to find out. He had already fought a personal battle on these issues during his time at Southeastern Seminary, and he was not about to let that take root here. He had heard that there was a group of liberals that met on Sunday nights, and very soon, one of the men approached him.

The man who invited Fred to lunch had also gone to Southeastern Seminary. He was the man who had told Fred that he had become so disillusioned there that he would study with a gun on his desk. He needed to find out just how committed Fred was to a conservative view of the Bible.

"Surely, Brother Fred, you don't believe that the stories of the

Bible actually happened, do you? You certainly don't believe that the miracle accounts are literal!"

"Why, yes," Fred replied, "I do."

"But you can't seriously accept the veracity of the Biblical record. Do you mean to tell me that you still believe that the Bible is without error?"

"Yes," said Fred, "that is exactly what I believe. I believe that the Bible is the actual Word of God, that it was given by inspiration of the Holy Spirit, that it means exactly what it says, and that it can be trusted without reservation. Anything else?"

Fred's lunch companion was silent. There was nothing else.

Fred was convinced that the old wineskin would not be able to hold the new wine that God was bringing. Eventually, as the church grew, those who were theologically liberal saw their influence diminish. Some left. Some stayed a long time. Some were changed.

On the Sunday evenings of April 2nd and April 9th, 1972, Cottage Hill Baptist Church cancelled the evening services to allow everyone to attend the James Robison Crusade at the Mobile Municipal Auditorium. At the age of 28, James Robison had already become one of the most popular evangelists in America, having launched full time into television ministry four years earlier with the help of Billy Graham. In fact, it was being said that James just might be the man to one day inherit Graham's mantle as America's Preacher.

Two buses left from Cottage Hill each night that week for people who wanted to ride downtown with others in their church family. Fueled by the excitement of having a new pastor and the evident growth of his first few weeks, the buses filled each night as Cottage Hill members of all ages met to attend the Crusade.

In his April 16, 1972 column, Brother Fred referenced the previous week's meetings: "The James Robison Crusade here in

Mobile has been tremendous. Almost 2,000 people have publicly committed their life to Christ. We rejoice in what God has done! Many of the members of Cottage Hill have been revived! This Crusade has been and will be a blessing to our church."

But the James Robison Crusade was also the catalyst for conflict and change in a way that no one had foreseen. On Sunday, April 16th, sixteen people who had given their hearts to Christ in the crusade meetings made their way forward at the altar call to publicly confess their decision, and to join Cottage Hill. One of those was a young man named Mike Washington. And Mike was black.

Most of the people were accepting toward Mike from a genuine heart of the love of Christ. But, it was still only 1972. Racial tensions were high across the country. The Equal Opportunity Employment Act had been passed only three weeks earlier, and many were still trying to hold on to the "separate but equal" way of life, with the key word being "separate." On April 18th, one of the men in the church came to Brother Fred and said, "Listen, Pastor, we're glad he got saved, but now he needs to go to his church. There is even one right down the road where we know he will be welcome."

"He's welcome here," said Fred. "This is his church. He wants to be baptized here, and I'm going to baptize him."

The man looked down and shook his head. "Well, I guess I'll just tell you. If you do that, it's gonna cause a lot of problems."

"Then let it cause problems. That doesn't bother me. I'm going to obey God."

All Mike Washington knew was that he had found new life in Christ, and he had found it here, through Cottage Hill Baptist Church. Fred baptized him, along with the others, the next Sunday night. He came to every church meeting, sat on the front row, listened eagerly to the sermons, and joined the choir, where he sang with all his heart. Almost everyone accepted Mike with warmth, and in fact, the younger generations were proud of the fact that their church was forward-thinking and loving to everyone. Still, though, the holdouts were circling their wagons. Before long, Brother Fred received word that a group of people, mostly senior adults, wanted to meet with him. Fred agreed, and they set a date to meet in the chapel.

About 140 people came to the meeting, and it was, in fact, all about Mike Washington. They expressed their unease about having a black man attending Cottage Hill Baptist, much less becoming a member. In response, Fred referred them to the tenth chapter of Acts. "When Peter was on the rooftop," he said, "God lowered a sheet from heaven that carried all kinds of animals that were unclean to the Jewish people. But he told them to go ahead and eat them, and Peter said, 'No, Lord, I have never eaten anything common or unclean!' And the Lord said to him, 'What God hath cleansed, that call not thou common.' Now, I'm here to tell you that God has cleansed Mike Washington. And we are not going to call 'unclean' someone whom God has made clean."

A man stood and said, "Now, I'm not doubting that God has saved him, but those people have their own churches. That's where they need to go!"

Fred would not be intimidated. "Everybody is welcome who comes through the doors of Cottage Hill Baptist Church," he said, "and they will be, as long as I'm the pastor. Jesus is the Lord and the Head of the Church, and He is Lord and Head of *this* church, and if we fail to accept everybody, then we grieve the Holy Spirit, and the word 'Ichabod'-- the glory has departed-- will be written over the doors. Now, we are not going to compromise on this. Every church comes to a point where they are tested. They either obey God and go on, or they disobey God and they keep meeting, but the presence of God has left. Those churches are everywhere. They are scattered all over our land, and we will not become one of them."

Fred was not alone in his assessment, and those who stood with him held the line. In the end, only about twenty people left the church, but the color barrier had been broken and the issue was settled. The doors would continue to swing open to anyone who wanted a relationship with Jesus and who wanted to find Him at Cottage Hill.

CHAPTER 6

THE TEAM COMES TOGETHER

Ed Keyes had only briefly met Fred Wolfe when Fred asked Ed if he would fill in at his church on a Sunday morning, when his own Minister of Music was going to be out of town. Ed was happy to do so, and they had a good service.

That being the extent of Fred Wolfe and Ed Keyes' acquaintance, Ed was more than just a little surprised when, one night in the early part of 1972, Ed answered the telephone to hear Fred Wolfe's voice on the other end. It had been at least six years since they had last spoken, and Ed was happily serving as Minister of Music at Trinity Baptist Church in Memphis, Tennessee, so he was not quite prepared for the offer that came down the line: "Hello, Ed, this is Fred Wolfe. I have just taken the pastorate at Cottage Hill Baptist Church in Mobile, Alabama, and I want you to come down and be my Minister of Music."

Though Fred was confident that this was God's direction, he knew that the people needed that same confidence. One week after the end of the James Robison Crusade, Fred announced in the "It's On My Heart" column for April 23rd that Cottage Hill would be holding revival services from May 7-12. Fred would be preaching each night, and the music would be led by Ed Keyes of Memphis, Tennessee, who would be singing and "leading a Great Choir."

The "New Life in Christ Revival" was a great success for Fred and for Cottage Hill in a number of ways. It gave Fred an opportunity to stretch a little bit beyond Sunday morning messages in sermon subjects and material, and to further demonstrate his heart to the people. It also introduced and endeared Ed Keyes to the people of Cottage Hill, who, when the week was over, found themselves wishing he could stay. Ed's warmth, soothing voice, and obvious love for the Lord had fit in well with what God was already doing at the church.

About a week later, Fred would write in his column that "Truly the words of the song, 'There's a sweet, sweet spirit in this place' expresses the atmosphere of our Worship Services. We praise God for what he is doing and give Him the glory and praise! This past Sunday night, we had the privilege of baptizing 23 who had put their faith and trust in Jesus Christ. Our Revival was a tremendous success. People came every night, confessing Christ as their Saviour and Lord, trusting and being obedient to Him. The attendance during our Revival was excellent. Praise the Lord for what He is doing."

Even though the new ministry at Cottage Hill was going well, Fred had not forgotten what the Lord had taught him at Woodlawn Baptist in Decatur. In March, Fred had floated the first balloon in an effort to gauge the congregations's willingness to adopt a bus ministry like the one that had so impacted Woodlawn. In his column, one of his goals for 1972 was that "Within this year (1972), our Church becomes involved in a ministry of Bus Evangelism. We must reach out into the community for unchurched children to bring them to Sunday School and Children's Worship Services. In turn, through these children, we must reach their parents. I would like to see our Church begin running three buses, providing this ministry within the next six to eight months."[2]

Anticipating the success of his campaign for a Bus Ministry, Fred also recommended calling and hiring Len Turner as the Associate Pastor, with special emphases on Outreach, Evangelism, and Bus Ministry. Len was another graduate of Southwestern Seminary in Fort Worth, and was serving as the pastor of Greenwood Baptist Church in Weatherford, Texas at the time of his seminary graduation in May of 1972. Even though he was only 25 years old, he had already held over 75 revivals throughout the Southern Baptist Convention, and had a reputation for invoking a favorable response to the gospel among young people. Fred had hosted Len while he was pastoring Woodlawn, and was impressed with the young man's gifts and personality. What's more, while Len was serving as Pastor in Weatherford, he had bought a bus and was successfully running a full time bus ministry there. To Fred, this combination made Len the perfect catch for Cottage Hill. On May 17, just days before his graduation, Cottage Hill voted to call Len for the Associate Pastor position. Eleven days later, The Cottage Hill Baptist announced that he had accepted the call. His total compensation package would be $10,500 per year, plus Social Security taxes.

By the end of that same week, the newsletter announced another new arrival. Ed Keyes had accepted the call to serve as Minister of Music, and would begin his new ministry on July 1st. In his June 4th column, Fred wrote, "My heart rejoices over the two wonderful staff members the Lord has sent to us. Len Turner will begin his duties on June 15, and Ed Keyes will begin July 1. They will be great assets to our Church. Their families will be a blessing to us!"

The Cottage Hill Baptist officially became *The Challenge* on July 21, and Fred continued to express his optimism about the life of the church: "God continues to pour out His blessings on our Church. I rejoice in the wonderful Spirit and unity that are throughout our Fellowship. Great things are happening and are going to happen. A real spirit of cooperation is among our people. As we get ready to launch our Children Worship Services August 14 and our Bus Ministry September 10, already workers are volunteering and things are falling in place." Len Turner and Ed Keyes joined Brother Fred in the first issue of *The Challenge* with their own glowing reports about the music and outreach ministries.

On Wednesday, July 26, 1972, Fred called the church into special conference regarding the Bus Ministry. At that meeting, Fred lined out in detail how the ministry would work. The church would begin looking to buy three used buses, model years 1964-66, for approximately $1,500 each. Each bus would be staffed by four people: a driver, a bus captain, and two teenagers, who would play games, sing, and work with the children to help them have fun in this new environment. The recommendation was brought to officially put the Bus Ministry underway. It passed with no questions or comments.

Len Turner and Fred Wolfe had a special bond. When Fred had invited Len to preach a youth retreat at Monaghan in 1969, they had stayed up all night long talking. It was clear from that night forward that Fred was not just some random stranger in Len's life, but that he would have a significant role in Len's life and ministry.

One day, not long after arriving in Mobile, Fred invited Len, or "Lenwood," as Fred liked to call him, to go with him to a Lion's Club meeting at which Fred had been invited to speak. Len was quick to agree, wanting to make the most of every minute with his new mentor.

As the emcee introduced their guest speaker for that day's luncheon, he told the audience that they were privileged to have with them Dr. Fred Wolfe and Dr. Len Turner. Len was fresh out of seminary, the ink on his Master's degree diploma still drying, and he was visibly taken back by the mistake. He certainly didn't want to pretend that he was something he wasn't, and knowing that neither he nor Fred had doctoral degrees, he felt confident that when Fred stood to speak, he would gently correct the man and straighten it out.

Fred never mentioned it. He spoke well and faithfully to the Lions Club, but he ignored the flub. Len was bothered by the whole thing, and when it was over, on the way to their car, he asked Fred about it. "Preacher," he said, "why didn't you correct that man in there? Why didn't you tell them that we aren't doctors?"

"Well, Lenwood," said Fred, "we ought to be, so let's just let them think that we already are."

As the summer ended and fall came in, Fred and his new staff settled into their roles and relationships. In 1972, church attendance and participation was still something to be admired and expected in America, so the consistent calls for increased faithfulness in attendance and giving were not out of place for the people of Cottage Hill. It was not unusual for whole families to arrange their week around whatever may be going on at the church. Consequently, Brother Fred's excitement about the church's future seemed to reflect everyone's sense that God was doing something good among them.

In his October 6 column, at the end of the reporting year, which ran from October through September, Fred presented the people with a look at the State of the Church. In it, he reported that total church membership was at 3,254, with 146 baptisms, which was a one-year record for Cottage Hill. "What about the Future?" he wrote. "Well, here are some words to describe the State of our Church:

1. Growing- In every area.

2. Growing Pains- Rooms are crowded--Teachers are needed--Praise the Lord for growing pains.

3. United- Praise the Lord for the unity of purpose, the oneness of Spirit in our Church.

4. Praising- Praising the Lord-- not man or men, not Staff-- for what God is doing.

5. Expecting- We all come every Sunday expecting God to work and speak in a mighty way. A spirit of expectancy pervades our services.

6. Singing- Praise the Lord for a singing Church, great Choirs, great Music.

7. Anchored- The Bible is our authority and guide. We test everything we say or do in the light of what the Bible says. Ministering to the space age but anchored in the Bible."

As Brother Fred's first year neared its end, Cottage Hill was gaining momentum and Fred was enjoying the most significant time of leadership in his life to date. In his column of November 10, 1972, Fred exclaimed, "Wow! Wow! Praise the Lord. That's the only way I know to describe last Sunday-- 1300 in Sunday School, 15 new members, 11 of these for baptism, and the largest weekly Budget Offering in the history of our Church- $9,571.80. That's tremendous."

Tremendous things were happening, and Fred was grateful. But with tremendous success came tremendous pressure. And 34-year-old Fred Wolfe had no idea what that would look like in the years to come.

CHAPTER 7

FAMILY MATTERS

Fred Wolfe was well aware of what he now had on his hands. Cottage Hill Baptist Church had already been well known in Alabama, but it was rising quickly in the Southern Baptist Convention as a church on the move. Fred had gone from pastoring a church of 600 or so in a town of 20,000 to pastoring 1500 people-- adding more each week-- in a city of 400,000, and gaining notoriety among all 13 million Southern Baptists.

As the church grew and the name Fred Wolfe was spoken more and more around the Convention, Fred began receiving offers to speak at other churches, conferences, and meetings. He gladly accepted most of those invitations, while being careful not to spend too much time away from his home church. But, he had a strong preacher in Len Turner, and no shortage of willing men who would be happy to preach from Cottage Hill's rock pulpit if Fred needed to be gone. Soon, due to Fred's popularity among the congregation, the pattern developed of the members being much less likely to show up for a service if they knew ahead of time that Fred wasn't going to preach. Eventually, the church wasn't always given advance notice that Fred would be gone on any given weekend.

Beginning in 1970, the Southern Baptist Convention entered a period of great conflict that came to be called the "Conservative Resurgence." Its detractors referred to it as the "Fundamentalist Takeover," but those on both sides knew it as the "Battle for the Convention." In short order, Fred Wolfe became a favorite spokesman for the conservative camp, championing the inerrancy of Scripture. Fred still felt the sting of his earlier exposure to liberal theology, and he was glad to be called on to defend the integrity of the Bible. The battle raged throughout the 1970s, culminating in the 1979 Houston Convention meeting, where Dr. Adrian Rogers, from Bellevue Baptist in Memphis, was elected President, and most Southern Baptist agency leaders were replaced with representatives who held to the inerrancy view.

During those years, with the future of his denominational home at stake, and the church growing in his own front yard, Fred's time was not his own. Typically, he would find that from right before church on Sunday morning, to the time Prayer Meeting was over on Wednesday night, he had already worked 60 or 70 hours. And the week was only half over.

This level of responsibility was new to Fred, and there was no one he could think of who had gone before him and could help him bring balance to his schedule. He was studying and delivering three different full-length sermons every week, and eventually leading three Sunday morning services every weekend. The staff was growing with the church, so more staff meetings were necessary, both at an executive level as well as leading the support staff, which included secretaries and assistants. And, as more and more people named Cottage Hill their home church, and Fred Wolfe their new pastor, it meant more people coming to him for help. By the time the Wednesday night service was over, Fred had conducted about fifteen different counseling sessions. And then he would do two more when Prayer Meeting ended. Each one of those sessions would run just under an hour. On top of that, he would normally take between 50 and 75 calls from Monday morning through Wednesday night.

It began to be frustrating to Fred as he realized that some of those who were coming to him didn't really want his help. He began to notice them coming back, again and again, with the same problems. He was giving them the best, most prayerful, most Scriptural advice he could, yet they never moved into any kind of victory. It was years before he realized that some of those people just wanted his attention. The counselor down the street might charge them $100 for a session, but since he was their pastor, he was free. After two or three visits, it dawned on him that he was just giving them the attention they craved. And yet, how could he turn them away?

The pressures that landed on Fred of pastoring a fast-growing megachurch and the responsibilities he felt to his denomination began to take its toll. When Anne was younger, she handled the place of dutiful pastor's wife pretty well. After the postpartum depression, she was more fragile than before, but now, with Fred away from home almost every minute of the day, her ability and willingness to shoulder the load at home was crumbling.

To complicate it even more, the ethics of the situation were murky, at best. Fred found himself feeling as married to the church as he was to Anne. After all, wasn't this work, this calling, of eternal importance? If God was opening doors and issuing invitations, who was he to refuse the opportunity? How could he draw a line between hours off and hours on? When people needed help, they needed it right then. How do you turn them away?

The phone rang, and Fred answered. Sure, there were other staff members, but no one else would do. Fred found that for too many people, no matter how many friends and other staff have loved them in their moment of crisis, until the pastor comes to see them, they haven't been seen.

And so the church thrived. And Fred's wife and sons practically lived without him. Anne would protest, sometimes verbally, sometimes passively, but it was always a losing battle. Not because of any hard-heartedness on Fred's part, but if all of this is God's doing, if He is demanding this, how do you argue with Him? How do you fight for your family if you are fighting against God?

Fred did what he could to protect his family from the pressure. As Cottage Hill continued to grow and the services began to be broadcast across the region on a weekly television program, Fred knew that it couldn't be easy to be growing up in Mobile as the son of Fred Wolfe. Mark and Jeff were just teenagers, and Fred tried to make sure that they had some chance to live a normal teenage life. If that included them trying to establish their own identities, so be it, even if they did so inappropriately at times.

Mark and Jeff saw at home, the same Fred Wolfe that everyone else saw at church. There was no discrepancy between the two, and his sons knew that he was always going to be genuine, especially with them. Years later, Mark would say that his father was always humble and not judgemental toward his sons, and though Fred made the same mistakes that every other parent makes, he was always quick to own up to them and ask his sons for forgiveness. It was this atmoshpere of honesty, confession, and forgiveness that would allow the whole family to heal in the years to come.

As for Anne and her involvement in the life of the church, Fred made it very clear when he began as pastor, that Cottage Hill Baptist Church was not getting a two-for-one deal. They were paying him, not her.

Fred also made sure that Anne knew this and helped her not to feel any internal pressure to perform. "You are not the assistant pastor," he said. "You are my wife, and the greatest thing that you can do for this church is to love me and for us to build a strong marriage. You do, in the church, whatever you feel comfortable doing. Do not feel any pressure to do anything. Just operate in the gifts God has given you in whatever way you want."

The people of Cottage Hill were gracious to Anne. They were aware of her battles with depression, made worse by two painful and debilitating neck surgeries, and they allowed her the room that she needed, however she needed it. There was really only one incident where someone crossed that boundary with Anne. She had taken a position teaching a Sunday School class of five year olds, and she loved it. She laughed with them and played with them. She saw them grow in their understanding of who Jesus is, and watched their love for Him flourish through the lessons, songs, and activities. And in turn, they gave her something to look forward to every Sunday. They made her happy.

One day, one of the men of the church approached her and decided that he knew better where she ought to be. "When are you gonna stop teaching them five year olds?" he demanded. "When are you gonna start teaching those adult women like you're supposed to?"

Anne was crushed. Deeply wounded by his words, she wondered if she really was in the wrong place. Was she really not doing what she was "supposed" to do?

Fred could not let this stand. He knew that if he rebuked that man, that it would seem heavy-handed and unloving, but it was a risk he was willing to take. However, he had two men who had already told Fred that if he needed something like this handled, to let them handle it. "Don't fight your own battles," they told him, "let us do it." One of those trusted men was Bill Rubley. Fred reported the confrontation, and Bill Rubley took the matter in hand. He went to the offender. "Listen," he said, "let me tell you something. Don't you ever say anything again to Brother Fred's wife. Don't you do it."

Fred never had to say a word to him, but neither that man nor anyone else spoke like that to Anne again.

The constant imbalance between pastoring a growing church, trying to be a husband and father, and answering the call to fight a righteous battle for the soul of a denomination began to spin out of control like a demented merry-go-round. One of the ways that Fred escaped from the pressures of church and family was to take more outside engagements. Especially in those days of fighting for the convention, it was nothing for Fred to be gone five to seven days each month. Arriving back in Mobile, Fred would realize that being gone only meant that there was much to catch up on. The pressures of pastoring never stopped, and they were all waiting for him to get back into town.

Riding the coattails of all of those invitations, was the inevitable ego building that came with them. Who wouldn't feel important when being invited to be the keynote preacher for the Southern Baptist Pastor's Conference in Tennessee, or to address the entire state of South Carolina-- their own home state-- at the Evangelism Conference? Fred found himself a favorite in the lineup of speakers at conferences held by Bailey Smith, the powerful evangelist and influential pastor of First Baptist Church, Del City, Oklahoma. Fred was a featured preacher at approximately twenty Bailey Smith conferences across the country.

Soon, Fred also found himself as the Chairman of the Executive Committee of the Southern Baptist Convention, the most powerful committee in the denomination, and arguably the most powerful group of men in American evangelicalism. He served in that capacity for two years, which also required him to be in Nashville, Tennessee for those meetings, for days at a time, at least three times a year, sometimes more. But, eventually, as the years moved by, the ego and the urgency of all of those invitations wore thin. Fred got tired. It occurred to him that he was sacrificing the things that would ultimately be the most important. And he knew that if he didn't rein it all in, the price he would pay might be far higher than he had ever bargained for.

For the first twelve years of his pastorate at Cottage Hill, Fred Wolfe's weekly schedule was out of control. Eventually, though, he came to realize that as a pastor, if you don't set your schedule and let people know what it is, then fleshly, needy people will set it for you. Fred was tired of his family only getting the leftovers of his time, so he set a new schedule and made sure that everyone knew it.

"As your pastor," he said, "please know that I am always available to you in an emergency. But you should also know that I am going to determine if it's an emergency. Having said that, here is my schedule: from Sunday through Wednesday, I am available for preaching, meetings, and limited counseling. On Thursday morning, I am studying. Thursday afternoon, I will do something for myself, maybe play some golf. Friday morning, I am studying again. But come Friday at noon, and all day Saturday, my time belongs completely to my wife. We will do whatever she wants to do. If I perform your wedding on Saturday, understand that I won't be at rehearsal on Friday night. That is Anne's time, and hers alone.

"If you come to me for counseling, I will be happy to see you. But after our meeting, I will probably give you a book that I think will greatly help you. If you want to see me again, you'll read the book. If you don't read the book, I will know that you are not serious about receiving help and being healed."

At the beginning of 1973, though, these lessons were still yet to be learned. And, even as the whirlwind of the coming years was just about to begin, God would show Himself faithful in the life of Cottage Hill, taking the church deeper and further than they had ever dared to imagine before.

CHAPTER 8

ACCELERATION

In the first week of January, 1973, while the schools were still on Christmas Break, Len Turner led a youth and college retreat at Citronelle Baptist Assembly. Somewhere between 200 and 300 youth were there, and it proved to be a powerful event. All through the week, young men and women were getting saved and getting right with God. One of the young men who was changed by God at that retreat was Wayne Dorsett.

Wayne was only a year out of high school, with no real direction. He was attending classes at Mobile College, but everyone could tell that Wayne was restless and aimless. He was not a bad young man, but he was also usually involved when mischief was afoot. Wayne had grown up at Cottage Hill, but until now, he had never quite been captured by the gospel.

Fred had been preaching on the Lordship of Jesus Christ since he had arrived at Cottage Hill, but on Wednesday, January 3rd, there in a small chapel heavy with the scent of varnished pine and old pews, Wayne Dorsett understood. His heart broke with conviction, and he wept as he gave his heart to Jesus for good. Wayne went forward at the altar call that night, and Fred, who was there at the retreat to get to know the kids better, prayed with him. It was a sweet and precious time.

Wayne returned to his seat and had great peace for about five minutes. Soon, he had a realization that God was also calling him to preach. He went forward again and took Fred's hand.

"Pastor," he said, "I think God is calling me to preach."

Fred had now been at Cottage Hill for almost a year, which was plenty of time to become familiar with the attitude and antics of Wayne Dorsett. Even though he was understandably a bit skeptical, he did not dissuade Wayne from this sense of a call, and he didn't put him off.

"Well," said Fred, "here's what I want you to do. I want you to pray about this for the rest of the week, and let's see what God says."

Wayne did just that, and as the week went on, his certainty grew. On Sunday night, January 7, Cottage Hill took the whole evening service to hear testimonies and reports from the youth who had been to Citronelle. And, once again, during the invitation at the end of the service, Wayne walked the aisle and told Fred that he still felt called to the ministry. "Alright, then," said Fred, "we need to tell the church."

When the music ended, Fred called Wayne up and said to the congregation, "Wayne Dorsett has come, and he has something he wants to tell you." Wayne, a bit surprised by this sudden spotlight, adapted and adjusted, and he succeeded in giving testimony of his call to the ministry. After the service, all the people that had known Wayne came up to him, hugged him, and encouraged him. And from that moment on, Fred Wolfe stood ready to encourage and equip anyone who wanted to preach.

On January 28, 1973, Fred's vision for staff hires neared its realization as Dr. Bob Rowell and his family visited Cottage

Hill. Another South Carolina native, Fred and Bob had met at Southwestern and become fast friends. As with Ed, Fred determined then that as soon as he got the chance, he was going to hire Bob Rowell as his Minister of Education. After the visit the Deacons and Personnel Committee recommended him to the congregation. He accepted the call.

So, one year after his arrival, Fred's prediction to Anne about whom he would have with him had been accomplished. His dream team was in place. In his column of February 23, he said: "This Sunday I begin my second year as your Pastor. Without question, this past year was the greatest in my life. God blessed me and my family in a wonderful way. Thank you for your love, prayers, encouragement, and support. It is a joy and privilege to be your pastor, and I thank God for leading me to serve with you. I am praying God will give me many years of service with you as Pastor... As we face another year, may we move ahead. Much needs to be done, so we cannot be satisfied. We must grow spiritually and win many to Christ in 1973."

Fred was feeling well enough established, now that his first year had passed successfully, to bring in another life-changing element from his days at Woodlawn. From March 18th through the 23rd, Miss Bertha Smith came to Cottage Hill and led the Christian Life Conference. Fred had been powerfully impacted by her life and ministry, and he was eager for this new and promising church to reap the same benefits. Fred knew her message well, and even though he had been preaching the Lordship of Christ, it was time for them to hear directly from Miss Bertha how to be filled with the Spirit. He was well aware that the message of the Spirit-filled life wasn't really being preached in the Southern Baptist Convention, but it was time to take the Holy Spirit out of the closet and invite

Him to be Himself at Cottage Hill.

Miss Bertha was just as powerful at Cottage Hill as she had been at Woodlawn. It was as if she hadn't aged a day, and she certainly hadn't slowed down or backed off. A little old lady with a flannelgraph was transformed by the presence of God into a little bundle of fire, holiness, and prayer before the hundreds of people who came to listen. Just as before, she encouraged the people to make their sin list, confess their sin, then burn the list, thanking God that they had been cleansed, then ask to be filled with the Holy Spirit. And, as before, many people were radically changed as they opened up to the indwelling Spirit of God for the first time.

During the week of the conference, Len Turner wrote in his column about how God had used her in his life. "I praise the Lord," he said, "for the way He is using Bertha Smith. One of the greatest highlights of my life has been to kneel and pray with her. Because of the way the Lord has used her in our Church this week, he is going to do great things in the upcoming days in our Fellowship."

After Bertha Smith's visit, the words "Spirit-filled" became part of the everyday vocabulary of Cottage Hill Baptist Church.

On Easter Sunday, April 22, 1973, Cottage Hill saw its highest attendance to date, with 1,739 in Sunday School and 2,300 in worship services. A fourth and fifth bus were added to the Bus Ministry, and Hayes Wicker was called as Youth Minister for the upcoming summer.

The Jesus Movement was in full force, and it had steadily and powerfully made its way east to Mobile since arriving on the Southern California coast three years earlier. On June 21, 1971, *Time* magazine had featured the "Jesus Revolution" as their cover story, in an article titled: "The New Rebel Cry: Jesus Is Coming!" In it, the writer seeks to describe what was making this movement, this revival, different from what was happening with the same demographic—hippies—who were not connecting to Jesus: "There is an uncommon morning freshness to this movement, a buoyant atmosphere of hope and love along with the usual rebel zeal. Some converts seem to enjoy translating their new faith into everyday life, like those who answer the phone with 'Jesus loves you' instead of 'hello.' But their love seems more sincere than a slogan, deeper than the fast-fading sentiments of the flower children; what startles the outsider is the extraordinary sense of joy that they are able to communicate."[2]

Hayes Wicker stepped into the serendipity of Cottage Hill's momentum at a pivotal moment, and capitalized on this youth revival that was changing a generation. This worked well in conjunction with Fred's vision and direction. Fred, himself, was only 35 years old, and Ed Keyes was only 30. Neither of them was far removed from the teenagers and young adults that were filling Cottage Hill's buildings, youth camps, and retreats.

Hayes saw it as his duty to effectively bridge what little gap there was between the staff and the youth group. So, he communicated the heart of the staff in the words of the next generation. For instance, in his column in *The Challenge*, "Talking Straight" for June 24, he wrote: "Listen to what some have to say about Youth Camp:

Robin Hood: 'It's a steal!'

The Three Blind Mice: 'It's outta sight'

Sleeping Beauty: 'It's a real sleeper'

Fred Wolfe: 'Can I make a statement... That baby's right.'"

"Super Summer '73" saw more increase for the people of Cottage Hill Baptist Church. Even during a season that for most churches is a slowdown, they averaged over 1,200 in Sunday School and over ten new members to the church weekly. The Bus Ministry was also breaking records. The summer season saw the first anniversary of the arrival of Len Turner and Ed Keyes, as well as the birth of Len's son, Kevin Blake. He joined his sister, Stacy, in the Turner home, and the Cottage Hill family grew by one more.

In August of 1973, Fred Wolfe began to make use of his platform and his influence to speak into culture. His first foray into that arena in Mobile seemed to be a viable threat to the youth revival that had captured the attention of the nation, so on August 31, Fred's article was a response to the Andrew Lloyd-Weber musical, *Jesus Christ, Superstar*. "I am no judge on the quality of the music in the opera, *Jesus Christ, Superstar*," he wrote, "but it is very clear that the Jesus of *Jesus Christ, Superstar*, is not the Jesus of the Bible at all." He went on to list seven aspects of the musical that he found Biblically inaccurate, with number seven being, "The final insult is that it leaves Jesus a corpse-- dead!

"I conclude, therefore, that the Jesus of *Jesus Christ, Superstar*, is not the Jesus of the Bible, but is a man-made, plastic Christ who cannot save and who cannot give abundant Life. I predict that after the American people have made the producers rich, they will look back and realize that *Jesus Christ, Superstar* was Jesus Christ, Superhoax!

"I would say to all to beware and search the Scriptures for themselves."

The 1973 church year closed with 399 professions of faith and 808 new members. Cottage Hill led the Alabama Baptist Convention with 346 baptisms. That year also saw the first salvo of young men being called into full-time ministry from under Fred's leadership, including Jerry Sutton, Terry Bryant, and Wayne Dorsett. Hayes Wicker reflected fondly over his experience with Fred and the people of Cottage Hill. "This is the last article from your 'Talking Straight' Summer Youth Director," he wrote. "I want to thank God for His blessings, and I also want to thank everyone at Cottage Hill for the best Summer I've ever had. It is I, not you, who has received the most from our time together."

As 1974 began, Fred and his staff began to find their rhythm. Attendance continued to rise, new members were added practically every week, baptisms increased, and an overall spirit of excitement and expectancy pervaded the congregation.

In March, Fred continued the practice of bringing in speakers who had something important to share with his people. For the Revival services scheduled April 14th through the 21st, Dr. Vance Havner arrived to preach. Fred had recommended him as "truly one of God's great servants in our generation," and the people loved him immediately.

Born in 1901 in Jugtown, North Carolina, Vance Havner was already 72 years old when he came to Cottage Hill. He was one of the most beloved, most often quoted preachers of the 20th century. Known for his humor and his pithy but pointed one-liners, when he arrived at Cottage Hill he was still grieving the loss of his beloved wife, Sara, a few months earlier. Dr. Havner hadn't married until he was 39, and now the death of his wife had been a blow. Shortly after, he wrote what some consider to be the best of his thirty-eight books, *Though I Walk Through the Valley.*

Describing him later, Fred said, "You would look at him, small, short, thin and think, 'Who in the world is this?' But he had a unique walk with God and was a powerful spiritual man. His way of presenting the gospel was so different from other men. He had a blend of humor and truth, you'd be laughing, but God would be cutting you to the heart. People were drawn to the anointing on him.

"He had a way of exposing the shallow religiousness of the day. In 1953, The Southern Baptist Convention's motto was 'A million more in '54.' To which Vance Havner said, 'Well, if we get a million more like we already got, we're sunk.'

"Vance Havner preached a Deeper Life message. He called people to surrender. He was a man of great courage. He preached for me at Woodlawn in Decatur, preached on the Lordship of Christ and said, 'Are you ready to confess Jesus as Lord? If so, just stand one at a time and confess, "Jesus Christ is my Lord." One guy stood up and started talking about something else, going off in another direction. Vance told him to sit down and be quiet. He was gentle and bold at the same time.

"Part of Dr. Havner's message to the church was that Christianity as we're seeing it is not what it ought to be, we have to go on with God. He had a unique way of presenting the gospel with humor that if any of the rest of us preachers tried to do it, we'd fall flat on our faces. You can use his truths, but you can't preach his sermons. I remember he said, 'My daddy would say to me, "Son, do your best to get home before dark." My goal in my walk with Jesus is, I want to get home before any darkness touches my life.'" After Dr. Havner's wife died in 1973, the consensus among his friends was that he almost grieved himself to death. Fred remembered, "People would say, 'Vance, what are you doing since your wife died?' And he would say, 'I'm just walking a little faster. And I'll get there a little quicker.'"

April of 1974 also saw the arrival of an energetic young Youth Minister as Malcolm Stuart signed on to the Cottage Hill staff. Having grown up in Hawaii, he was an instant favorite among the youth of the church, and that status was cemented the first time he wore his famous banana-yellow leisure suit on a Sunday morning.

Malcolm soaked in everything he could in his time with Fred and Ed and the rest of the staff. Everything he was hearing about the Lordship of Christ and being filled with the Spirit was intriguing and exciting, so he hungered for more. On one particular trip with the staff to the Alabama Evangelism Conference, Malcolm found himself under a heavy sense of the Holy Spirit, and he knew that he needed to do business with God. At the altar call, Malcolm took his burden to the altar and knelt, weeping. As he poured out his heart before the Lord, he sensed someone kneel down next to him and put his arm around his shoulders. He glanced over to see Brother Fred, head bowed, not speaking, just being there. Malcolm would remember that moment for the rest of his life. The quiet power of a spiritual father's presence and support taught him more in a few seconds about real leadership than he would ever learn from a classroom or a book.

The programs of Cottage Hill Baptist Church reached into every avenue of family life, and 1974 sped by like a freight train. Easter Sunday saw the largest attendance in the history of the church, and new Youth Minister Malcolm Stuart connected with the youth group easily and quickly. The summer was a time of camps, retreats, conferences, and more buses added to the Bus Ministry.

On Sunday morning, November 3, 1974, Fred Wolfe preached what became one of his most well known and most talked about sermons for years, called "Christianity Cafeteria Style." In the message, Fred proclaimed with passion that neither God nor His Word can be approached with an "I'll take this but I don't want that" attitude. Again, his life's message was preached from the Cottage Hill pulpit: Jesus Christ is Lord of all, or He is not Lord at all.

In his column in *The Challenge* for the next week, Fred made it clear that he was well aware of how important that message had been. "Heaven came down and glory filled my soul!" he wrote. "What a day, this past Sunday. Never before have I experienced such an outpouring of God's Spirit at CHBC. Tear-filled eyes, broken hearts, confession of sin, and surrender to Jesus as Lord. The invitation went on for some 40 minutes as scores of people made things right with God. To God be the glory for the great things He hath done. Our Church will never be the same after Sunday."

From that moment on, it seemed that Cottage Hill was in a state of revival that lasted for years. Each Sunday, each month, barreled into the next, every one of them seemingly more successful and more expansive than the one before. The people kept coming, Fred kept preaching, the choirs kept singing. And God kept moving among them.

a Sermon

❈

The Holy Spirit in Today's World

THE HOLY SPIRIT IN TODAY'S WORLD

by
Fred Wolfe

Jesus had much to say about the Holy Spirit. In John 14:15-17, Jesus said, "If ye love me, keep my commandments. And I will pray the Father, and he shall give you another Comforter, that he may abide with you forever; Even the Spirit of truth whom the world cannot receive, because it seeth him not, neither knoweth him: but ye know him, for he dwelleth with you, and shall be in you."

The difference between the Old Testament saint and the New Testament Christian is: In the Old Testament the Holy Spirit dwelt with people, but at Pentecost the Holy Spirit came to live in people. Jesus said in verse 17, "He dwelleth with you, and shall be in you." Jesus spoke further about the Holy Spirit in John 14:26, "But the Comforter, which is the Holy Ghost, whom the Father will send in my name, he shall teach you all things, and bring all things to your remembrance, whatsoever I have said unto you."

Jesus spoke again of the Holy Spirit in John 15:26, "But when the Comforter is come, whom I will send unto you from the Father, even the Spirit of truth, which proceedeth from the Father, he shall testify of me." Then in John 16:7-8, Jesus talked of the Holy Spirit,

"Nevertheless I tell you the truth; It is expedient for you that I go away: for if I go not away, the Comforter will not come unto you; but if I depart, I will send him unto you. And when he is come, he will reprove the world of sin, and of righteousness, and of judgment." In John 16:14, Jesus testified of the Holy Spirit,

"He shall glorify me: for he shall receive of mine, and shall shew it unto you."

Dr. Stephen Olford made a statement that genuinely startled me when I heard it. But I am convinced it is true. Dr. Olford said, "If the sin of the Old Testament was a rejection of God the Father, and the sin of the New Testament age is a rejection of God the Son, the sin of our day is the rejection of God the Holy Spirit." This is tragic. I believe that the normal Christian life is one lived under Christ's control and in the fullness of the Holy Spirit. Vance Havner commented, "We have been abnormal so long that, when a person becomes normal, we think that they are abnormal." I think he is correct.

I have been a Southern Baptist all of my life. It is the only church I have ever been a part of. I believe exactly the way Southern Baptists believe about the Holy Spirit. I don't believe it just because Southern Baptists believe it, but because I believe it is true to the New Testament. What about Southern Baptists and the Holy Spirit? I believe, to some degree, the person and work of the Holy Spirit has been neglected in Southern Baptist churches. Let me tell you why I believe this is true.

In 1900, the Pentecostal movement first swept across America. There were about three facts associated with the Pentecostal movement. It put a great deal of emphasis on the Holy Spirit, speaking with "unknown" tongues, and an excess of emotionalism. Southern Baptists looked at the Pentecostal movement and saw this emphasis on the Holy Spirit. They beheld this unscriptural emphasis on speaking in tongues, and the excess of emotionalism, and it greatly influenced us. Subconsciously, we felt "If emphasis on the person and work of the Holy Spirit produces this excess emotionalism and overemphasis on unknown tongues, this is not for us." Sadly, we began to shy away from preaching and teaching and emphasizing the ministry of the Holy Spirit. I believe with all my heart Southern Baptists have the truth about the person and work of the Holy Spirit. In these next pages we will examine these wonderful truths about the Holy Spirit and power for service.

First, what about the Holy Spirit and Jesus? One of the most exciting truths in the New Testament is the relationship of the Holy Spirit to Jesus. In John 15:26, we read, "But when the Comforter is come, whom I will send unto you from the Father, even the Spirit of truth, which proceedeth from the Father, he shall testify of me." The Holy Spirit testifies to the reality of Jesus. In John16:14, Jesus says, speaking of the Holy Spirit, "He shall glorify me: for he shall receive of mine, and shall shew it unto you." One of the exciting things about the ministry of the Holy Spirit in our lives and in our churches is that, when the Holy Spirit is in control of a life and a church, we preach about Jesus, sing about Jesus, talk about Jesus— we exalt the Son of God. When the Holy Spirit takes control of a life or a church, they do not spend all of their time talking about the Holy Spirit. If all a church talks about is the Holy Spirit, something is wrong, for the Holy Spirit came to glorify Jesus and to testify to his reality.

What about the Holy Spirit and the unsaved person? We need to see what the Bible says about that subject. Jesus says in John 16:8, "And when he is come, he will reprove the world of sin, and of righteousness, and of judgment." No person is ever saved apart from the work of the Holy Spirit. We must live in the fullness of the Spirit, and the Holy Spirit must be free to work in our churches, because no one is ever saved apart from the work of the Holy Spirit. The Holy Spirit convicts a sinner of his sin. The Holy Spirit draws the sinner to Christ. The Holy Spirit removes the spiritual blindness from the sinner's eyes. The Holy Spirit brings the sinner to the place where he can receive Jesus Christ. However, he doesn't even arrive there unless he is ushered there by the Holy Spirit.

What about the Holy Spirit and the Christian? There are five transactions which happen between a person and the Holy Spirit the moment that person is saved. These occur in the heart of a person when they are born again through faith in the Lord Jesus Christ. What are these five things? The Bible says we are born of the Spirit. What did Jesus say to Nicodemus? "Nicodemus, ye must be born again." Nicodemus said, "How can I be born again? Can I enter a second time into my mother's womb and be born?" Jesus said, "That which is born of the flesh is flesh, and that which is born of the Spirit is spirit. Marvel not, Nicodemus, that ye must be born again." You see, the miracle of the new birth is worked in one's life by the person of the Holy Spirit. We are born of the Spirit. In simple faith we trust in Jesus as our Savior and Lord, and the Holy Spirit works the miracle of new birth in our lives.

Also, we are baptized by the Spirit into the body of Christ the moment we are saved. At the instant of a new birth you are spiritually baptized by the Holy Spirit into the body of Christ. First Corinthians 12:13 says, "For by one Spirit are we all baptized into one body." The Holy Spirit takes us and immerses us spiritually into the body of Christ. The Bible teaches that at salvation we are indwelt by the Holy Spirit. The Bible says in 1 Corinthians 6:19-20, "What? Know ye not that your body is the temple of the Holy Ghost which is in you, which ye have of God, and ye are not your own? For ye are bought with a price: therefore glorify God in your body, and in your spirit, which are God's." Our body is the temple of the Holy Spirit.

The Holy Spirit comes to live in us.

The Bible teaches that at conversion we are sealed by the Holy Spirit. Ephesians says, "Grieve not the Holy Spirit whereby you are sealed unto the day of redemption." It is by the Spirit of God that we are sealed in Christ.

Also, the Bible says of the believer that the Holy Spirit becomes the earnest of our inheritance until the redemption of the purchased possession. The Holy Spirit is God's down payment in our lives to guarantee that what God has promised us, God is going to fulfill. He is the earnest of our inheritance.

While all of this is true of the Christian and the Holy Spirit, God commands us in Ephesians 5:18 to be filled with the Spirit. "Be not drunk with wine, wherein is excess, but be filled with the Spirit." The normal Christian life is one lived in the fullness of the Holy Spirit. Ephesians 5:18 in the Greek language consists of two imperative commands. An imperative command is one that begins in the past and continues into the present. The first command is, "Be not drunk with wine." God commands us in the past and it continues into the present. "Don't be drunk with wine." The other command in this verse is, "be filled with the Spirit." That is an imperative command. The same God who commanded us not to be drunk with wine also commands us to be filled with the Holy Spirit! I didn't understand for a long time why God put that verse together as he did. Has it occurred to you, "What has being drunk with wine got to do with being filled with the Holy Spirit?" Think about that for a moment. Have you ever noticed how wine, when it takes control of a person, affects him. When a person is drunk with wine, it controls his mind, it controls his tongue. It also affects the way one thinks. The wine controls every part of a person who is drunk. What God was saying through Paul is, "I don't want your behavior to be controlled by wine, but I want your behavior to be controlled by the Holy Spirit. I want the Holy Spirit to control your mind, your eyes, your tongue, and all of your being. Do not be controlled by wine but be controlled by the Holy Spirit."

There are three reasons why every Christian ought to live in the fullness of the Holy Spirit. I know God commands it. That is reason enough alone, but there are three other reasons why you and I need to live in the fullness of the Spirit. First, we need to live in the fullness of the Holy Spirit because the Holy Spirit gives us the power to know. How do you receive the power to know the Word of God? This Bible is a spiritual book. All Scripture is given by inspiration of God. The Bible has God as its author. It is a spiritual book filled with spiritual truth. How can you know this book? Jesus tells us that the power to know the Word of God comes from the fullness of the Holy Spirit. In John 14:26 Jesus says, "But the Comforter, which is the Holy Ghost, whom the Father will send in my name, he shall teach you all things, and bring all things to your remembrance, whatsoever I have said unto you." In John 16:13, Jesus tells us again that the power to know the Word of God comes from being filled with the Spirit of God: "Howbeit, when he, the Spirit of truth, is come, he will guide you into all truth." The Bible is a spiritual book. We can only understand it, digest it, and make it a part of our lives as we are taught it by the blessed Holy Spirit of God. First Corinthians 2:14 states, "The natural man receiveth not the things of the Spirit of God: for they are foolishness unto him: neither can he know them because they are spiritually discerned." However, a Christian living in the fullness of the Holy Spirit has the power to know the Word of God. If the Bible is a closed book to you, and you never read it, you need to be filled with the Spirit of God. The Spirit of God makes the Word of God come alive in a Christian's life.

Second, we need to be filled daily with the Holy Spirit because the Holy Spirit gives us the power to be. Several years ago as a young pastor of the Eastview Baptist Church right outside of Rock Hill, South Carolina, I heard that Evangelist Hyman Appelman was preaching a revival in Lancaster, about twenty-seven miles from Rock Hill. I took one of our deacons and we drove over to hear Appelman preach. Hyman Appelman is a Russian Jew. However, he found Jesus as his personal Savior and was transformed by the power of Christ. God soon called him to preach the gospel. When his family heard he was a Christian, his mother and father disowned him, and his mother said to him, "Hyman, I would rather you be dead than be a Christian." And she said, "Hyman, I want you to know that when I die the family is not to let you know of my death. As far as I am concerned, Hyman, you are dead." It cost Hyman Appelman everything to know and to follow Jesus. It cost him his family.

As I heard Appelman preach that night, I will never forget the question he asked. "How many of you in this auditorium are not satisfied with the Christian life you are living?" That went straight to my heart. I knew I was not satisfied with the Christian life I was living. I didn't mind his asking that question, but do you know what he asked us to do? He said, "If you are not satisfied with the Christian life you are living, raise your hand." Well, it was one matter if I had been alone, but here I was the pastor of a church, and beside me was one of our laymen. What was I going to do? "If you are not satisfied with the Christian life you are living, raise your hand."

I was too proud to let that deacon see me raise my hand. I thought to myself, What am I going to do? Then I realized he was sitting on my right so I thought I will sneak up the left hand. That's exactly what I did. As I was sneaking up my hand, I looked at the pulpit and I saw something I cannot forget. There stood Hyman Appelman, this converted Jew who had left everything to follow Jesus. You know what? He had both hands raised all the way to heaven and he was weeping. Tears were running down his cheeks; he was weeping openly before God and men. He had both hands raised toward heaven and he said "I am not satisfied with my Christian life because I am supposed to be like Jesus." That pierced my heart.

The question is, How in the world can you be like Jesus? People say, "You need to be like Jesus." I agree, but it is not easy to be like Jesus. Jesus said, "Love your enemies." I even have trouble loving my neighbors. Jesus said, "If a man wants you to go one mile, go two." I don't even want to go a hundred yards. Yes, we need to be like Jesus, but how? How can you ever be like Jesus? You reply, "When I became a Christian, God took all those big sins out of my life."

I am glad, but do you ever have any trouble with the little sins? I have plenty of trouble with those little sins. For example, I have trouble with selfishness. Now, I am easy to live with when everything goes my way, but when it doesn't, I can really be selfish and upset. Sometimes I am just plain old irritable. Are you ever irritable? Was Jesus ever selfish? No. Do you think Jesus was ever irritable? No. It is the little sins in your life that keep you from being like Jesus. Selfishness, self-centeredness, self-will, self-pity, self-righteousness, irritability, harshness, unkindness, criticism, faultfinding. Jesus was never any of these, but we are often like that. We are not like Jesus. Really, there are no little sins.

I never will forget one day I was going to the hospital in Mobile, and we had a shut-in in our church by the name of John Stacy. He had rheumatoid arthritis. For fourteen years he had been bed ridden. His knees were locked, swollen. His wrists were twisted, and the bones were sticking out. He had not walked for fourteen years. He was a wonderful Christian man. I went by there and knocked on the door. Mrs. Stacy came to the door and said, "Brother Fred, I am glad you have come by. John is dying." I said, "Mrs. Stacy, I didn't know that." I was startled. I said, "Dying?" She said, "Yes, it is some kind of problem with his lungs. They are not even going to put him in the hospital. It is only a matter of time." I tried to comfort her. I went in that big high ceilinged room, pulled an old hard bottomed chair up beside John Stacy's bed, and began to talk with him. He said, "Brother Fred, I'm going to die." I attempted to comfort him. He replied, "Oh, I'm going to die. I know I'm going to die. Let me tell you what happened last night." John looked at me and said, "Over the morning God revealed himself to me. I heard singing like I have never heard before. The reality of Jesus, an awareness of his presence, gripped me. I wanted to go home to heaven."

He was crying as he told me; it really moved me. John had been so visited by God that night, he was wanting to go, and was ready to go, to heaven. Then John said to me, "The closer I get to heaven and the closer I get to Jesus, the bigger those little sins are in the sight of God." That convicted me.

How do you overcome those little sins. Where do you get the power to overcome the little sins in your life, the power to be like Jesus? I believe that I have discovered from the Word of God how to have the power to be like Jesus. Galatians 5:22 says, "The fruit of the Spirit is... "The fruit of the Holy Spirit. Galatians 5:22 names these fruit of the Spirit. The fruit of the Spirit is love. No one ever loved like Jesus. The fruit of the Spirit is joy. No one ever had joy like Jesus. The fruit of the Spirit is peace. Jesus was called the Prince of peace. He said, "My peace I give unto you, not as the world giveth, give I unto you." The fruit of the Spirit is long suffering. That word means bearing up under adverse circumstances. No one ever bore up like Jesus did. Another fruit of the Spirit is gentleness, and no one was ever as gentle as Jesus. Also goodness. No one was ever as good as Jesus. Also faithfulness. No one was ever as faithful as Jesus.

Another fruit of the Spirit is meekness which means selflessness. No one was ever as selfless as Jesus. And the word temperance means self-control. The fruit of the Spirit is the life of Jesus. When we live in the daily fullness of the Holy Spirit, the Holy Spirit produces his fruit, and the fruit of the Spirit is the life of Jesus Christ. The power to be like Jesus comes from being filled with the Holy Spirit. A person says, "I am filled with the Holy Spirit." Well, if he is, he will have the fruit of the Spirit which is the life of Christ. The Spirit will produce his fruit, and the fruit of the spirit is the life of Jesus Christ. The way to be like Jesus is to be filled with the Spirit of God. That is the normal Christian life.

Let me illustrate this—I walk into an apple orchard. As I enter this apple orchard, I notice an apple tree that is having a nervous breakdown. I mean, it is going to pieces, falling apart. It is wrinkling its leaves, twisting its limbs, chipping its bark, falling apart. I go over and put my arms around that apple tree and say, "My dear apple tree, what is your problem?" And the apple tree replies, "I am struggling, and I am striving, and I am going to have apples if it kills me." I say, "Wait a minute. Hold it. An apple tree doesn't have to struggle to have apples. The natural fruit of an apple tree is apples. Relax and just bear fruit."

You go into the average Baptist church and there he or she is. They love God. They love the church. They are faithful, but it is evident they are very tense and often frustrated. They are wound up like a rubber band. You can tell they are uptight, and you go over to that dear brother or sister and ask. "What is your problem?" They reply, "I am struggling, and I am striving, and I am going to be like Jesus if it kills me. I reply, "Wait a minute. You don't have to struggle or strive to be like Jesus. You just need to be filled daily with the Spirit of God. When the Spirit of God fills and controls your life, he will bear his fruit, and that is the life of Jesus. The power to be like Jesus comes from living in the fullness of the Holy Spirit every day. The fruit of the Spirit is the life of Jesus in the believer.

As we are filled with the Spirit, we have the power to *do*. The power to do God's work. Where do you get the power to pray? Ephesians 6:18, "Praying always with all prayer and supplication in the Spirit." The power to pray comes from being filled with the Holy Spirit. The Holy Spirit takes the prayer that is in the heart of God, and he puts it in your heart, and you send it back by way of the cross.

Where do you get the power to witness? Acts 1:8 says, "Ye shall receive power, after that the Holy Ghost is come upon you: and ye shall be witnesses unto me." The power to witness comes from living in the fullness of the Spirit.

Where do you get the power to preach? Paul said, "That my speech and my preaching shall not be with enticing words of man's wisdom but in the demonstration of the spirit and of power with godly sincerity and plainness of speech." The power to preach, to teach, comes from being filled with the Holy Spirit.

Where do you get the power to be a deacon? Acts 6:3 says, "Look ye out among you seven men of honest report, full of the Holy Spirit." The power to be a deacon comes from being filled with the Holy Spirit. Yes, the power to do God's work emanates from the fullness of the Holy Spirit.

How can you be filled with the Holy Spirit? There is a daily filling of the Holy Spirit. There is no once-and for-all filling of the Holy Spirit. It is a daily filling of the Spirit. How can you experience a daily filling of the Spirit? First of all, if you are going to be filled with the Holy Spirit, you have got to be empty. What have you got to be empty of? You have to be empty of your sins. It takes only one unconfessed sin to quench or grieve the Holy Spirit. You say, "That is not true." Yes, it is. If Holy God could have something to do with one sin, he could have something to do with all sin. But because God is holy, he can have nothing to do with sin. One unconfessed sin grieves the Holy Spirit. One unconfessed sin quenches the Holy Spirit. We must keep our sins confessed up to date.

Secondly, we must not only be empty of our sins, but we must be empty of self. Jesus said, "If any man would come after me, let him deny himself, and take up his cross daily, and follow me." As long as self is on the throne of one's heart, the Holy Spirit cannot fill one's life. We must say no to self and deny ourselves. When you are empty of your sins and empty of yourself, you can crown Jesus Lord. Jesus, not self, ruling in your life. "Jesus, be the King of my heart, Lord of my heart, Master of my heart, Ruler of my heart." Jesus is crowned Lord in your life. You make him king of your heart, and when you are under his control, then you can ask the Father to fill you with the Holy Spirit. He is already indwelling your life; now he can be free to fill your life.

When your sins are confessed, when self is on the cross, when Jesus is Lord of your life, the Holy Spirit is free to fill and control your life. Then there will be the power to know God's Word and we'll have the power to be like Jesus and the power to do God's work.

The power for service comes from being filled with the Holy Spirit. Ask God to fill you with his Spirit now as you meet his conditions.

CHAPTER 9

GOING DEEPER

Ricky Cagle had been a prominent fixture in the life of Cottage Hill Baptist Church for a number of years, especially as a favorite worship leader at various youth camps and retreats. He had assisted Hayes Wicker during Super Summer '73, and was easily one of the most popular members of the Cottage Hill youth group. So, it was no surprise when he became the first of Fred's "preacher boys" to surrender his life to the call of full time vocational ministry. This call culminated in his being the first young man to be ordained under Fred's leadership on June 25, 1975. Many more men and women would follow Ricky Cagle in giving their lives to the gospel ministry under Fred at Cottage Hill. A legacy had begun.

During the first week of July, Fred took his family on vacation for rest and relaxation, but also to visit his ailing father. They spent two weeks together in Rock Hill, and it would prove to be his last visit. By mid-September, Fred Wolfe, Sr. passed away after being in critical condition in a Rock Hill hospital for a number of weeks.

Fred said later of his father, "He was truly a remarkable man. He was a strong leader in our home. I could not be a 'delinquent.' My father would not let me, for I knew he meant business about right, moral living.

"He was a great provider. Miracles still happen. He provided for seven children on the salary of a policeman. When I reflect upon nine people living in that three bedroom, one-bath home, I still believe in miracles... I am glad that I can say that he was saved as a young man, and Christ lived in his heart... It is humanly difficult to give him up, but I have not lost him. Who knows, maybe Hebrews 12:1-2 applies to him. Could he be looking over the portals of heaven and being a part of every glorious service we have at CHBC as we worship and serve our risen Lord? Praise the Lord for Jesus and eternal life."

Within the next few weeks, Fred was required to walk through his first real staff transition as Len Turner accepted a call to become the pastor of Colonial Heights Baptist Church in Jackson, Mississippi. He would begin on October 1st. Len would point out quickly that he was just leaving one CHBC to go to another CHBC. Len would write his last "Just Between Us" column for the September 26 issue of *The Challenge*. "Thank you for a wonderful three years and three months," he wrote. "Thank you for your prayers, encouragement, cooperation, hard work, and love. Never have I worked with such a wonderful group of people. You are, and have been during these years, an inspiration to me... Remember to serve the Lord in the power of the Holy Spirit. Allow Christ to be constantly enthroned in your heart, and permit the Holy Spirit to fill you continuously and Jesus Christ will be glorified in your life and in this Church."

When Fred had arrived at Cottage Hill Baptist Church in

February of 1972, around 800 people gathered for worship each Sunday. On October 19, 1975, less than three years later, the attendance in the morning worship services on a High Attendance Sunday, was a record 3,548. At least 280 professions of faith had been recorded the previous twelve months, and 242 had been baptized, with almost half of them over eighteen years of age.

1976 and 1977 continued along those lines of growth, both in numbers and in spirit. Worship attendance continued to reach close to 3,000 per week regularly. Cottage Hill acquired a local lake, and Joy Springs joined the collection of facilities that the church would use to minister to families in various ways. Staff members came, some went, and it seemed that all of them were grateful for the two or three or more years that they experienced under Fred Wolfe's leadership.

One of those staff members joined the team on March 1, 1976. Terry Sutton officially became the Director of Christian Activities, though only sixteen months later he would assume the expanded title of Director of Youth and Activities. Terry remembers his time on the CHBC staff with great affection, especially the occasional staff ice cream fellowships.

At one of those, six or seven of the men had brought homemade ice cream, and each of their freezers stood ready, waiting for everyone to taste each family recipe. Fred brought some, too, and as people began to gather, Fred was calling them over to his can, giving them a sample of his wares. "Come here, Terry," he said, "taste this. That's good, isn't it? Here, Ed, try this. Isn't that fantastic?" And there was no doubt about it, the consensus was that Fred's ice cream was, in fact, fantastic. That's when Anne came up behind him and said over his shoulder, "Well it ought to be fantastic. He just stopped at the store on the way over and filled this thing with Blue Bell!"

As the year went on, more and more young men and women gave their lives to vocational ministry and were licensed, ordained, and recommended to seminary by Cottage Hill.

Celebrities and sports figures spoke at church gatherings and celebrations, as billboards appeared all over Mobile proclaiming that "There's Plenty of Room in the Family!"

All of the choirs saw explosive growth and led worship with profound depth through the sincere and heartfelt leadership of Ed Keyes. Musicals like "Alleluia," "Celebrate Life," and "Living Witnesses" were performed by the Adult and Youth Choirs to packed houses each time. The album "Worthy is the Lamb" was added to the Cottage Hill catalog to join its predecessors of the previous few years, "The King is Coming" and "God's Choir."

On September 4, 1977, at 6:00 PM, the church dedicated its new Education-Administration Building, erected in one of the only spaces available for building, the east courtyard. Fred led the people in a responsive reading that expressed their collective willingness to see God use this building "for the winning of those who are burdened with sin; for the teaching of the Word of Truth; and for the extension of the Kingdom of God to the ends of the earth."

Earlier in the year, from March 13-16, 1977, Cottage Hill hosted a man who would prove to be one of Fred's favorite speakers and good friends, Peter Lord. Peter had been pastor of Park Avenue Baptist Church in Titusville, Florida, since 1966, and they had been experiencing a genuine move of God for some years. Peter was a native of Jamaica, and his almost-British accent endeared him to the people of Cottage Hill quickly. His theme for the meetings was "The Abundant Life."

During one of the services, Peter Lord asked the congregation, "How many of you here today think that you are as righteous as

Jesus?" No one raised their hands. "Anyone?"

Peter turned to Fred, who was seated behind him on the stage, and said, "Pastor, this is an amazing thing. You have a church full of people here who don't believe the Bible!" The shock of that statement regarding a pastor and church as conservative as Cottage Hill Baptist made everyone sit up and listen more closely. "The Bible says," he went on, "that we have been made the righteousness of Jesus Christ. It is a gift from God. It has nothing to do with your behavior, and everything to do with how God sees you, robed in the righteousness of Jesus Christ." Peter went on to explain how the Abundant Life is available because of what Jesus has already done for us, not because of what we can do for Him.

In another service, and with Fred's prior approval, Peter found a woman in the congregation and gently pointed her out in an illustration of what he termed "Soul Care." "Here is a woman," said Peter, "who has really beautiful hair. May I ask you a question, Madam? How often do you go to the beauty salon to have your hair done?"

"Well," she said, "I guess once a week or so."

"Once a week," said Peter. "That sounds about right. If I may, madam, how much time do you usually spend getting your hair right each morning? On the average?"

"I suppose about an hour," she said.

"And this morning, before you came to church?"

"The same," she said, "about an hour."

"I see," said Peter. "And how much time did you spend preparing your soul to worship and to receive the Word of God before you came to church today?"

She had no answer. "Of course," said Peter, "I am not trying to embarrass this beautiful woman. My point is that every one of us probably spends more time each day making the outward man presentable, than we do preparing the inner man to meet with God."

Peter Lord also was one of the only preachers who was speaking with authority and credibility on the subject of hearing the voice of God. He encouraged every believer that they could, indeed, hear God speak to them if they would just "tune in" to the correct frequency, which was the presence of the Holy Spirit. Peter encouraged everyone to get alone with God until He spoke to them.

Fred was quick to put Peter's advice to the test. "Lord," he said, "I need a word from you, and I'm not getting up from here until I have one."

In short order, God spoke to Fred, and gave him one of the most profound moments of his life. It was only three words, but it changed him forever: "I know you."

Peter's dual message of "soul care" and "hearing God" made a great impact on Fred. His message underscored the vital importance of prayer in the life of a Christian and the church. Fred encouraged every member of Cottage Hill to get a copy of Peter Lord's guide to a daily quiet time, the *2959 Plan*. The title was based on the assumption that if you would spend thirty minutes a day with God, it might take you one second to open the notebook, leaving you twenty-nine minutes and fifty-nine seconds with God.

Peter Lord's visit and his ongoing friendship with Fred paid dividends for years to come. He would come back a number of times through the years, and his ministry to the people of Cottage Hill would be a lasting one.

Another agent of change in Fred's life and the life of Cottage Hill Baptist Church arrived in November of 1973 to lead a series of meetings. Major W. Ian Thomas, spoke twice daily from November 13th through the 17th, including special lunch meetings at noon and full services each night. Ian Thomas, originally of London, England, introduced another vital insight into the successful Christian life that took Fred even deeper into his relationship with God.

After giving his heart to Jesus at the age of twelve, Walter Ian Thomas took his Christian commitment seriously. By fifteen, he had surrendered his life as a missionary, and began to train and study in the medical field. Just a few years later, he was convinced that, no matter how hard he tried, he was going to be unable to live the Christian life the way that God seemed to be demanding. He knew that, in his own strength, it was a losing fight.

Then, through the revelation of the Holy Spirit, he discovered the principle of allowing the life of Christ in him to live the life of Christ through him. Major Thomas went on to explain this truth in enduring classic books such as *The Saving Life of Christ, The Mystery of Godliness*, and *If I Perish, I Perish*. This distinction between the self-life and the Christ-life helped Fred to understand more completely what Miss Bertha had introduced years earlier-- how to live in the fullness of the Holy Spirit. Fred knew right away that the message of Major Ian Thomas was going to be a great help to him and his people on their journey.

Spring Break 1975 brought more than college kids and beachgoers to Mobile and the surrounding area. From March 10th through the 14th, Cottage Hill Baptist Church hosted the Gulf Coast Conference on Revival with Bertha Smith, Manley Beasley, and Jack Taylor. Meetings were held at 10 and 11 AM each day, and 7 and 8 PM every night. The school vacation helped to increase the attendance of the young people who were hungry to attend.

Fred was, of course, very familiar with Miss Bertha, and the people of Cottage Hill welcomed her back with great enthusiasm. Jack Taylor was new to Cottage Hill, but Fred had known him since they were young men. When Fred was attending Southwestern Seminary, in 1966, he attended a retreat at Falls Creek, a Baptist encampment in Oklahoma. Jack was the speaker that week, and the way he preached about the Lordship of Christ and being filled with the Holy Spirit connected deeply with Fred's own heart. One day that week, while on the ball field, Fred approached Jack and said, "You know, Brother Jack, the message you're preaching isn't preached a lot."

"Well, Fred," he said, "it isn't being preached by Southern Baptists, and I hope it hasn't passed us by." From that moment on, Fred knew that he and Jack would be knit together. By 1975, Jack had been the pastor of Castle Hills Baptist Church in San Antonio, Texas, where they had seen a great move of God. His bestselling book, *The Key to Triumphant Living*, echoed perfectly what the people had already been hearing from Fred and others about the Lordship of Christ and the Spirit-filled life. Together with the success of other books, like *Much More*, and *After the Spirit Comes*, Jack Taylor had become the number one selling author for Broadman and Holman Publishers.

Manley Beasley was also new to the church, but he added another dimension of teaching that would impact Fred for the rest of his life. Manley was more of a mystic than Fred had ever met. Manley heard the voice of God like no one else. He was sick often, but continued to be healed from life-threatening illnesses. Still, Manley taught people how to hear the voice of God through the Bible. There was a difference, he said, between the *logos*-- the written word-- and *rhema*-- the living and active word that your heart receives directly from God. Manley encouraged people to make decisions and direct their lives based on *rhema*, letting God speak to their heart by causing the Scripture to come alive in a unique way, then having received it, standing on it with confidence.

Manley had learned to hear God so intimately that he lived on a different spiritual level than anyone else. He also knew that people sometimes said and sang things that they didn't mean. During one visit, Manley and Fred sat next to each other on the platform while a duo of men in the church sang the popular song, "Whatever It Takes." Manley listened as they sang:

For whatever it takes to draw closer to you Lord
That's what I'll be willing to do
For whatever it takes to be more like you
That's what I'll be willing to do

Fred saw Manley start to squirm. Then the singers delivered this verse:

Take the dearest things to me
If that's how it must be
To draw me closer to thee
Let the disappointments come
Lonely days without the sun
If through sorrow more like you I become

I'll trade sunshine for rain
Comfort for pain
That's what I'll be willing to do
For whatever it takes for my will to break
That's what I'll be willing to do

Manley Beasley leaned over to Fred and punched him in the ribs. "They have not got a clue what they're saying," he said. But Manley knew. He had already settled it. He had already walked through a number of valleys of shadow, and he knew what the song really meant.

Manley Beasley would challenge the people to believe God like never before in their lives. "What is it," he would ask, "that you are believing God for, that if He doesn't come through, you're sunk? If there isn't anything, then you aren't walking by faith yet. You may say, 'Well, I don't want to get out on a limb.' I understand, but what you don't know, is that's where the fruit is!"

Fred Wolfe would take to heart Manley's message and apply it for the rest of his life. He might hear correctly, and he might not, but from then on, Fred would always wait for a *rhema* word from God before making a major decision.

As the Gulf Coast Conference of Revival came to a close, it was evident that the pastor and people of Cottage Hill Baptist Church had gone to a deeper level with God.

CHAPTER 10

RAVENHILL

In March of 1978, a four-year-old girl recognized Fred while he was out eating breakfast, and asked if she could pray for him. After praying, she looked at her mother and said, "We better pray for Brother Fred every day or the devil will get him." For Fred, truer and more welcome words had never hit his ears.

Ever since the aftermath of Miss Bertha's first visit with him at Woodlawn, the concept of a strong prayer life had been driven deeper in him every year. Prayer was an absolute for Fred, a non-negotiable. "The church moves forward on its knees," he said, and he was committed to seeing that proved out at Cottage Hill Baptist Church.

Four years earlier, on February 6, 1974, Fred had established at Cottage Hill a Prayer Room at the church, with Dot Martin serving as the Prayer Coordinator. Dot and her husband, "Jiggs" Martin, had just returned from a visit to Castle Hills Baptist Church in San Antonio, Texas, where they had observed the prayer ministry there in great detail. The San Antonio church, pastored by Jack Taylor, was experiencing a phenomenal move of God, and it was agreed that focused and consistent prayer was a key factor in that revival. From that moment on, the emphasis on prayer and the recruitment of Prayer Warriors was a constant and intentional thread that was woven through the fabric of every part of Cottage Hill's life.

Less than a year later, Fred met with everyone who had signed on as a Prayer Warrior on January 19, 1975. The growth of the prayer ministry and use of the prayer room had been steady and powerful, and they launched a plan together to fully staff a Prayer Room that never closed, and that would be staffed with someone interceding there 24 hours a day, seven days a week, throughout 1975. By 1978, about 125 volunteers were occupying the Prayer Room at every hour of the day and night, praying for an hour or more over 2,500 prayer requests and answering the Prayer Line telephone.

The Prayer Room was not the only available avenue of focused personal and corporate prayer, though. By this time, there was also at least one early morning prayer time each week at the church, from 6:00 AM to 7:00 AM for anyone who wanted to come. Then, others gathered to pray every Saturday night for two hours, crying out to God for revival and for the services that would follow the next morning. And with every lifted voice, the golden bowls of heaven were filling with the prayers of the saints. Soon, they would be poured back out on Cottage Hill in an unprecedented way.

In November of 1977, a young evangelist came to preach a Youth retreat for Cottage Hill. While he was in town, he visited old friends Melvin and Libby Badon. The Badons had been members of the church in Little Rock, Arkansas that his father had pastored. During the visit, he mentioned that his family had just had an encounter in prayer that had changed them forever and had "straightened a lot of things out."

Soon, the Badons found themselves in Little Rock, getting the whole story directly from the yong man's mother. After reading a book called *The Adversary* by Mark Bubeck, the pastor's family began praying for his mother, and she was immediately and dramatically delivered from years of deep demonic influence and oppression. Melvin and Libby had never heard anything like it, and they were floored by the details, but they were convinced.

On returning to Mobile, Melvin took a copy of Bubeck's book to Brother Fred and asked him to read it. Fred was intrigued, and he began to read *The Adversary*. As he read, he came upon one particular story in the book that stunned him almost into shock. In the book was an account from someone whose experience exactly mirrored what had happened to Fred that night in his college dorm room. The near-paralysis, the anxiety, the persistence of it--- it was all the same.

At that moment, Fred finally found out what had come on him all those years ago. He had been attacked by a spirit of fear. He hadn't known what to call it then, and he had seen it defeated as he continually sought God, but for a year he had been under severe spiritual pressure, and now he knew why. It had been nothing less than demonic.

No one had to convince Fred of the validity of this kind of spiritual warfare. In fact, he knew he had to help the people of Cottage Hill understand. Almost as quickly as Fred closed the back cover of *The Adversary*, he wrote a letter to Mark Bubeck and asked for his permission to use some of the warfare prayers outlined in the book as a handout to the people of Cottage Hill.

"Use it any way you like," came the reply from Bubeck, and Fred had the church produce a booklet called "Warfare Praying." That book kept going out about as quickly as it could be reprinted, and many years later, some people-- including Melvin Badon-- still pray those prayers over themselves and their families daily. In the years to come, Fred would give out more than 30,000 copies of the "Warfare Praying" booklet.

Fred's style of accessible and honest leadership continued to impact staff members in ways that would follow them for years. On June 1, 1978, Terry Bryant returned to Cottage Hill Baptist Church to take over the responsibilities of Evangelism, Discipleship, and Bus Ministry.

Terry had just finished serving on a church staff in another state, where the senior pastor had serious control issues. He was harsh and manipulative, constantly berating those ministers who worked with him. When Terry came to the CHBC staff, he was still hurting from the wounds inflicted on him there, and he was a little apprehensive, hoping that this new "inside look" behind the curtains of Cottage Hill would not undo the years of respect that he had built up for Fred Wolfe.

At the first staff meeting that Terry attended, Fred had just returned from a preaching trip, and on the way home, he had bought a small, rubber band-powered balsa wood toy airplane in the Atlanta airport. All during the staff meeting, even as they discussed the various programs, vision, and goals of the church, Fred led the meeting while simultaneously flying the little wooden airplane around the room. The juxtaposition of responsibility and playfulness showed Terry something that he had never seen before. Fred was actively demonstrating that even though we take the gospel very seriously, we should never take ourselves too seriously. Terry breathed easy that day, and his time at Cottage Hill became one of the greatest joys of his life.

In the latter half of 1978, Fred was on the way out of his house on Huffman Drive when his eyes fell on a book that was sitting on a shelf. When he noticed that it was written by a man named Leonard Ravenhill, the Holy Spirit spoke to him and said, "I want you to invite him to Cottage Hill." So Fred did what he had learned from his friend Manley Beasley, and he responded to the Lord. "I'll do it," he said, "but you're going to have to confirm that I am hearing you correctly. If you want me to have him at Cottage Hill, have somebody speak to me about him."

Fred closed and locked the front door and picked up Herb Fisher to accompany him to a preaching engagement. About two blocks down the road, Herb turned to Fred and said, "Brother Fred, have you ever heard of Leonard Ravenhill?"

Fred had, in fact, heard of him. Leonard Ravenhill was born in 1907 in Leeds, in Yorkshire, England. He was educated at Cliff College under the leadership and teaching of Samuel Chadwick, the famous Methodist preacher of the late 1800s. Ravenhill became known as one of the most fiery of outdoor evangelists in England in the early part of the 20th century. In the 1950s, he and his wife Martha moved with their three sons to the United States, where he cemented his reputation by writing books like *Sodom Had No Bible*, *America Is Too Young To Die*, and the classic, million-copy bestseller *Why Revival Tarries*. In the 1980s, Ravenhill moved to Lindale, Texas, where he became a mentor to a number of influential Christian leaders, from Keith Green to Charles Stanley to David Wilkerson.

Fred understood that God was confirming that he needed to invite Leonard Ravenhill to Cottage Hill. In 1978, Ravenhill was still living in Seguin, Texas. Fred contacted Ravenhill and arranged to come out and meet him to talk to him about coming to Mobile. He flew Delta Airlines out of Mobile, which required him to change planes in Houston in order to catch a connecting flight to San Antonio.

Something in Fred told him that this invitation was more important than even he knew. So, even en route to Houston, Fred was asking God to confirm again that he was doing the right thing.

Arriving in Houston, Fred wasn't sure where to go to catch his connection. He approached a Delta ticket counter and walked up to a young woman in a Delta uniform. "Excuse me," he said, "but I'm not sure where to go for my next flight. Can you help me?"

She smiled at him. "Of course," she said, looking at his ticket. "Your gate is just down here," she said, pointing down the concourse and giving him directions.

"Thank you," said Fred, as he began to walk away.

"Oh, and by the way, when you get to San Antonio," she said, "Seguin will be about forty miles east of there."

"Thank you," Fred said over his shoulder. A few steps later, though, it hit him. He looked at his ticket again. *Mobile to Houston to San Antonio.* He turned it over and examined it carefully. *Mobile to Houston to San Antonio.* Nowhere on the ticket was there a mention of Seguin. He hadn't said anything about Seguin. How could she have known?

Fred had to know. He quickly turned around and walked back to ask her. But she was gone.

Arriving in Seguin, Fred spent time getting to know Leonard Ravenhill. When Fred asked him to come and speak at Cottage Hill for two weeks, Leonard said, "You meet early in the mornings to pray at the church, do you not? And you have a meeting for prayer every Saturday evening. You have a prayer room that is open and available twenty-four hours a day. You have over seventy men who pray for you in teams of seven every Sunday morning during the preaching. You have women who do the same on Sunday evenings. Any church that is that serious about prayer is certainly serious about revival. So, yes, I will come."

Leonard Ravenhill first stepped behind the pulpit at Cottage Hill Baptist Church on New Year's Eve, December 31, 1978. He preached a message at a Watchnight service, and then led the congregation in Communion as the first minutes of 1979 arrived.

Ravenhill not only preached on praying and wrote books about it, he was a man of prayer. His message of pursuing revival was grounded in a call to earth-shattering, life-changing prayer. Close on the heels of that, though, was his conviction that the effectiveness of that prayer life was directly connected to our desire to live a life of holiness and godliness. Ravenhill did not tread lightly on the issues of the lukewarm state of the church in America. His messages were bold and convicting and they cut to the heart of the matter when it came to dealing with the shallowness and the lifeless prayer of the average Christian. He believed that revival was imminently attainable, but that it would require the people to be focused on the seriousness of a sold out commitment to Jesus Christ as Lord of everything.

This new and deeper exploration into the Lordship of Christ appealed to Fred quickly, and he saw right away that it was yet another dimension to the truth that had changed him so many years ago. When Leonard Ravenhill preached, Fred was usually the first to respond to the invitation, often on his face before God in the atmosphere of holiness that pervaded those services for the first two weeks of January in 1979.

Ravenhill's preaching was so fiery, though, that it presented challenges to Fred for the first few days. Ravenhill was so bold, that Jack Taylor called him America's only prophet. It took some getting used to. Ravenhill was committed to be at Cottage Hill for two weeks, but three days into it, Fred was thinking he might need to cut it short and end it there. He resisted the urge, though, and God began to reshape Cottage Hill in profound ways.

Although Leonard Ravenhill was a bold lion in the pulpit, he was a humble gentleman when he was out from behind it. He never did anything in a church he visited without a recognition of the authority of the pastor of that local congregation. God was moving in that series of meetings at Cottage Hill, and real revival was stirring. After one of the services, Leonard came to Brother Fred and said, "Pastor, some of the people are asking me to lay hands on them and pray for them, but I will not do so without your permission. Do I have it?" Fred said that he did, and the revival went to another level.

The Ravenhill Revival presented other, more unique challenges to Cottage Hill. As the word of the move of God began to spread throughout Mobile, others flocked to the nightly services, as well as the Tuesday through Friday noon sessions. Especially interested were those in Mobile who were aware that Ravenhill was not afraid of a more Charismatic style ministry, and in fact embraced anything that would be an avenue of the power of God.

By the third day of the meetings, the level of "non-Baptist" activity had increased to a level that made Fred uncomfortable. After the service on the third night, Fred let God know what he was thinking on the way home. "Lord," he prayed, "I don't think I can deal with the level of demonstration of the Spirit we're seeing this week. If this is revival, I don't want it."

But by the time he awoke the next morning, he had come to his spiritual senses. "I didn't mean what I said last night, Lord," he said. "Whatever You want to do among us, whatever it looks like,

I just want You. Please don't let revival pass us by just because it makes me uncomfortable."

In the days to come, Fred would have to communicate this same resolve to the people of the church. Some of the people of Cottage Hill were more than a little unnerved by the "infiltration" of "the Charismatics." They seemed to all know each other, waving to each other from across the auditorium, and some Cottage Hill members began to suspect that they were dividing in order to conquer. And so they looked to Fred for guidance. But Fred Wolfe was not disturbed by them. The hunger in his life for all of God was so evident, that it quickly became clear that no matter who raised their hands, or shouted, or even danced in the middle of the message, none of it really mattered. What mattered was the Lordship of Jesus Christ, even at the expense of his own sense of decorum.

One of the most vivid examples was Arthur Rose. Arthur was well known in Pentecostal-Charismatic circles in Mobile, and he would attend every service, sitting on the front row. When Arthur got excited, he stood, waved one arm above his head, and shouted his agreement before sitting back down. Once he became so excited that he ran across the front of the church. Very soon into the two-week engagement, Ravenhill affectionately dubbed him "Athletic Arthur," and that is how he was known for years to come.

Area Charismatics were not the only non-Cottage Hill people who came through the doors while Ravenhill was teaching. The two-week meetings advanced Fred's role, not just as a pastor *in* the city, but also as a pastor *to* the city. Nan Smith, a member of Cottage Hill Presbyterian Church, just down the road from CHBC, wrote a letter of thanks to the church that reflected the growing influence that Fred and Cottage Hill Baptist seemed destined to extend. "Dear Brothers and Sisters in Christ," she wrote, "I just wanted to thank you all for giving us the opportunity to hear Leonard Ravenhill. I can't tell you how much his messages stirred and challenged me. Praise the Lord!

"There were quite a few of us from Cottage Hill Presbyterian who were so blessed to see the Lord working so beautifully in your Congregation. I praise God for the dedication and prayer life of all your ministers and their faithfulness to Christ. I am so glad God is pouring out His Spirit on you and is gracious enough to let the blessings fall on visiting Presbyterians also... My Christian walk has been renewed because of you! The Lord bless you!"

All during the late 1970s, the Charismatic Renewal was in full force across much of the United States, leaving no denomination untouched. In Mobile, Dick Braswell was pastoring Lott Road Baptist Church when he was joyfully swept along into a fuller experience of the Holy Spirit. It didn't take long for the denominational hammer to fall, and Dick found himself alone in the city, not quite knowing who he was anymore, with no one to talk to about it. Lott Road Baptist Church was invited to become an ex-Southern Baptist Church by the local Association, and they became just Lott Road Church. The men that Dick had counted his friends, men he had attended seminary with and fought alongside in the trenches of pastoring, now turned on him and turned away. Except for one.

Fred Wolfe had heard what was happening at Lott Road, so he invited Brother Dick to lunch. They sat down, ordered their meals, and Fred said, "Tell me the whole story. I want to know everything that is happening with you." Dick didn't hold back, and he told Fred that even though he didn't understand everything that he was moving into, he was confident that the Lord was in it.

Fred listened to the whole story, and said, "Sounds like God to me." He never questioned the legitimacy of Dick's experience, never doubted the integrity of what he was doing. Fred Wolfe was the only man to embrace Dick Braswell and tell him that it was going to be alright. He spoke at their church, and spoke at their school. Fred walked beside Dick, unashamed and unapologetic.

And, it was the hyper-Charismatics in town who then came down the hardest on Fred. They wanted him to do with Cottage Hill what Dick had done at Lott Road. If he was so approving of the modern operation and gifts of the Holy Spirit, why didn't he, too, have the nerve to make the change?

But what Fred knew, and what Dick Braswell knew, is that as a pastor, the people who like to give you advice don't have to live with your decisions. "But you are marked by your decisions," says Dick, "and they aren't. Doesn't cost them anything to tell you what to do, but you know that it is your job to hear from God for the people whom you pastor, and to lead according to what the Holy Spirit tells you. I will always admire Fred Wolfe," he says. "He was my friend when others had walked away, and he led his people with integrity and compassion. He is a dear friend indeed."

Friday night, January 12, 1979, was the last of the Ravenhill meetings. By then, it became clear to Fred Wolfe that Cottage Hill Baptist Church had swung on a hinge. Those two weeks had challenged the church, smashed their preconceived ideas of who God is and what He is doing in the earth, and defined them in a way that nothing and no one had done before. It proved that here was a church that was going to go wherever God led them, no matter the cost.

Fred H. Wolfe

Fred Wolfe Ordination Set Sunday

Above: Anne Heath, the soon-to-be bride of Fred Wolfe, in high school.

Left: A young Fred Wolfe is ordained in preparation for his first pastorate.

Below: 2-year-old Fred with his parents and four older sisters.

The Wolfe family home in Rock Hill, South Carolina.

Fred with his sisters and their mother.

Fred's parents in their later years.

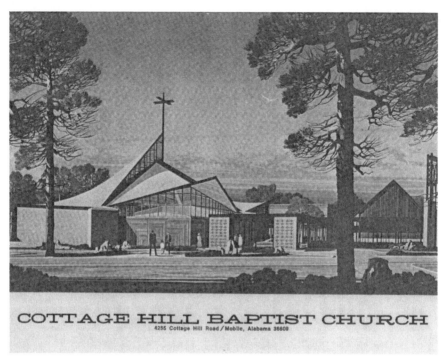

Front of a Welcome Card from Cottage Hill Baptist Church, circa 1972.

Fred Wolfe preaching from the rock pulpit in Cottage Hill's
1600-seat sanctuary.

Above: Brother Fred visits a Preschool Sunday School Class.

Right: Praying at the 1983 Pastor's Conference in Pittsburgh.

Below: Ed Keyes sings at the "Giving From God's Hands" service in the Mobile Municipal Auditorium. Fred and Ed have served together for over forty years.

Above: Fred and Anne with their two sons, Jeff (left) and Mark (right), their wives, and the first three grandchildren in 1987.

Right: The article from the Mobile Press Register announcing Fred's resignation from Cottage Hill in December, 1996.

The Rev. Fred Wolfe

Register file photo

Fred Wolfe to leave Cottage Hill

▶ Baptist congregation surprised by decision from prominent minister, who was approaching 25 years with the church

Left: Fred Wolfe with his mother, Margaret.

Right: Fred with all six of his siblings.

Left: Fred and Anne with their five grand-children and spouses.

Above: Brother Fred and Dr. Levy H. Knox (center) with Dr. Mark Wyatt (left)

Left: Dr. Fred Wolfe speaking at Dr. Mark Wyatt's Ph.D. ceremony.

A living legacy: Some of the many men and women who went into ministry from under Fred's leadership, along with long time friends and staff members, as they celebrate Brother Fred's 70th birthday at Gulf Shores, Alabama in December of 2007. Dr. Ricky Cagle is on the far right of the back row.

a Sermon

❧

Heart Cry for Revival

HEART CRY FOR REVIVAL

by
Fred H. Wolfe

I want you to open your Bible this morning to the book of Isaiah 64. "To whom much is given, much is required." Now think about that, to whom much is given, much is required. You had no choice where you would be born. No choice who your parents would be, you could have easily been born in Kenya, where there is a great drought going on now and thousands are dying every day. You could be born in a place where there's nothing but darkness, where the Gospel of Jesus had never been preached. You see, we really are where we are, by the sovereign grace of God. But I just have a sense that to whom much is given, much is required. So just think about that. You know, have you ever felt this way? I'm desperate. You know, desperation is not necessarily a bad thing, not at all. Being desperate can be a blessing. You know why? Desperate people pray. That's right, desperate people pray. Desperate people look outside of themselves. They look outside of themselves for help. You know, I looked up that word desperation, it means having a great desire. So if you are desperate, you have a great desire or a great need.

By the way, and talking about desperation, the dictionary said, it causes one to act recklessly."

Did you know that eighty percent of the people that we have a record of in the New Testament that came to Jesus were desperate? The centurion servant was dying, he was desperate. The woman with the issue of blood pressed into the crowd so she could touch the hem of the garment of Jesus, because she'd spent all she had and still was no better. She was a desperate woman who did reckless things.

Eighty percent of the people in the Bible, who came to Jesus were desperate. These are desperate days in which we live. Or, very much so, desperate times. You say I don't believe that, well then you missed it. I'm telling you, these are desperate days. These are desperate times. Let me just make this personal to some of you. I mean, you're sensing in your heart desperation this morning. You have a great desire or a great need. Some of you are experiencing desperation because of some sickness in your body. I have noticed that people will just be going along in their lives and then someone that they love, someone close to them will get a news about illness that is "incurable" by men and terminal, and I'm telling you I've noticed that everything about them will change. Everything about their family will change. Their routine will change.

Let me tell you what happens to them. When the word comes about the sickness, they become desperate people. They have a great need and sometimes they just do desperate things. Some of you this morning are experiencing desperation because your children are in a hard place, they may be running with the wrong crowd and they may be making wrong choices and you know the path they're going down. But they're not listening to you right now and I'm going to tell you something. What you're feeling in your heart is that you're desperate. There's a desperation here and it calls you to change you the way you live and the way you think.

Let me tell you something, some of you are desperate this morning about your marriage. I never would've guessed how many times I've seen people that I didn't know, just came out of nowhere and show up at church which I was glad and then later they would say, "We came today because our marriage is in trouble and we're desperate." That's good, because when you're desperate you pray, when you're desperate you look outside of yourself, you look outside of yourself. So some of you today may have been without a job a while or it may be that financially you're in a crisis, but I am telling you where you are, you're desperate. But that can be a blessing because desperate people pray. Desperate people look outside of themselves for help.

Now how many times have we read or heard 2 Chronicles 7:14? It says, "If my people, who are called by my name, will humble themselves and pray, seek my face and turn from their wicked ways, I will hear from heaven and forgive their sin and will heal their land." Great verse. "My people, humble themselves, pray, turn from their wicked ways, seek My face, I'll heal." But you know what the verse before that says? Do you know what 2 Chronicles 7:13 says? If there is famine, if there is pestilence, if there is disease, what it's saying, if it's desperate times, read that 2 Chronicle 7:13, he says, "if it's desperate times." Are you listening? "If it's desperate times," then it says, "In the light of the desperate times, if my people, who are called by my name, will humble themselves and pray, I will hear from heaven, forgive their sins and heal their land."

This morning I want to show you the prayer of a desperate man. Look at Isaiah 64. We're going to look today at the heart and the heart cry of a desperate, desperate man; a man of God whose name was Isaiah and I am telling you, he was desperate. Let me ask you a question: Why are we having 10 days of prayer and fasting? Is it just because we need to do something to look spiritual? It is just because we need to do something because we don't want to feel guilty before God? I'll tell you why. These are desperate days. These are desperate times, I promise you. A lot more desperate than God lets you and I know. What do Christians do in desperate times? They pray. That's exactly what they do. That's exactly what we're doing, recognizing we're desperate, these are desperate times and it calls for drastic reckless action by the people of God. We're saying what we'll do is we'll just set apart ten days and we'll pray and fast and we will cry out to God because these are desperate times.

I want you to look at the cry of a desperate man. Of all the passages of the Bible that reveal of the heart of a person, I can honestly look at the heart of Isaiah when I read this, and I can feel the emotion of his voice. I want you to listen to the prayer of a desperate man. I'm just going to read the first 3 verses, then I will tell you why he is desperate.

Isaiah 64:1 "Oh that you God would tear open the heavens and come down. And would you invade our lives and invade this country and invade the nation. Oh, God would you tear open the heavens that you would come down, that the mountains might shake at your presence." He said, "God if you come even the mountains will acknowledge your ear, the mountains will shake at your presence." And he goes on-- listen to his heart cry. He said, "Lord as fire burns brushwood and as fire causes this water to boil, make your name-- God's name, not the Baptist name or the Methodist name, or the Presbyterian name-- he said, "to make your name known to your adversaries. God let them know, make your name known to your adversaries that the nations may tremble at your presence." You see, he is crying out for the presence of God. He wasn't crying out for a new program or a new plan. He wasn't crying out for a new gimmick. He was crying out for the Presence of God, because the only thing that will shake those mountains was the Presence of God and the only thing that was going to startle the adversaries of God was the Presence of God. So, his heart cry was for nothing other than the invasion, an invasion of his life, an invasion of the nation of Israel, of the Presence of God Himself. This is the cry of a man who said, "Our only hope is the Presence of God, our only hope is that God would come and shake the mountains, our only hope is for God to come and let his adversaries know what His name is, that's our only hope. And the only way that the nations are ever going to tremble is when God comes in His Presence and His power. Then he said, "You did awesome things Lord. I know what You've done in the past, You did awesome things for which we did not look. You came down. Hallelujah! I know when you came down Lord, You came down and the mountain shook at your presence."

Did you know that the days in which Isaiah lived, were just like the days in which we live? You see, Isaiah saw the mountains and they were not physical mountains. There were four mountains that he saw, that he knew would never be shaken and never come down unless God almighty invaded those people and those nations. First of all, Isaiah was fully aware of the fact that he was living in a desperate time. Why was he crying out like that? Why was he calling for God to tear open the heavens and come? What was going on with Him? Why was he so desperate? Because of four reasons:

First of all, he was living in a time of moral insanity. Look at chapter 4 and I want you to drop down to verse 5. You see, the day in which Isaiah lived was a time of absolute moral insanity. How do I know that? Because he tells us in the last part of verse 5. Listen to what he says about the people of Israel. He is asking God to come down into nations around him. "You are indeed angry for we have sinned. In these ways we continue. God you are angry because we have sinned and we continue in our ways. In these ways, we continue and we need to be saved." He was crying out. He was living in the midst of moral insanity. Listen to verse 6: "We all are like an unclean thing. All of our righteousness is like filthy rags. We all fade like a leaf, Lord, we are fading like a leaf." Listen to this, "and our iniquities like the wind have taken us away." You know why Isaiah was desperate? Because he was living in a time of moral insanity. Can I say something to you? We are living in a time of moral insanity. My heavens, abortion on demand. Moral insanity.

Mine and Anne's grandson, Stephen, with his wife Lindsay just had a little great grandchild for us, a few weeks ago and you know, you can send pictures on the internet. So they had some kind of picture of an ultrasound and I am telling the honest truth. It was about two months before Reagan was born, but I could see her nose, I could see her eyes, and I could see her face. I said my Lord I am looking at my great grandchild's face. But they say, "Oh no, they are not alive, they are not a person." Only when they actually come outside of the womb. That is gross stupidity and gross wickedness. It is moral insanity.

We are living in the day of every type of sexual perversion. I am telling you it is unbelievable. Things that use to make us blush no longer make us blush. You know child pornography, can you believe that? Pedophilia. The child is innocent. The child didn't have a choice in these matters. But see we are living in the day of moral insanity and these are desperate, desperate days. I mean, we are living in the days of homosexual marriages. These are desperate days. Do you understand? Every moral perversion that calls God to destroy Sodom and Gomorrah we live with every day and people are lobbying to make it legal. These are days of moral insanity. These are desperate days, but why isn't the church of the Lord Jesus Christ desperate?

You know, there are probably more people living together who aren't married than those who are living together now, who are married. It's amazing. I read the statistics not long ago. People don't get married anymore. I mean, people don't get married anymore, now they just move in. It's amazing. They just move in. Well, a preacher friend of mine went to see this couple that was visiting his church and he said, "How long have y'all been married?" They said, "Well, no, we are not married. But we've been living together for a couple of years, but now that we've been coming to church we're really thinking about getting married". He said, "I didn't know what to say." He said, "I was caught totally off guard."

These are times of moral insanity. And these are desperate days. Drugs, crystal meth, every form of alcohol. 80% of all crimes are committed by people under the influence of alcohol or drugs. Eight out of ten that go to prison committed that crime when their mind was neutralized or nullified by alcohol or drugs. These are days of moral insanity. 65% of the people in America do not believe in a moral absolute-- nothing's always right, nothing's always wrong. We have believed the lie of humanism, of situational ethics. The situation determines if it's right. No, that's a lie. God determines if it's right, and God determines if it's wrong.

Isaiah was living in a day of moral insanity, and that is exactly what we are living in. And let me tell you something; the Bible says when you get to the place that you don't want to retain God in your knowledge – are you listening to me? When you get to the place you don't like to retain God in your knowledge; in Romans 1:28, the Bible says, "God will give you over to a reprobate mind." "I don't want anything to do with God, I don't want to hear anything about God, I don't want any part of God, I don't want any part of God in my life, I want nothing to do with His Word."

Here's the second reason that Isaiah was desperate. He was living in a day of ungodly government. Look at the 10th verse. You know, the capital and the center of everything that went on in Isaiah's day was Jerusalem. And in many ways it was the center not only of religious government, but of civic government. Would you read what he says? "Jerusalem is a desolation." Can I rephrase that? Washington is a desolation. Let me give you a verse. "When the righteous rule, the people rejoice. When the wicked rule, the people mourn."

Anybody that knows anything about America's roots, and anybody that knows anything about our heritage, and anybody that knows anything about where we are and where we are headed. Do you know what they're doing? They're mourning. They're mourning over the loss of their country. And I'm telling you these are desperate people. Isaiah was desperate because he was living in a time where there was unrighteous and ungodly government. Now, you know, I've just got to be totally honest with you. This nation is not governed by righteous Godly principles now. This nation is controlled by greed and by covetousness. That's all it is. It's all about money. In the house and the senate, it's all about money. Is my district going to get the money? Because if I get the money there's a chance I'll get re-elected. Let me tell you something, we have sat back and watched Fannie Mae and Freddie Mac absolutely bankrupt this country and instead of sending them to jail where they should've gone, they got bonuses. God have mercy on our soul! Instead of causing businesses to be accountable, instead of letting them face the reality of their sin, we gave a stimulus, to get them out of the mess they created. That is insanity! It's insanity. And it's all because of greed and covetousness that control this nation. And I am telling you right now, there has got to be a moral and spiritual awakening or it'll never change.

I mean, I believe there are some saved people in the Senate. I believe there are some saved people in the House. But I am telling you friend, we do not just have an economic problem, we have a spiritual problem. Ungodly people are going to be ungodly. No wonder Isaiah was desperate, because he lived in a time of moral insanity. He lived in a time of unrighteous, ungodly government. He lived in a time of dead and lifeless religion. Look at Isaiah 64:10. You talk about a picture of religion in America, this is it right here; he said in the tenth verse, "Your holy cities are a wilderness." I'm talking about all the beautiful, empty buildings in Europe. All the empty buildings that used to be magnificent church structures, the only problem is those big buildings are there now, but they're museums. They are there now, but they have guides to show you through them, because there's nobody there. You see, the holy cities are a wilderness. They are a wilderness. Zion is a wilderness, the center of worship.

You say, "Brother Fred, why are people, in this crisis we're living in, why aren't they going to church?" You want me to tell you why? They've been there before, and when you go and there's no life, there's no power, there's no presence of God; if you go and get pop psychology and lifeless religion and rituals, why do you want to go back? You can get pop psychology from Dr. Phil on TV. Why should you go to church? And I promise you, lifeless and meaningless rituals will never cause anybody to have an encounter with a living God.

Isaiah was desperate because he was living right in the middle of lifeless, dead religion. You know, they were going to the synagogues like they always did. They probably have bigger crowds than they always have. Now, we're living in the day when somebody says, "We got a big crowd!" So what? They got a big crowd down at the bar, too.

Who can ever judge what God is doing by the size of the crowd? God is not impressed by the number of people. God is impressed with righteous and Godly people. Isaiah was desperate because he was living in a time of lifeless, dead religion. That's probably our greatest need in America-- for God to turn around the Church. But that junk I'm talking about is not the Church. I'm talking about the Body of Christ. Here was the fourth reason he was desperate.

This is why he was crying, "Oh God, Oh God , would you tear open the heavens? Would you come down? Let the mountain of moral insanity shake at your presence. Oh God, would you come down? Let the mountain of lifeless, dead religion shake at your presence? Dear God, would you come down and let the ungodly and unrighteous government in Jerusalem be changed. Dear God, if you don't come down, I've seen no hope Lord," and so he was crying for God to tear open the heavens and to shake and destroy the mountains and to bring life. He was praying, "God, please intervene."

But I'll tell you another thing that stirred him up. Because of the apathy and the indifference and the prayerlessness. Now, I want you to look at verse 7. I want to tell you something. This is an indictment. Why are we having 10 days of prayer? We ought to have more than that. We ought to be crying out for God day and night, every one of us. Because you see the reason Isaiah was so desperate was because he saw the apathy and the indifference and the prayerlessness.

Would you look at verse 7? These were critical times. Critical. "There is no one who calls on your name." What? Isaiah, I mean y'all were in a horrible place. What are you saying? "There's no one who called on Your name. Who stirs himself up, to take hold of You?" Isaiah said, "What makes me so desperate? I don't hear anybody stirring themselves up to take hold of God. There's no one who calls on Your name, Lord. Israel ought to be on their face, and there's no one that calls on Your name. There's no one that stirs himself up to take hold of You.

You've probably heard this story. This is one of the most remarkable things that I have ever encountered. It was time for me to change the oil in the car. I usually change my oil at the Super Lube on Cottage Hill Road. But for some reason, I was over close to the Providence Hospital. This has been 15 years ago, maybe 20. And I decided, I had about 15 minutes, so I decided to pull in to the Super Lube on Airport Boulevard and to get my oil changed. And, you know, it was kind of little break. You know, you pull in there and they say, "We're gonna get this changed in 15 minutes." It never happens.

They got a nice little room. They got books, they got magazines, and they even got a snack machine. I said, "I don't care if it takes 20 minutes. I'm just going to relax, and enjoy the little waiting room here. Well, this guy comes in and I am telling you he was wired for sound. He walked in, he said, "Brother Fred, Am I glad to see you!" I said, "Oh dear Lord, here we go."

"Am I glad to see you. I have been wanting to see you for a number of years. I mean, I'm so excited about seeing you!" I said,

"Well wonderful, wonderful". But then he told me why. Under God, this is exactly the way it happened. He said, "Do you remember a few years ago, when you were preaching on the fact that there was no one who called on God's name? And no one who stirred himself up to seek God?" He said, "I'm going to tell you something. I was sitting at home in my den watching television. I was lost and didn't know Jesus, but you kept saying there was no one who was calling on God's name and no one who would stir himself up to call on God and I said to God, 'If nobody else will do it, it might as well be me!'" True story. And he said, "Shortly after that I got saved, Brother Fred, and I just got back from a mission trip overseas." I said, "Well, glory to God!" This man's not only going to go to heaven, he's going to overshoot it because of his zeal for the Lord.

But let me tell you something you think God didn't convict me, he was a lost man who heard the voice of God speak and said, "well if nobody else will stir themselves up to take hold of God, it might as well be me." Thank God, he got saved. I guarantee you he's still stirred up, too! You see, one reason Isaiah was desperate was because of the apathy, the indifference, the prayerlessness.

Well, I want to talk to you about the cry because of his desperation. "Oh God, would you come down? Would you shake the mountains? Would you cause the nations to tremble before you? Lord, Lord, Lord, would you make your name known to your adversaries? God would you just come and Lord shake and destroy that mountain of moral insanity. Oh God come and shake and destroy that mountain of unrighteous government. Oh, God come and strike, destroy and pull down that mountain of lifeless religion. Oh God come down and pull down and destroy that mountain of apathy and indifference." The mountains he was talking about weren't physical mountains, they were spiritual mountains. I'm telling you, we look them in the face. Every day, we're looking at these mountains and we say "Well, if we can elect the right person, they'll tear that mountain down." I want to elect the right person, but there ain't no man that can tear those mountains down. I'm telling you, we need an invasion of the living God! "Oh, Lord you tear open the heavens!" Now, here's my most important point. We've got to make a commitment to make a difference. We got to get desperate, because these are desperate times and if you're desperate about personal things in your life, I'm glad. Cry out to God for them. They are important.

We are desperate about moral insanity and all the junk that is going on, the lifeless religion, the government and apathy. It is a desperate thing, but you've got to make a commitment to make a difference. I want to show you some verses and I just want to look at Isaiah 64 and I want you to look at verse 8. He makes a statement here that changes everything. He has been talking about the mountains, but then he says—and this is where our hope comes in-- no matter how big the mountain is, our God is bigger than the mountain. He says in verse 8, "But now Lord, You are our Father." Oh, He's the God who cares. He is the God who is involved in our lives. He is the God who is our Father through personal faith in Jesus Christ. He is not a distant God, an uninvolved God. No, if you know Jesus Christ, if Jesus Christ lives in your life, if your life has been changed by the power of Jesus Christ you can say, "Oh Lord, you are my Father."

Listen to this: "We are the clay and You are the Potter. We are all the work of Your hand. Don't be furious, Oh Lord. Don't remember our iniquity forever. Indeed please look, listen to this, we are all your people." You see he realized that God had made a covenant with Israel. God was a covenant making, covenant keeping God. He says, "But now Lord, You are our Father and we are Your people. Now Lord You are the potter and we are the clay and Lord we just ask You to remember that we are Your people."

So God is not looking into Washington, God is looking into His people. That's where the desperation needs to come, that's where the commitment needs to come. If God is our Father, and we are truly saved by the shed blood of Jesus, and we do belong to him. If we are God's people then there has to be a commitment on our part to repent of all of our sins. Look at Chapter 4, 5, 6 & 7, you say," Well I don't have any sin to repent of." Oh yes you do, you just don't know what they are. You aren't in heaven yet, and the only perfect person was Jesus. So listen to Isaiah 64:5-7: "You are indeed angry, for we have sinned and these ways we continue. We need to be saved. We are like an unclean thing, Lord. All our righteousness, oh God is like a filthy rag. We all fade as a leaf and our iniquities, like the wind, have taken us away. You have hidden your face from us; you have consumed us, because of our iniquities." Now listen, all I know to do is to say, "God I want to be a desperate man. We want to be a desperate church. We don't want to live in desperate times and be apathetic and prayerless. So God, would you convict us of our sin and Lord, we know that our righteousness is as filthy rags. Lord, we know that we fade like a leaf and we know our iniquities, Lord, just like the wind can carry us away. So God would you search me, would you know me and would you try me and would you show me any wicked way in me so that I can repent of the sin that is in my life?" Listen you get quiet with God for a while and you be honest with God and you just ask the Lord to search you and to know you, and to reveal the innermost part of your heart. I'm telling you, God is faithful. And folks listen, if the Church was pure and the church was holy then the Church would be powerful. So, as we become pure and holy by the blood of Jesus, we will be powerful. So, I'm telling you, we've got to make a commitment to live in repentance. And by the way, repentance is not just confessing our sin, it's turning away from them, "Hey, God I want to confess my prayerlessness. I repent." Well then, you're going to pray. "Well, I want to confess my lack of study of the Word. God, I have been indifferent towards Your Word. I repent. So what I'm going to do, I'm going to get in Your Word. And Lord I want to repent that instead of standing strong, I have begun to look like the world and talk like the world and act like the world so I want to repent, Lord, that I'm not salt and I'm not light." And so you repent and you become salt and light. We have to make a commitment to walk in repentance of our sin.

Secondly, we have to make a commitment to come before God in total surrender. God uses surrendered people. God doesn't use people that are not surrendered. He uses surrendered people. Now let me tell you why I know that's in here. In chapter 64 he, "We are the clay and You are the potter." Okay, now you know what the potter does with the clay? Whatever he wants to do. The potter would put a lump of clay on the wheel and he would begin to mold it and he would begin to shape it and he'd look at it and there would be something there that he didn't like so he would start over. The clay was surrendered to the hands of the potter. The clay had no choice. All he did was respond to what the potter did. And, so, I mean we're the clay and He is the potter so we just come before Him and surrender and God puts us on the wheel and He begins to mold us and to make us and He gets this out of our life and that out of our life and He adds this and soon He is making a vessel of honor, set apart and ready for the Master's use and prepared for every good work. A vessel of honor, a vessel that reflects the very life of Jesus Christ and the very character of Jesus Christ so we come. We make a commitment to walk in repentance. That's being a desperate person, but we make a commitment to walk in surrender and saying, "God, just mold me and make me into the person that You have made me to be." And we're clay in the potter's hand, that's called "A commitment to surrender."

There is a third commitment; a commitment to repent, a commitment to walk in surrender, and a commitment to action. You say, "I am going to be that man, I'm gonna be that woman. I am going to stir myself up. Now here is what it is, I am making a commitment to action. I will call on Your name. By the grace of God, by the power of thw Spirit, I will repent, I will be clay in the potter's hand and by the grace of God, I will call on Your name. I will stir myself up to take hold of You. The Spirit of God is speaking this to me right now. I long, I have a passion for godly leaders, a godly president, I long for that, I long for godly people in the House and Senate, who are selfless and who live not for their own good, but who have a love for the people and the country at their heart, I long for that. But God is saying to me, "You have been looking long enough for a man or a group of men to deliver you. That will not happen, you better get your eyes off man and you better get your eyes on Me; I can raise up the man, I can do that, but you do not look for the man, you look for the living God." And He is speaking that strongly to me, as much as I long to see Godly people, who care about this country and care about you and it is not about themselves, I am telling you only God can raise them up. So, I am not looking for them, I look to God and say, "God you better do it or it won't get done." Does that mean we're silent? No. Does that mean we do nothing? No, but it means our focus is not on any man, our focus is on the living God. So, there is a commitment to action: "Lord, I will call on your name, I will stir up myself to take hold of You."

Then the last thing, there is the commitment to believe. You see, some of you are giving up hope, but I want you look at verse 3 and 4 now. There is the commitment to repent, there is a commitment to surrender, there is the commitment to action, I will call on Your Name and I will by the grace of God, stir myself," but then there is a commitment to believe.

Look at verse 3. This ought to encourage you. "You did awesome things, for which we did not look. God, You did more than we could ever ask or think. You did awesome things for which we did not look, You came down." Hey God answered his prayer! "You did awesome things for which we did not look, You came down and the mountains shook at Your presence, Hallelujah! God, You did more than we could ever ask, You came down Lord, You did awesome things, for which we did not look and the mountains shook at Your presence."

Verse 4: "For since the beginning of the world, men have not heard, nor perceive by the ear, nor has any eye seen any God beside You, who acts for the one, who waits for You. You are the only God that acts for the people that wait for You, You are the only one. No other God does. You meet him (that's us), You meet him who rejoices and does righteousness, who remembers You in Your wait. You meet him, You meet her who rejoices, who does righteousness and remembers Your ways."

Desperate times: some of you are fighting desperate battles personally in your own life. I care about that. We care about that. Don't fight those battles alone. Let us pray with you. Let us pray for you. Let us encourage you. I would not minimize the personal battles that some of you are fighting in this room today. Listen to me, I know you are fighting some battles and I know you are desperate, and that's why you are here and I want you to know that God hears your cry. Don't let unbelief be brought back. God hears your cry. Cry out to God. Take hold of the hem of His garment. Be like the widow who persistently cried out for God.

Cry out to God. Let us cry out with you. We care, but let me tell you something now corporately. We've got to cry out to God. We've got to get desperate for the city, we've got to get desperate for the state, desperate for our nation, desperate for the multitude of lost souls who are hanging by a thread over a devil's hell. Listen, these are desperate times and we have got to start crying out to God to come down. "Lord, tear down that mountain, let the adversaries know Your name. God let the mountains shake with You!" See? We've got to do it now. There is a call to action and it is a call from God. I can't do it for you; all I can do is encourage you. God can use His people. He always has used His people to make a difference.

The Civil War was the bloodiest war in American history. Right before the Civil War, Jeremiah Lanphier started a prayer meeting in New York City. First day, four people showed up. Soon, they were so many, they had to go to another room. Soon, there were about a hundred different prayer meetings all over the city of New York. Then it began to spread, and a man said, he travelled all the way from New York City to Chicago and in every city, there were people that were meeting at noon to cry out to God and out of that, came the great prayer revival before the Civil War. About a million people came into the Kingdom of God during that prayer revival of Jeremiah Lanphier. He was just one man. God will use you; He will use you to make a difference. If you will come before Him in repentance and surrender absolutely and absolutely say, "God, I'll answer Your call to action."

CHAPTER 11

OUT WEST AGAIN

The meetings of January 1st through 12th started 1979 on a high note at Cottage Hill Baptist Church as the echoes of the Ravenhill Revival sounded throughout Mobile. Attendance, baptisms, and enthusiasm were all riding high in the wake of the powerful meetings, and Fred Wolfe was firmly entrenched as one of the most influential men in the city. On February 23, 1979, as he began his eighth year as pastor, Fred wrote, "Many times when a Church grows a great deal and the Pastor and People love each other as we do, people sometimes say that the Church is 'personality' centered. Well that is certainly true of CHBC. The person we are all centered around is Jesus Christ. Our eyes are on Him, and He never changes and never fails. Praise His Name-- Jesus Christ is Lord!"

Seven wonderful years had been completed. Fred Wolfe was without question the most well-loved and successful pastor that Cottage Hill Baptist Church had ever seen. It was the optimal convergence of excitement, vision, growth, and loyalty between pastor and people.

Until the first crack appeared.

On February 28, 1979, Fred sent a letter to every member of Cottage Hill. What he had to say was more important than just his regular "It's On My Heart" column. This was big, and everyone needed to hear it.

"This is a very important letter," he began. "I have just made one of the hardest, yet more important decisions of my life.

"I have now completed seven (7) years as your Pastor-- seven wonderful years. God has given me the assurance that he wants me to continue as your Pastor for many years to come.

"I have been prayerfully considering for over a month a call to a fine church in Texas. They are wonderful people. The church has a wonderful opportunity. The decision I have made was, by far, the most difficult of my life.

"In the beginning, I felt led to go to Texas. Then barriers came up, and I felt led not to go. Then God showed me those barriers were put up by Satan. So those came down, and again I felt led to go to Texas. Then another barrier came up and I said, 'No, I cannot go.' That barrier came down, and the door was open for me to go. I was moving full speed ahead. All this time I was praying that God's will would be done. I told God I would rather die than be out of His will. Monday, February 26, and Tuesday, February 27, a barrier was erected, a final barrier, and this was God confirming to me that I was not to leave CHBC, but to remain for years to come. The matter is eternally settled!

"What God has started here at CHBC, He is going to complete. He gave me a promise in Psalms 90:17 that 'He is going to establish the work of our hands.' I praise Him for this. God has taught me many things during this very difficult time.

"1. He has taught me some things about myself and my own spiritual needs.

2. He has taught me many things about my own family. He has used this to draw Anne, Mark, Jeff, and myself much closer together. There have been tears shed in these past few weeks.

3. He has drawn our Staff and families here at CHBC closer together, given us a new unity and purpose that only He can give.

"Needless to say, I am physically, mentally, and spiritually exhausted. Thursday - Saturday, I am going to get away with my family for a few days.

"I look forward to seeing all of you Sunday, March 4, for a new beginning together of some wonderful years of service. We love you in Jesus. Thank you for loving us! Thank you for praying for us.

"My prayer is that God will make CHBC a source of revival for Alabama, the Gulf Coast, and around the world. God is able! Let's be available.

Jesus Christ is Lord,
Bro. Fred"

Panic and relief flooded the congregation simultaneously. *Fred wanted to leave?* was followed closely by *Thank God he didn't!* In the next couple of weeks, Fred and the staff set out to make sure that no sense of instability took root in the minds of the people. By March 16, Fred touted the "Days of Glory and Grace" that he and the staff felt were just ahead for Cottage Hill Baptist Church. Fred issued a three-page "Vision for the Future" that included the possibility of three Sunday morning worship services, three Sunday Schools and two Sunday evening worship services before they could build the additional space that was needed.

March 25th through the 29th, Fred's old friend, Manley Beasley, returned and led in a strong week of meetings. That Sunday, twenty-three people joined the church.

On Easter Sunday, April 15, three Sunday School schedules

ran concurrently with three worship services in the morning, with baptisms, the Lord's Supper, and a message in the evening service.

A week later, Fred and four other men traveled to Tokyo to conduct revival services. Meanwhile, the people were asked to pray for the leadership as they drew a Master Plan for a new auditorium and other future buildings.

And as 1979 went on, the prospect of Fred having left was forgotten, as crusades, witnessing programs, mission trips, musicals, and vision for the future continued to bloom before them.

Late on the evening of September 12, 1979, Hurricane Frederic made landfall as a direct hit on Mobile. A strong category 3 with sustained winds of 135 miles per hour, the storm barreled up Mobile Bay and caused an estimated 6 to 9 million dollars of damage to the port city. Frederic blew all through the night, into the early morning hours of September 13, and hardly a square foot of the greater Mobile area was spared. Power was out across the region for two weeks or more. Many people on the Gulf Coast traveled as far as New Orleans for a block of ice and a loaf of bread.

The sweltering September heat was exaggerated by the lack of power for air conditioning. Most residents unavoidably had two weeks off of work either because of no power in the workplace or storm damage to be cleaned up, whether in their own yards or in tandem with friends and neighbors. Cottage Hill Baptist Church was empty and dark the Sunday after Frederic, as everyone tended to their own homes and families.

Church services resumed at the Cottage Hill facilities on September 23, but with a low attendance. The weekly budget requirement was $23,000, and the offering for that day was $6,000. The next Sunday made up the difference in the giving, and

Fred reminded everyone of what really matters: "We praise God for sparing our lives, and for all He has taught us as a result of this experience. Material things can be changed and gone in a matter of an hour. But Praise God He is eternal, Jesus is the same and in Him our lives are founded on 'The Solid Rock.' No Hurricane can move that."

For Fred Wolfe, though, Hurricane Frederic did more damage than he knew at the moment. The powerful winds didn't only uproot trees and take the roofs off buildings, it also laid bare a fatigue that had been building slowly in Fred since he first arrived in Mobile. Fred had been faithfully at the helm of a ship of change for almost a hundred hours each week for almost eight years, and it was finally coming for its pound of flesh. The devastation of Frederic had been discouraging on many levels for everyone in Mobile, and the certainty of the hard work of rebuilding stretched out in front of Brother Fred. The church in Texas was calling again. They would not take "No" for an answer, and he had told them "No" twice. It was a large church, sure, and there was work to be done, but maybe not as much work as he had done for the past seven plus years at Cottage Hill. Fred was happy here, Anne and the boys were happy here, and they were all loved. But with Cottage Hill still growing faster than seemed possible, there was no end in sight that would promise some kind of real rest. More growth meant more to oversee, more to prop up, more for which only Fred would be ultimately responsible. He was exhausted just thinking about it.

And so it came to be that on Monday, November 12, 1979, Fred Wolfe wrote the following letter to the people of Cottage Hill Baptist Church:

Dear Fellow Christians,

In February of 1972, God led me and my family to be your pastor.

God has blessed us with seven wonderful years and ten months together. He led us to Cottage Hill from a good church in Georgia where God was blessing and doing a wonderful work. I came to be your pastor because the Holy Spirit led me to Cottage Hill.

The same God who led me by His Holy Spirit to Cottage Hill in 1972 is now leading me to become pastor of the First Baptist Church of Lubbock, Texas. I am resigning as your pastor for only one reason-- The Holy Spirit has led me to do so. I know without a shadow of a doubt, it is God's will for me to go to Texas to minister to those people.

Some will say, "Well, if we had supported Bro. Fred more, he would not have left us." That is not true. No church could have loved us, prayed for us, supported us, and encouraged us more than you wonderful people. The reason I am leaving is because it is God's perfect will!

I know you have questions. This Wednesday night, November 14, I will share in detail how I came to this decision. I will answer your questions. I ask you to be present so you will know first hand how God has led.

My resignation will be effective November 26, 1979. I realize this is only two weeks, but separation from loved ones is painful, and to prolong it would be unwise.

Thank you for your prayers and understanding. Jesus is Lord, and this wonderful church is in His hands! The future of CHBC is as bright as Jesus who is Lord!

Jesus is Lord,
Fred H. Wolfe

The staff was informed by telephone the night before the congregation received the letter. Ed Keyes was especially devastated. He had come to Cottage Hill just months after Fred in 1972, and these had been the best ministry years of his life. Ed and Fred served and ministered as one. Ed rarely disagreed with Fred on anything theologically, and even then it was never anything of any real consequence. He had also learned to trust Fred's leadership, especially his willingness to change his mind on any given idea if it didn't look feasible later. Ed knew, though, that he still had a job to do here, with these people. If anything, Cottage Hill would need him more in the coming days than they had in the last seven plus years.

Sunday, November 25, 1979, became "Pastor Appreciation Day." One of the greatest testimonies to Fred's effectiveness and influence for the past seven years and ten months was the outpouring of love on his leaving. The people were deeply saddened, but they had learned over the years to accept the plan of God with gratitude, and wait for Him to show His faithfulness in it all. The Sunday School attendance broke all records that day, as people gathered to sign a Declaration of Love in each Sunday School department. Everyone was invited to contribute personal or family letters that would then be included in one volume and bound for presentation to Brother Fred.

From the time of his arrival in 1972 to his departure, Fred Wolfe baptized 2,110 people at Cottage Hill Baptist Church. 5,100 people joined Cottage Hill during that time, while the average Sunday School attendance went from 950 to over 2,100, and the annual budget grew from $300,000 to over $1.3 million.

Fred preached his final message after almost eight years at Cottage Hill Baptist Church that evening at 5:00 PM. The Pastor Search Committee was also announced that night. It would include Bill Rubley, Jerry Benson, Herb Fisher, Charlie Jackson, Pat Moore,

Herb and Charlotte Reynolds, Mal Roebuck, and Harlan Taylor.

But on the evening of November 25, 1979, as gifts were given, good-byes were said, and tears rolled, no one there could have predicted the surprises that were in store for those committee members over the next few months-- especially not Fred himself.

PART III

CHAPTER 12

LUBBOCK IN THE REARVIEW

Fred arrived in Lubbock as Christmas lights adorned the West Texas city. The historic stone buildings of Texas Tech stood like ornaments on the barren landscape. The scrub trees were bare for the winter, but Fred had a feeling that they wouldn't look much different when summer came.

As he drove past the enormous eleven-story bell tower adjacent to the worship center at Broadway and Avenue V, the sky was dark, but Anne's mood was darker. Mark was in his junior year back in Mobile College, and they had left Jeff in Mobile with friends, to finish his senior year of high school. Both of their sons and all of their friends were more than 900 miles away, and Anne could feel every inch of it.

Fred began his ministry at the 10,000-member First Baptist Lubbock as 1979 drew to a close, and he was looking forward to a fresh start. He could hardly believe that just one year ago, he was preparing to host Leonard Ravenhill, and now here he was, halfway across the country, with a group of people whom he didn't know at all. It had been the most difficult year of his life. Hearing God had never been harder, and he still hoped he had heard correctly about this move. There was nothing for it now but to forge ahead.

So much had been poured into Fred in the last eight years. Bertha Smith, Jack Taylor, Manley Beasley, Peter Lord, Leonard Ravenhill. The Spirit-filled life, hearing the voice of God, soul care, praise and worship, prayer, and revival. Where would he start with the people in Lubbock?

He would start where it all started with him. And he would see just how hungry they were.

The people of FBC Lubbock were kind and gracious, and they received Fred and Anne with warmth and love. They responded to Fred's preaching with gusto, and the Lord began to move among them right away. They had heard of all that God had done under Fred's leadership at Cottage Hill, and they were eager to see if He would do the same here.

Fred could see how they were receiving easily what was on his heart, so he gave them a test. He scheduled a meeting where he would teach on how to be filled with the Holy Spirit, and he would invite them to ask God to fill them. He would preach with everything he had on what it means to know Jesus as Lord. And he would have that meeting on the evening of Super Bowl Sunday.

On January 20, 1980, the Pittsburgh Steelers and the Los Angeles Rams faced off in a championship contest watched by millions around the world. The game would feature such football legends as Terry Bradshaw, Lynn Swann, Franco Harris, and Vince Ferragamo. The Rose Bowl Stadium in Pasadena, California was packed out. So was the chapel at First Baptist Church, Lubbock, Texas. It overflowed and was standing room only.

The people had responded to Fred's invitation with a hunger that surprised him. It was a turning point in many lives, and the life of the church. By the time the meeting was over, many people had prayed and asked God to fill them with the Holy Spirit and to make Jesus the unchallenged Lord of their lives.

Not everyone was happy with Fred's direction for the church, though, and as the days passed, a few began to make it clear.

Fred had so enjoyed serving with Ed Keyes, and together they had fought the "worship wars" of the 1970s. Arm in arm, Fred and Ed had stood their ground and helped the people of Cottage Hill into unprecedented freedom in the arena of praise and worship. They had seen great victory as people opened their hearts and hands to the Lord like they had never done before. Not only was it gratifying to see the people of Cottage Hill embrace the presence of God, it was deeply satisfying for Fred as well, and he knew that he never wanted to take a step backward into a form of worship that didn't allow for at least some sense of expression.

Shortly into his tenure, he suggested to the Minister of Music some of the songs that he would like to see them start singing. They were songs that had ministered to him at Cottage Hill, and he was sure that the people at FBC Lubbock would appreciate them, too.

After the first Sunday of what Fred thought was a powerful time of worship, he received a letter from a prominent lawyer in the church. "That kind of music is not acceptable, and it's not going to work here," the man said. "We don't want to go that direction."

Soon after, Fred began to get to know the leaders more deeply, and he realized that the lawyer's thoughts represented more people than he had thought at first. This was going to be more work than he had anticipated. This was going to be a real struggle. *Okay*, he thought, *I guess we have a way to go. It will probably take about ten years for God to change this church, but I'm here now. I have the time. Let's get started.*

By February, the Pastor Search Committee of Cottage Hill was frustrated. They had begun following up on 65 recommendations, they had heard 17 of them preach, and had received interested responses from seven, but they had no clear sense of direction.

Things at Cottage Hill were going very well. Dr. Roy Fish, the popular Professor of Evangelism at Southwestern Baptist Theological Seminary, was flying in every weekend to preach as interim pastor. It was a natural fit, especially since Dr. Fish was the man who had recommended Fred to Cottage Hill exactly eight years earlier. Roy Fish's style of preaching was easy and effective, and his heart was full of love for Jesus and for people. The church continued to grow, even in a time when most churches don't. The people still prayed every day for Fred and for the people of First Baptist Church, Lubbock. They had been taught well that their strength is not from a man, but from the Lord.

Still, the Pastor Search committee could gain no ground. During that time, one of the committee members, Herb Fisher, passed through Lubbock as part of a trip, and he visited his old friend. That day, Herb asked Fred if he would be interested in coming back. The response was firm and clear. "No," Fred told him, "I'm here now. I'm staying."

On April 16, 1980, the presence of God permeated the Easter Sunday services at First Baptist Lubbock. More than a dozen people responded to the altar call to give their lives to Jesus. The church was beginning to enjoy and appreciate who God had sent them in their new pastor.

One day after Easter, Fred was sitting in his study, praying and thinking about where he was and what lay ahead. As he was thinking, he noticed a plaque that had been given to him years before, that had gone with him wherever he went. He had never really thought about it too much, but for some reason, now it was as if God was speaking directly to him through the words of a plaque that he had casually read hundreds of times. It said, "Idolatry is trusting people, position, or possessions to do for you what only God can do."

The Holy Spirit spoke to Fred's heart, and it would not have been any clearer if it had been audible. "Fred, you have committed idolatry. You have trusted something other than Me. People encouraged you to come to Lubbock because it would be important in the 'Battle for the Southern Baptist Convention,' and you believed them. You made this move because you were trusting that this position, or these people, could do something that only I can do. You only left Cottage Hill because you got restless and stopped trusting Me."

Fred understood immediately that it was true. He hadn't realized that had been in his heart until God revealed it, but there it was. He knew right away that he was in the wrong place. "Lord," he said, "I'll do whatever you want me to do. I'll go back to Cottage Hill, or wherever you want."

Fred made a phone call to Herb Fisher, who had approached him in February. "If you still want to pursue this with me," he said, "I would be open to it, but only if the search committee is unanimous, and only if every one of you has a *rhema* word from God on it."

Within a few weeks, the Cottage Hill committee confirmed that every one of them would like to see Fred return, and that every one of them had tested it against Scripture and had a *rhema* word from God in confirmation.

Fred Wolfe was about to do the hardest thing he had ever done. First, leaving Lubbock was going to be traumatic. He had only been there less then six months, and the ministry was going well.

The Lord seemed to be moving, and in general, the people were responding to Fred's leadership in most things.

Second, how do you return to a church that didn't want you to go but you convinced them that it was God's will? Especially after such an outpouring of love and an enormous sendoff?

Fred knew that there was only one way that he was going to get through this. He would have to bury his pride in the deepest ditch he could find, and just go forward one step at a time.

On May 7, the Pastor Search Committee of Cottage Hill Baptist Church brought a report to the congregation and told them that they were unanimously pursuing a prospective pastor. They asked the people to pray for them for the next two weeks.

On Wednesday, May 21, the Search Committee shared with the congregation that their choice for Pastor of Cottage Hill Baptist Church was Fred H. Wolfe. They explained how they believed God had led them to that conclusion, and testified of following the leading of the Holy Spirit over the past five and half months. The congregation enthusiastically supported the invitation for Fred to preach in view of a call at Cottage Hill— for the second time— that coming Sunday, May 25th.

When the official invitation reached Fred in Lubbock, he told his Associate Pastor what was happening. "I won't be here this Sunday," he said. "I'm going back to the church I came from to preach in view of a call as their new pastor. Then I'm going to resign."

"Well," said his colleague, "you can do that if you want, but I'll tell you something. You're finished. You're finished in leadership in the Southern Baptist Convention, and you are finished in this denomination."

"That's okay," said Fred. "If I'm finished, I'm finished. I'll be alright."

On Sunday morning, May 25, 1980, Fred Wolfe stepped back into the familiar pulpit at Cottage Hill and preached on the "Pearl of Great Price." That evening, he would have another chance to address the people before they voted.

On Sunday afternoon, Fred felt sure of what was about to happen. He called the Chairman of Deacons at First Baptist Lubbock. "I've written a letter," he said, "a resignation letter. It's on my desk in my office. They haven't voted on me here yet, but I know I'm coming back to Cottage Hill. But, I'll come back and be there next Sunday to resign publicly before the church."

"Well," said the deacon, "I'll be frank with you. It would probably be better if you didn't."

On Sunday evening, Fred spoke to the people of Cottage Hill Baptist Church. Not surprisingly, even among the excitement of the prospect of Fred returning, they were trying to understand how all of this could have happened in the first place. Fred referred them to the story of Abraham and Isaac in Genesis chapter 22. "You know," he said, "God told Abraham to take his son, Isaac, to a mountain that he would show him later, and to sacrifice his son there. Abraham didn't understand, but he trusted God and obeyed him. Then, on the mountain, God stayed Abraham's hand and stopped him from actually performing the sacrifice. It looked like a contradiction from where Abraham stood, but he didn't have to understand it, just obey. We stand at this place today, and if we try to understand the events of the last six months in light of today, we are just going to get confused. But, as with so many other things in our lives, the important thing is not that we understand. It is that we obey what we know to do in this moment in which we stand."

The auditorium seating capacity of 1,600 was pushed to capacity and beyond that evening with almost 1,900 voting members. Four overflow areas with television monitors were packed. When the ballot count was finished, only fifteen people had dissented. The vote of approval was higher than ninety-nine percent. Fred was overwhelmed.

On June 15, 1980, Fred returned to the pulpit of Cottage Hill Baptist Church as Pastor. Two days earlier, he had resumed his column, "It's On My Heart," in that week's issue of *The Challenge*. "This Lord's day we begin our journey together again," he wrote. "The six months apart were used of the Lord to teach us many things. As your Pastor, I believe the same is true of CHBC as a Body. As we begin again, let me share with you some things I believe are vital and necessary if God is to have His will in this Church and in this City:

1. Let us keep our eyes on Jesus. He is the Author and Finisher of our faith. Hebrews 12:1-2.

2. Let us give all praise and glory to God for what He does.

3. Let us enlarge and intensify our prayer life. God does nothing apart from prayer but everything in response to believing prayer.

4. Let each one seek his/her place of ministry in this Body of Christ. Not one of us is to be a spectator, but all are involved in the place of ministry God has for each of us.

5. Let us gather expectantly in anticipation for God to move mightily in our midst.

6. Let us love one another unceasingly with a fervent love.

7. Finally, let us intensify our efforts to carry the Gospel to every person in this City. If we faithfully sow the seed, God will give the harvest.

I love you in Jesus. It's a joy to be your Pastor. Pray for me and my family as you have never prayed before. Remember,
Jesus is Lord!
Bro. Fred"

CHAPTER 13

BACK TO THE FUTURE

Fred settled quickly and easily back into the role of Pastor of Cottage Hill Baptist Church. The fellowship had continued to grow and prosper under the interim preaching of Dr. Roy Fish. Excitement was high and participation was higher. Cottage Hill experienced a new growth spurt immediately after Fred's return.

In August of 1980, the church staff met for a retreat in Memphis where whey prayed and talked together about what would be next. They agreed that the mandate to reach more people in Mobile was still operational, so after the retreat, they unveiled the new plan: five services every Sunday.

Three regular Sunday morning services were already filled almost to capacity at 9:30 AM, 11:00 AM, and 7:00 PM. The leadership now planned to add another morning service at 8:00 AM, and a 5:00 PM evening worship service to encourage Sunday night growth. Fred would preach two of the three morning services and both evening services, with an associate pastor handling the other morning service. He would rotate between all three morning meetings as the weeks went on.

The parade of spiritual giants who spoke into the life of Cottage Hill continued from October 19-24 as Roy Hession came to speak. An internationally known revivalist from Great Britain, Hession quickly became one of the church's favorite guests. A short and stocky man, Roy Hession was so genuinely full of sincere love for Jesus that it would have been difficult not to listen to him. It was not unusual for him to spontaneously lead the congregation in singing with great gusto a chorus that he had written, waving his arms with controlled abandon as he worshipped.

After having come to Christ at the age of 18, Roy Hession soon submitted his life to the work of evangelism, and had subsequently experienced a new reality and understanding of grace which changed his life and ministry. He unashamedly gave out the grace of God wherever he found himself. He was an integral part of what became known as the East African Revival. Once, while walking down a dirt road in Africa, he encountered a new convert walking the same road. "Hello, young man," said Roy, "how are you today?"

"I am not well," said the young man. "I have failed God. I have sinned."

Hession stopped him in the road and looked him in the eye. "Let me ask you a question," he said. "Has the blood of Jesus lost its power?"

"No," said the man, "of course it has not."

"Then you have believed a lie, my friend," said the evangelist. "You have been told that because you have taken many steps away from God, that it will be a long way back. But I tell you, no matter how many steps you take away from God, it is always just one step back to Him. That is the grace of God."

Roy Hession made another statement that had a great impact on the many preachers who heard it. "I have heard thousands of sermons in my lifetime," he said. "Most of them have been good advice. Not many have been good news."

By the time Roy Hession arrived at Cottage Hill Baptist Church, his most well known book, The Calvary Road, had sold a million copies and had been translated into fifty languages. A later book, My Calvary Road, was his own story of how he had found and experienced grace and revival.

By the dawn of 1981, it had become as clear to the people of Cottage Hill as it was to Fred and the leadership, that holding five Sunday services every week was merely a stopgap measure and not the solution to the problem of not enough space. Cottage Hill had baptized 336 people in 1980, which ranked number one among churches in Alabama, and it showed no signs of slowing. On January 25, three CHBC members funded a church-wide dinner as part of a one-night, whole church gathering at the only place in Mobile that was large enough to accommodate all of the people of Cottage Hill at one time-- the Mobile Municipal Auditorium.

Fred preached that evening a message called "Where There Is No Vision," in which he made it clear that unity in gathering was important to unity of purpose. If Cottage Hill Baptist Church was to continue to grow and impact the city of Mobile, more worship space was needed on campus so that more people could meet together at one time. This was not a fundraising meeting, and no offering was received that night. But the mandate was clear. Cottage Hill needed to build.

At the banquet that night, Fred cast his vision, based on Isaiah 54:2: "Enlarge the place of thy tent, and let them stretch forth the curtains of thine habitations: spare not, lengthen thy cords, and strengthen thy stakes."

"I can see," Fred told the people, "an adequate but not ornate auditorium with a 300-voice choir, and a congregation of 3,700 people all together and singing praise and bringing glory to God! What a witness of His power and glory! I can see our church with room to reach more and more people for our Lord Jesus. I can see people coming to Him, following Him, and reaching out to others in His name."

And the meeting closed with faces set forward as they sang the hymn that marked the night: "Lead On, O King Eternal."

Vance Havner returned for the week of April 12th, 1981, and though now in his eighties, he was still as strong and clear as ever, maybe even more than before, as he drew nearer to being "Home Before Dark." In anticipation of a powerful week of meetings, Fred was once again driven deeper into a desire for Christlikeness in every area of his life, and he hoped that the same desire was making its way through the people under his care. In his column of April 10, he implored the congregation to examine their own hearts even as he was examining his. "Am I," he wrote, "consciously or unconsciously creating the impression that I am better than I really am? Am I honest in all my acts or words, or do I exaggerate? Can I be trusted? Am I a slave to dress, friends, work or habits? Am I self-conscious, self-pitying, or self-justifying? Did the Bible live in me today? Am I enjoying prayer? When did I last speak to someone with the object of trying to win that person to Christ? Do I pray about the money I spend? Do I insist upon doing something about which my conscience is uneasy? Am I defeated in any part of my life, jealous, impure, critical, irritable, touchy, or distrustful? How do I spend my spare time? Is there anybody whom I dislike, disown, criticize, hold a resentment toward or disregard? If so, what am I doing about it? Is Christ real to me?"

This level of spiritual introspection was a constant companion to Fred as he opened his pulpit and his heart to the teachings and the influence of those who had something fresh from the Lord to say. This same characteristic of being constantly teachable would be caught by dozens of men and women who would go on into ministry themselves, taking with them an open and listening heart.

At the end of April 1981, Fred and Anne finally went on a honeymoon, just 25 years late. To celebrate his ninth anniversary as pastor and their 25th anniversary, Cottage Hill had presented Fred with a gift of money that would allow them to take a few days off. On April 27, they left for Ocala, Florida, where Fred preached at First Baptist Church of Ocala Monday through Wednesday before having some time alone with Anne. They spent a week at St. Thomas in the Virgin Islands. The dramatic change of pace and scenery was a welcome interlude.

Cottage Hill had already begun its foray into broadcast media with a live radio airing of the 11 AM and 6:15 PM worship services each week. WMOO, Mobile's most powerful AM station at the time, pumped 50,000 watts behind Fred's sermons every Sunday, and the response had been positive. However, it was generally agreed that if they could secure television time, that would be even better. And so, after about five years of asking God for an opportunity to broadcast on television on Sunday morning, the local CBS affiliate, WKRG Channel 5, came knocking.

Beginning on September 21, 1981, Fred Wolfe stepped into living rooms all over the greater Mobile area each Sunday morning from 10:00 to 11:00 AM. Having been encouraged and inspired by the television ministries of other churches like Bellevue Baptist in Memphis, North Phoenix Baptist, Roswell Street Baptist in Marietta, Georgia, and Castle Hills Baptist in San Antonio, Fred had no doubts and no fear as he led the charge into the world of video.

George Harris, pastor of Castle Hills, had said to Fred that "If God opens the door for your church to go on television, my suggestion is go! God does not give this ministry to every church, only to a select few who have the kind of ministry that the world needs to hear."

For a total cost of $1,425 per week, Remote Units of WKRG came out on Wednesday night to tape the service. Fred and the leadership team made slight changes to the Wednesday night format to make it look and feel more like Sunday mornings, when it would air. The TV station survey indicated that at least 52,000 homes would be tuning in, which brought the cost of the program to 2.8 cents per family. Telephone counselors would be trained and provided at the end of the broadcast to pray with callers. "It is the deep conviction of your Pastor and Staff," Fred wrote to the church, "that God has answered our prayers and opened this door. We wholeheartedly and enthusiastically recommend that we take advantage of this God-given opportunity."

On June 17, 1981, the congregation joined the staff with their approval to launch the TV broadcast in September.

In July, the congregation was invited to submit possible names for the TV program, something that would connect with the viewer's sense of need, rather than a statement from the church. Suggestions flooded in. Two keywords that kept reappearing were "life" and "issues." So, the telecast was named in keeping with the phrasing of Proverbs 4:24: "Keep thy heart with all diligence; for out of it are the issues of life." And so, on September 20, 1981, *Issues of Life* premiered in an estimated 52,000 homes at 10:00 AM. Replays of the telecast were made available on Sundays at 5:00 PM in the Chapel so that Cottage Hill members who attended Sunday morning services could see what the people of Mobile were seeing on Channel 5.

At the same time that further growth was expected through the TV broadcast, Fred realized that the newly extended Sunday schedule of five services was not working for him. The decision was made to return to one evening worship service. They continued the three morning services with Fred preaching all three. Fred had never given over one of the three morning worship services to a preaching associate, as was his original plan. He felt it was important that everyone who came to Cottage Hill on Sunday morning should hear the same message, and they needed to hear his heart. Preaching three services on Sunday morning and two in the evenings was taking its toll on Fred physically, emotionally, and spiritually. "I just cannot hold up to this for the next two or three years," he wrote, "until our new auditorium is completed. I thought I could, but I realize it is just not wise."

The Prayer ministry of Cottage Hill Baptist Church was still going strong, as volunteers continued to staff the 24 hour Prayer Room and Fred sought other avenues to bring prayer to the forefront of the lives of the people. To that end, Fred brought in Don Miller from Fort Worth, Texas, to lead a seminar entitled "If My People Will..." Don Miller had founded Bible Based Prayer Ministries as a result of a life-threatening ordeal in which he faced death in multiple operations in 1976. Afterward, he gave his life to God for the cause of prayer. With more than thirty years experience in preaching and leading churches, Don came to Cottage Hill in August of 1981 to train Prayer Warriors. More than a thousand people showed up and committed themselves to prayer in a new and deeper way. Later, Fred said of the time with Don Miller, "Prayer is not us persuading God to do things our way. It is that time we spend with God, and He moves our spirit into oneness with His Spirit. We are thinking and seeing and choosing things His way. John 15:7 expresses this thought so clearly. Many of you moved into new dimensions in prayer life in the Don Miller Seminar. Let me urge you to continue to be faithful in your prayer life. This church will move no higher spiritually than the prayer life of its people."

And just a few months later, those prayers, especially the prayers for revival, would be poured back out on Cottage Hill like a fresh spring rain.

CHAPTER 14

GROWTH OPPORTUNITIES

1982 came in with a swirl of activity, from missions involvement locally and globally, to the growing response to the new television ministry and the problems of limited space. Sunday, January 10th saw the largest attendance since the previous Easter, and people were starting to leave before the worship services began because they had nowhere to sit. Fred was deeply troubled to hear that, and it strengthened his resolve to see a new auditorium built as soon as possible.

The worship services of the last Sunday in January and the following Wednesday were unusually powerful. Thirty-one people joined the church, and two callers gave their hearts to Christ after that Wednesday's service was broadcast. "Truly," said Fred, the "Spirit of God visited us and blessed us. Let me encourage you to lift up your eyes and look on the fields. There are thousands of people in Mobile who need to come to Jesus. God wants to use you and me to bring them to Christ." Commensurate with that end, on January 20, the congregation approved two architectural firms to serve as the architects of the proposed 4 million dollar new auditorium.

In February, Brother Fred and Cottage Hill Baptist Church celebrated ten years together. It was generally agreed that the Lubbock excursion would be considered merely a blip on the radar, and there was no need to start counting at zero again on Fred's return from west Texas. In light of the first ten years, Fred gathered up all of the revelation and the principles that had been poured into him over the course of his life, especially at Cottage Hill, and he used those to express his desire for the kind of church that Cottage Hill would always be. Running throughout the "1982 Prayer for Cottage Hill" were the many threads of the Christian life that had been deeply woven into Fred Wolfe over the years by Stephen Olford, Bertha Smith, Peter Lord, Jack Taylor, Manley Beasley, Leonard Ravenhill, and so many others. The evidence of how Fred was growing up even as the church was growing large rang clearly as he looked ahead:

"1. We Will Be A Christ-Honoring Church. I want us to love the Lord Jesus and exalt Him and magnify Him in all that we do. In every program, organization, and ministry, that Jesus Christ will be preeminent.

2. We Will Be Bible-Centered Church. Without apology, we believe in the inerrancy and infallibility of the Word of God. The Bible is our authority for all that we believe and practice.

3. We Will Teach and Practice the Spirit-Filled Life. That each of us would know what it is to deny ourselves and to say "yes" to Jesus in such a way that the Holy Spirit will empower each of us and that His love would permeate all of us.

4. We Will Be A Great Praying Church. That we will pray, intercede, and be mighty in prayer. We will never go beyond our prayer life as a Church.

5. We Will Be A Church Which Has the World in Its Heart. That we will have a world vision. We must have a heart that longs to

see the salvation of souls. We must reach our neighbor across the street and that person across the world. The bringing of people to Jesus, evangelism, needs to be our watchword. God gives us His compassion for souls.

6. We Will Be A Loving Church. While we will take a stand against what is wrong, we must have a spirit of love that will be conspicuous and contagious. For the people in Mobile and around the world to say, 'Behold, how they love one another.'

7. We Will Be A Holy Church. We must be a Church that adheres to the Biblical standards for separated living and godliness and that departs from all forms of sin and worldliness. A pure Church is a powerful Church.

8. We Will Be A Progressive and An Optimistic Church. God delivers us from a negative spirit. We have a great God, a great gospel, and a great commission to spread it. If God be for us, who can be against us?

9. We Will Be A Church Where Every Member Discovers His Spiritual Gifts and Puts Them to Work. No one should be idle. Everyone can do something. I want it to be truly said that everybody is a vitally involved part of this Body of Believers.

10. We Will Be A Church That is Steadfast and Unmovable. We must always abound in the work of the Lord, as we anticipate and expect the soon and imminent return of our Lord Jesus Christ."

"As we face the future," Fred continued, "we are so thankful that the future is in His hands. We are all aware that to continue to reach people, we must provide additional space... I know we will not go beyond the 2,500 to 2,600 in Sunday School and the present attendance in worship until we provide more space. The people are here. The fields are white. God forbid that we would miss our God-given opportunity by failing to provide space needed to continue to reach and minister to people."

But even as Fred and Cottage Hill set their sights on the daunting task of a multimillion-dollar building project, they were determined not to be distracted from the deeper spiritual realities that had given rise to the phenomenal growth to begin with.

So, in March, the 1982 Conference on Revival began.

The Conference on Revival began on Sunday, March 21, with five special speakers brought in the for the event, four of whom already had a relationship with Cottage Hill: Roy Hession, Jack Taylor, Bertha Smith, and Roy Fish, with Jim Hylton being the fifth. Jim was serving as Pastor of Lake Country Baptist Church in the North Fort Worth area, and was seeing a remarkable move of God in that church. He had also been the catalyst in an 18-week revival in a church in New Albany, Indiana called Graceland, with a pastor whose first name really was Elvis.

Over the course of the next six days, 54 messages were preached by this team, with three services each day, all three featuring three different messages from the speakers. The theme, of course, was revival, both personal and corporate, and as each speaker poured out their heart to the people, the fires of awakening and renewal were stoked. Every service was crowded, no matter the time of day.

By the end of the week, the atmosphere almost vibrated with expectation. The sense of hunger for whatever God wanted to do among them was at an all-time high for the people of Cottage Hill. Testimonies began to bubble up in every conversation, and by Sunday morning, even though the speakers had gone home, the Sunday School departments were buzzing with stories of how God was visibly changing the lives of the people who had been so impacted by the conference. That Sunday morning, on March 28, the worship service was saturated with an awareness of the presence of God. Brother Fred announced that services would resume again on Wednesday, the 31st, and would go through Friday, then pick up again the following Sunday and Monday.

Jim Hylton agreed to return to speak at those extended meetings, having sensed that God was doing something unusual and knowing that it was a special time. Mobile was not Jim's only destination, either. He was also conducting and overseeing a similar revival happening simultaneously in Dothan, Alabama. While these services in Mobile were going on, Jim flew into Mobile, then on to Dothan, then back to Fort Worth to preach at Lake Country.

The Conference on Revival was another key element in spreading and solidifying Fred's influence to pastors outside of the Mobile area and outside the denomination. After the meetings, Fred asked the church to pray not only that the revival would spread throughout Mobile during the continuing services, but also for the "148 pastors, missionaries, and Church Staff Members who attended the Conference... and for their churches in Alabama, Florida, Georgia, Louisiana, Michigan, Mississippi, Tennessee, Texas, and Virginia."

Fred's own journey and his desire to know God more completely was now being replicated in the lives of those who came into his sphere. The ways in which Fred had pursued God had now become the model for others' pursuit as well. A visiting pastor from one of those churches enunciated well the kind of influence that Fred was beginning to walk in as a pastor to pastors, in a letter sent to Fred after the March conference. "Dear Fred," wrote pastor Danny Graham, "once again I found myself in debt to the 'overflow ministry' of Cottage Hill Baptist Church. I have time and again been instructed, inspired, and enlightened because Cottage Hill is a church with no walls up.

"It was at Cottage Hill that God clearly reaffirmed His call on my life to Pastor. It was at Cottage Hill that God convicted me of my great need to enthrone Jesus Christ as Lord of all, and to allow His Holy Spirit to make such a commitment real in experience in daily living. It was in the Leonard Ravenhill meetings and the Don Miller Prayer Seminar that the Lord inspired and instructed me to be a struggler in Prayer.

"And when I find myself or my own ministry needing, it has many times been a need wonderfully met by the overflow ministries of Cottage Hill. I have wept and worshiped as the Lord Jesus has been marvelously magnified through music. As Bro. Ed and the many Choirs of Cottage Hill have sought to bear witness and praise to the Lord, I have found my life blessed by their devoted efforts. How thankful I am for their talents in lifting up Jesus through music.

"Now, again, I find my heart washed and healed through the preaching of the Word in this Conference on Revival held at Cottage Hill this past week. Thank you, thank you, thank you for being a Church with a concern and compassion for others, for your sister churches, and for your brother pastors. May our Lord continue to lead in His kingdom's work.

Danny Graham"

A few weeks later, on May 1, 1982, Fred's growing influence was recognized more formally as Mobile College conferred upon him the Honorary degree of Doctor of Divinity in special services at the Mobile Municipal Theatre.

Less than two weeks after that, Fred Wolfe's notoriety leaped to the international level as Trinity Broadcasting Network flew him to Santa Ana, California to appear on the *Praise the Lord* program. Once again, Fred testified to the effectiveness of all that God had poured into him in the areas of prayer, revival, being filled with the Spirit, and church growth.

Then, on June 14, Fred took another step into a wider realm of leadership, one that he had invested in for a long time. On that day, he was elected President of the Southern Baptist Pastor's Conference at the annual meeting being held in New Orleans. This position, Fred knew, would provide him a platform for speaking into the lives of every pastor of a Southern Baptist church in the country, and he could use that platform to further drive home the values that had been so important and fruitful in his own life and church. This office, he believed, was also a result of his efforts in the Battle for the Convention years ago, and now perhaps all that he had given there was coming back to him.

In September of 1982, Fred introduced Cottage Hill to another speaker who had a powerful impact on the church. Dudley Hall came to preach in revival services September 12-15, and it would not be the last time that he would occupy the pulpit at CHBC. Dudley was a uniquely gifted teacher who communicated the truth of Scripture in a way that was easily grasped, yet deeply profound. He spoke at noon meetings each day, as well as evening services at night. The gym was packed at each noon meeting, as people from all over Mobile would bring their lunches, find a seat at a table, and be fed in ways that they had not expected.

Dudley was the president of Successful Christian Living Ministries out of Euless, Texas, but his idea of success had nothing to do with the world's idea of success, and everything to do with the Lordship of Christ, the Spirit-filled Life, and prayer. Once again, Fred listened and learned as another speaker strummed the strings of his own heart by taking the issues closest to him and making them clearer than ever before. Dudley had served Roy Hession years before, so it was no surprise that his message resounded with notes of grace and the unconditional acceptance that God has extended to his sons and daughters. Dudley Hall's ministry that week was special, and it added to the legacy that Fred was building at Cottage Hill, a legacy of openness and a willingness to follow all that God was laying out ahead of him and Cottage Hill.

By November of 1982, the names of Fred Wolfe and Cottage Hill Baptist Church were well known, now not only in the greater Mobile area, but increasingly throughout the country and around the world. Fred remained very aware of the responsibility that accompanied that kind of influence, but he was grateful for the opportunity to see it used for the expansion of God's Kingdom.

Part of Cottage Hill's weight in the city came from the fact that the mayor, Gary Greenough, was a vital part of the church. As a direct result of all that Mayor Greenough had learned and experienced in his years at Cottage Hill, he unashamedly issued a proclamation for the city, designating the week of November 21-28, 1982, as "Bible Week" in Mobile. The clearly Christian wording of the proclamation gave no room for doubt about the mayor's stand:

"WHEREAS, we live in days of uncertainty, surrounded by international turmoil, inflation, rising crime rates and moral confusion; and

WHEREAS, the Holy Bible remains an indestructible foundation of truth and a source of inspiration all of us can turn to; and

WHEREAS, every person within his innermost being has a yearning and hunger for spiritual fulfillment with God, in His infinite wisdom has made provision for through the Holy Scripture; and

WHEREAS, the Laymen's National Bible Committee has developed materials and media messages around the slogan "THE BIBLE, READ IT FOR YOURSELF," to help people get into the Bible,

NOW, THEREFORE, DO I, GARY GREENOUGH, MAYOR OF THE CITY OF MOBILE, ALABAMA, hereby proclaim November 21-28, 1982, as "BIBLE WEEK" in Mobile and urge all citizens to participate in this annual observance by reading the Bible and becoming familiar with its teachings and principles."

In the first week of December 1982, Cottage Hill hosted a man who would have one of the most lasting effects on Fred Wolfe. Arthur Blessitt— "The Man Who Carried A Cross Around the World"— came to the church.

Fred was indelibly imprinted by the calm intensity of the man who had carried a cross through 60 countries and preached the gospel in 83 countries in the world. He had been covered by every major news outlet, including ABC, CBS, NBC, and appearing on Tom Snyder's *Tomorrow*, and NBC's *Today*. He had also been featured many times on Christian TV programs like *The 700 Club* and *PTL*. Fred was well aware of the reach of Arthur Blessitt's ministry, and he was eager to learn all he could from him.

And Arthur did not disappoint. At the end of their time together, Fred knew that Arthur Blessitt was more like Jesus than any man he had ever met.

When it came time for Fred to plan the Pastor's Conference meetings at the upcoming 1983 Southern Baptist Convention in Pittsburgh, Pennsylvania, he knew right away who he wanted to join him on the platform. The Pastor's Conference is held the two days before the actual Convention meetings begin, and it effectively sets the tone for what will follow as thousands of Southern Baptists from around the country gather.

Since Fred was president, he had the privilege of designing the program for those two days, and he began by featuring the music ministries of Cottage Hill that had flourished so beautifully under the leadership of Ed Keyes for the last ten years. Fred knew that many of the pastors come to the conference tired and discouraged, and he wanted them to experience the joy of knowing Christ that was so powerfully conveyed by the CHBC choirs every Sunday.

Next, Fred put together a lineup of speakers including Jim Hylton, Len Turner, Ron Long, and E.V. Hill, the popular African American pastor of Mount Zion Baptist Church of Los Angeles, along with his new friend, Arthur Blessitt. He also invited Dr. Stephen Olford as the keynote speaker, since Dr. Olford was the man who had been the greatest influence on Fred, and was, in truth, Fred's mentor.

Fred also invited a number of "unknowns" to join him in preaching the Pastor's Conference. He knew full well what it was like to be faithful in obscurity, where no one knows your name. One of the criticisms in the past had been that the same speakers were invited every year, and Fred wanted the crowds to hear fresh voices with fresh words, even if they were from smaller churches that no one had ever heard of before.

When Arthur Blessitt agreed to speak, Fred suggested that they carry the cross starting at Point State Park, a popular destination in the city of Pittsburgh where the Ohio River, the Allegheny River, and the Monongahela River converged. Knowing that there was going to be an art festival in the park that Saturday, Fred intended for the cross walk to be a focal point, hoping that it would entice people to come to the meetings in the arena.

Saturday, June 11, 1983, brought a beautiful, sunny day to the city of Pittsburgh, and hundreds of people filled the downtown area where the three rivers come together. Just before four o'clock that afternoon, the day before the Pastor's Conference began, Fred and

Arthur arrived downtown to carry the cross in Point Park. The walk had been publicized in pre-Convention materials, so a few dozen others had shown up to walk with them, along with most of the adult choir from Cottage Hill, who had made the trip at their own expense to support Fred and to minister to the pastors who would be coming. The walk would begin at the park, then go along an approved route through a section of downtown and end at the Civic Center. As they prepared to start the walk, Fred and Arthur noticed a number of people going into the park, carrying coolers and kegs, lunches and picnics. Fred and his contingent were positioned at the edge of the park, and would be walking away from it to their destination.

Arthur Blessitt, though, was not one to walk in the opposite direction of a crowd of people who needed Jesus. He looked at Fred and said, "We need to take the cross and go in there."

Fred looked in the direction of the Civic Center. Then he watched the people passing him, going into the park toward the riverside. He nodded, and told Arthur to lead on. Arthur lay down on the grass, and got on his face before God, praying in the direction that he knew they needed to go. In a few minutes, he stood, shouldered the cross, and began to lead the walkers into Point State Park. Fifty yards into the park, a Pittsburgh police officer held up his hand and stopped Arthur.

"Hold on, sir, you can't go in there with that," he said.

"But," said Arthur, "other people are carrying beer and all kinds of things in there. I'm taking this cross."

"But that's not your route," the officer said.

"I understand," said Arthur, with great calm and confidence. "But I'm just gonna tell you, I am going through there."

The officer looked at Arthur, and after a moment, stepped aside. Arthur turned around to the crowd that was ready to follow him, and said to them, "Everyone, listen. Let me tell you what you are going to see in there. Some people are going to mock us. They are going to call you names, and they are going to say horrible things about the Savior and the cross that you love. Others, though, are going to be curious and interested. They are going to ask why we are doing this, and they will want to talk with you. Still others, though, are going to fall under the conviction of the Holy Spirit and will want to be saved right there, on the spot. Are you ready?"

Fred was scared to death. He certainly didn't want to cause trouble in his first outing as president of the Southern Baptist Pastor's Conference, but he could not deny that this was an obvious moment where God was moving in an unusual way. He trusted God and he trusted Arthur. Yes, he was ready.

And they did see all three reactions. Some mocked, some asked questions and sought to engage them, in both curiosity and debate. But when they got to the center of the park, Ed gathered the 150 members of the Cottage Hill adult choir that were there, and they sang-- at the top of their voices, and with no instruments-- "I Will Glory in the Cross."

And the glory of God fell in a park in downtown Pittsburgh, Pennsylvania. Then they saw the third reaction, as people wept under the conviction of the Holy Spirit. A great number of people gave their hearts to Jesus that day, at a place where three rivers flowed with the redeeming love of God.

CHAPTER 15

MOVE OF GOD

At the start of 1984, Cottage Hill Baptist Church was growing in every way. The church's influence was felt all through Mobile, and now in wider circles, through broadcast media, evangelism, missions efforts, and Brother Fred's participation in various denominational offices. Worship attendance continued to rise, as did the budget, the giving, and the vision for the new building. A few months earlier, the congregation had approved the first numbers, with a new Worship Center expected to come in at just over $6 million.

The year continued smoothly, on a comfortable and predictable incline. Then, toward the end of summer, rumors began to swirl about one of Cottage Hill's more prominent and devoted members, and Fred soon found himself on the inside track of a national news story. In October of 1984, City of Mobile Mayor Gary Greenough was indicted on charges of perjury and conspiracy to steal city funds.

From 1911 to 1985, Mobile was run by a three-man city commission. The office of Mayor would rotate between the three men, so that each of them served as President of the Commission and Mayor of Mobile several times. In the 1970s and early 1980s, the Commission was made up of Lambert Mims, Robert Doyle, and

Gary Greenough. During Greenough's last rotation, though, two managers for the Mobile Civic Center had come under investigation for fraud. They were accused of skimming money from City Auditorium revenues generated from concerts and associated sales, and giving some of their illegal income to Gary Greenough in the form of campaign contributions. Greenough flatly denied having any knowledge of the actions of George Juzang and David Gwin and the skimming of funds. In turn, they accused him of lying about not knowing.

As December approached, Greenough was whisked away by the FBI to an undisclosed location in Mississippi, where they questioned him for two days. During the questioning, they indicated to him that they knew that he had nothing to do with it, but they were after someone else. If he would roll over on former Mobile County Commissioner Dan Wiley, they would drop the charges on him. Greenough said that he didn't know anything about Dan Wiley, that he had never had any dealings with the man. At the end of the two days, the FBI agents decided that Gary Greenough was lying to them, and they would make sure that he went down for the crimes he was being accused of, and that he would get the maximum sentence. Fifteen years later, in 1999, Wiley would plead guilty to federal tax fraud and money laundering connected to his telecommunications business.

It was common knowledge that Gary Greenough was not only a core member of Cottage Hill Baptist Church, but that he and Fred Wolfe were close friends. In all of Fred's experience, he had never had to deal with the media in a situation like this, but he chose to stand by his friend as Greenough continued to profess his innocence.

December 6, 1984, Gary Greenough was convicted on fourteen counts of fraud, conspiracy, and extortion. On January 4, 1985, he was sentenced by United States District Judge Brevard Hand to twenty-five years in federal prison.

The night before Greenough was to be taken away to prison, Fred and a number of deacons met at the Greenough home. Fred asked Gary if he could talk with him privately, and they went to a back room of the house. "Gary," Fred said, "you're going to prison tomorrow. It's all said and done, and nothing is going to change that now. So I want you to tell me something. I'm only going to ask you this one time, and I want you to tell me the truth, because it doesn't matter now. Did you do it?"

"No, Brother Fred," said Gary, "I didn't do it. I have maintained my innocence from the beginning, even when they offered me a way out, even in the face of a much too harsh sentence. But I did not do this thing."

Fred was convinced. "That's all I need to know," he said. "I believe you. And I want you to know something. You will not have to worry about your wife and daughters. We will make sure that they don't lack anything, do you hear me? We are going to take care of your family."

After Gary Greenough was transported to prison, Fred called an informal meeting made up of seven or eight others who had committed to stand with Gary's family. That night, they set up a fund whereby they would contribute, on a strictly volunteer, completely personal basis, to the well-being of Fran Greenough and her daughters. Fred knew that this could not and should not be done through the church, and so it never was. About a week later, City Commission candidate Walter Shorey made statements to the press linking Cottage Hill Baptist Church with money being given to the Greenough family. Fred responded: "The information given by Mr. Shorey in regard to the church's financial aid to Mr. Gary Greenough was totally inaccurate and untrue. No money whatsoever has been given through Cottage Hill Baptist Church to the Greenough family for Mr. Greenough's defense, or for the support of his family. None of this financial support has been given through Cottage Hill Baptist Church; it has been given directly by their friends to the Greenough family."

Fred continued to stand by Gary while he served the next six years. When he was released, he was welcomed back in to the Cottage Hill Family as if he had never left.

In January of 1985, yet another year brought another all-time high of giving, attendance, and involvement. In Fred's first year at Cottage Hill, in 1972, one Sunday they had received the highest one-day general fund offering in the history of the church, a little under $10,000. Now, in the 1985 budget of $3.1 million, that "highest-ever" offering would not be one sixth of what was required on any given Sunday. And, once again, Cottage Hill's 301 baptisms for the previous year ranked CHBC as number one in the top 50 churches in Alabama for baptisms.

In July of 1985, Fred and Anne took a few days off to get away and relax. On Thursday of that week, as they sat having lunch at the Original Oyster House in Gulf Shores, something amazing happened. There, in the middle of nothing overtly spiritual, the Holy Spirit fell on both of them with power. They both began to weep.

As they returned on Saturday, Fred listened to a tape relating the events around the Asbury Revival. During a typical chapel service one morning in 1970 on the campus of Asbury College in Wilmore, Kentucky, a great move of God swept through. What was typically a one-hour service went on for 185 hours, nonstop. It then continued intermittently for weeks, and had a dramatic and widespread effect across the country, then the world.

As Fred was listening to the tape, something struck him in his spirit and would not leave. What he heard was that one of the hallmarks of revival is a deep love for others. Immediately he connected with that revelation, and it spoke directly to a situation he had just encountered, one that had hit too close to home. He knew what he would preach on the next day.

On Sunday morning, Fred stood at the 8:00 service and delivered his message. He spoke with passion and conviction of the necessity of loving people with everything you are, not just being kind, but having compassion for hurting people that breaks your own heart. "A couple of weeks ago," he told the people, "a neighbor of mine came to my house. He was discouraged over some things in his life, and I listened, but I didn't feel any urgency about it. When he left, I didn't think about it anymore. A couple of days later, that neighbor of mine committed suicide." Fred's broken heart over his own lack of love showed in the tears that rolled down his face. "But, as God lives in me, that will never happen again. I will give my life for the love of others."

The Holy Spirit swept over the congregation in a massive wave of repentance. Immediately, the altars were flooded with people weeping and crying out to God for their own neighbors and family members, pleading with the Lord to use them to make a difference, both for now and for eternity.

Typically, when the 8:00 service ended, those attenders would pass the ones coming in for the 9:30 service. Except that this day, they didn't leave. They stayed at the altars, weeping and praying. Fred was in no hurry, either. This looked too much like revival to stop it, so he just let it run. The people who were poised to enter for the later service could see through the windows that something was happening. As they entered the sanctuary, they felt the presence of God immediately. With people still in the altars, they began the 9:30 service. The same thing happened again, and the altar was full at the end of the service. Now those who were planning to attend the 11:00 service came in to see the altar still filled with people. They moved ahead with the worship service. And, again, God moved in power as scores of people brought their all and laid it on the altar of God. All through the building, a cry went up to heaven. Revival had come.

That night, in the 6:00 evening service, the atmosphere was the same. The air was charged with expectation, and there seemed to be a holiness and an awe covering every pew. The service went on for two and a half hours, and no one wanted to leave.

At around eight-thirty, Fred, exhausted but exhilarated, said, "Well, everybody, I don't know exactly what to do here, but I think the Lord wants us to meet again tomorrow night. So, we'll be here at 7:00 for anyone who wants to come." And with that, the crowd slowly dispersed, and the lights went off.

By the time seven o'clock arrived Monday evening, the 1,600 seat auditorium was filling up, and people kept coming. Word had spread quickly around Mobile that God had "shown up" in an unusual way at Cottage Hill on Sunday, and now members of other churches in Mobile were coming to see.

Again, the air practically pulsed with expectation. Even the music portion of the service was unusually rife with a sense of the presence of God. No one was casually conversing with anyone else, no one was fidgety or bored. All eyes were on Ed Keyes and Fred Wolfe. After the singing, Fred preached again, a simple sermon that was saturated with power. And as the invitation began, the altars were flooded.

Just as the night before, no one wanted to leave. Finally, Fred repeated his words from Sunday evening. "I think we need to come back tomorrow night," he said.

And they did come back. Night after night in that first week of July in 1985, the crowds swelled, the tears ran, and people were saved, renewed, and awakened by the presence and power of God. By the time the next Sunday morning dawned, people were traveling in from surrounding states just to breathe the air of this revival. On that Sunday morning, about 3,000 people packed the three morning services.

For two weeks, they came every night, and the Holy Spirit was resident in power every night, too. Finally, at the end of the two weeks, Fred realized that he had no idea how long any of them could continue at this pace. So, with a tired but heavy heart, he decided that they would not return the next night.

Later, Fred referred to that decision as one of the few things he wished that he had done differently. "Do you know," he has said, "that revival was just as hot the last night as it was the first. People were still coming and it had not waned a bit. But I didn't know what to do. I didn't know anyone who had been down this road before me, I didn't have a pattern. I didn't know then that you could take a couple of nights off then come back. So we just stopped. If I could do it again, though, I would have adjusted the schedule, but I would not have stopped it."

CHAPTER 16

CHEST OF JEHOASH

On October 29th, 1986, bids for the new worship center were opened. Only two bids came in by the deadline, and they were both over $10 million. The church had already firmly decided to stay in the $7 million range, so more bids would be solicited.

In November, Fred found himself in a place of further influence when the two thousand pastors of Southern Baptist churches in Alabama elected him President of the Alabama Pastors Conference for the upcoming 1986 year at the annual meeting in Huntsville.

In June of 1986, Fred and Anne celebrated 30 years of marriage. Fred honored Anne by addressing her support for him in his column: "I'm so thankful that Anne has been a faithful part of this journey for the past 30 years. I have a deep and abiding love for my wife. She has seen me at my best and at my worst, but her stickability and her commitment to me and to our family have been tremendous blessings... I want to thank you as a Church for loving her, encouraging her and accepting her. Let me publicly express my love and commitment to her, and I pray that God will give us many more wonderful years together."

Cottage Hill had, in fact, accepted and loved Anne, but more than fourteen years after their arrival in Mobile, she was still something of an unknown entity to most people. Of the thousands who came to Cottage Hill every week, only a handful would have been able to pick her out of the crowd, and fewer still could say that they really knew her.

Anne was always sweet and quiet, and engaging when she had to be, but she still suffered deeply from clinical depression that had come back on her forcefully as she began to enter menopause. It certainly had not helped matters that she had also undergone two different and extensive neck surgeries to try and alleviate, if not eliminate, chronic neck pain. Even for the most emotionally healthy person, unending pain could be unbearable and lead to depression on its own.

Fred was open, if not public, about Anne's battle with pain and depression. Again, it had been determined early on that she was not a co-pastor, she was his wife. He felt it his job to protect her the best he could, both from any criticism that may come her way, but also from the more common struggles and disappointments that any pastor and wife will face. When some group of people would leave the church because they were disgruntled, or because Fred was not going fast enough in his pursuit of the supernatural, or he was going too fast and "going Charismatic," Anne would never even know that they had left. In a church of 7,000 people you can lose forty or fifty, and it doesn't rock the boat, so Fred would protect her from the inevitable discouragement that comes to a pastor and his wife when people walk away.

It was also a sense of protection for Anne that kept Fred from opening the curtain of his home life too wide for all but a select few. Anne's off-and-on struggle with depression caused some dark and difficult days in their home, especially when Mark and Jeff were younger. She was already starting from behind, emotionally, and with the added pressures of being a pastor's wife, plus the normal ups and downs of raising two young boys factored in, the result was sometimes disastrous and frightening.

One of the most difficult balancing acts that Fred maintained was to successfully fulfill his roles as loving husband, faithful father, and dynamic pastor of a growing megachurch. One of the ways he did this was to connect with friends in similar situations. Over the years, he became close friends with two other well-known pastors with national ministries, whose wives also suffered from clinical depression and bipolar disorder. Fred and those friends became more than just colleagues, but confidants. Their friendship for each other over the years helped keep all three of them sane, healthy, and responsible as they sought to love their wives and their churches in a way that honored Jesus at all times.

Fred and Anne's 30th Anniversary vacation came at a great time for them, and they returned from their trip refreshed and ready for whatever came next. And in July, Fred announced that the leadership had received an exciting offer from a contractor, and if all went well, they would break ground for the new worship center on August. 3rd.

On August 3, 1986, the people gathered at the site of the new building. TV news crews recorded the event as hundreds of CHBC members put a special offering in the shovel of a front-end loader, then circled the outline of the building and worshipped. Almost $60,000 was given that evening. Construction began the next morning, August 4th.

Cottage Hill Baptist Church had already been debt free for some time and had built a new Education Building in 1984, and paid cash for it. Now, they were committed to two things simultaneously: 1) to build a new, state-of-the-art 3,800 seat worship center, and 2), to remain debt free. That meant that they would have to pay for a $7 million dollar building as it was being built. The goal was to move into it debt free from the very first day.

This goal required a strategy. As with every other major decision that Fred made, he did not offer one until he felt he had a word from God about how to go about it. Then, once having received it, he would not waver from it.

On October 6, Fred outlined what he felt that he had heard from the Holy Spirit on how they were going to move into a $7 million building debt free. As he read the Scriptures, Fred was impressed about how many times the number forty is mentioned, especially the span of forty days. He mentioned at least eight different instances where God had chosen either forty years or forty days to accomplish His propose. So, Fred proposed that Cottage Hill enter into thirteen separate periods of forty days of giving.

"God has shown me clearly," Fred wrote to the church, "that we are to use the forty-day principle to trust Him for our finances. Forty days were very significant in the Bible. This is the way the forty day period of believing, building, and blessings, are to work: Days 1-5 of the forty days, you are to pray and ask God specifically what He would have you give to the building fund during that forty days. You are already a tither, you're already bringing to God the first fruits, now you are asking God during days 1-5 what He would have you give to this building-- above your tithes to the Budget-- during this forty-day period. From days 6-40 you pray specifically and ask

God to give you that amount of money to give to the Building Fund. God may show you where you already have that amount. He may show you where He has already provided it, and you can go ahead and give it. However, you may have no idea where this amount is to come from, only that it is to come from God, so pray specifically and daily and constantly that God will provide that amount for you to give for the building during the next thirty-five days. As soon as God provides, give that amount-- on that day-- to the Building Fund and write out a little testimony of how God provided it for you and pass it on to one of our staff members. It is going to be beautiful to see how God gives for us."

To collect the offerings, a special chest would be put on the altar at the end of every 40 day period, called the Chest of Jehoash, taken from an account in II Kings chapter 12.

On November 16th, the people gave a special cash offering of $76,738.88. It was less than what was needed, but impressive just the same. The journey of a thousand miles had begun with that one step.

By February 15, 1987, Brother Fred's fifteenth anniversary as Pastor of Cottage Hill Baptist Church, membership of the church was at 8,518-- more than ten times the average attendance when he arrived.

The Chest of Jehoash offering for May 31, when added to the previous forty-day offering, was almost $156,000. Fred wrote to the church, "Thank you for being a vessel through whom God can pay cash for this building."

These special offerings went on, and they continued to rise through the next three seasons, as people saw God providing. In

March of 1988, more than $400,000 was given to build the new worship center.

In April of 1988, Cottage Hill's Sunday worship services were being broadcast by television and radio at least six times each week throughout the Greater Mobile area, and Brother Fred's half-hour radio show, "Light for Life," was being heard every Monday through Friday in at least four metropolitan areas in three states.

That summer, Fred and Anne's oldest son, Mark, finished the required classwork toward a Doctoral Degree in Marriage and Family Counseling, and he moved, with his wife Margaret and their children, to Atlanta to begin working with Christian counselor Stephen Arterburn's Rapha Treatment Center.

Fred was being stretched thinner than he ever thought possible, as he continued to keep a growing and thriving church on mission while simultaneously motivating some 4,000 regular attenders to give more than seven million dollars in two and a half years, on top of the annual $3+ million normal budget. The money was constantly in front of him, whether he wanted to see it or not. What God was doing to fund this building was amazing, but there were times when they fell short.

By August of 1988, the people of Cottage Hill had given over two million dollars, almost half of which was above the budget and went directly to the new building. Still, they were going to be $55,000 short of the bills that would be due in ten days. And as soon as that was caught up, September would bring another $200,000 to pay, for the construction bills of August.

It was coming in, but it was wearing on Fred. He was uncomfortable in this position of having to focus on money, but he stayed motivated by the firm conviction that if they could do this thing, then God would get all the glory. He showed the people his heart even deeper when he wrote in September, "I realize that every week I have to come to you and talk about the new building and about our giving. You know, since I have been your pastor for seventeen years, that it is not my thing to talk about money at all. I just really don't like to do that, but God is giving me the grace to just remind you and to be faithful in doing this. Remember, on January 8 when we move into the new building and all the bills are paid, we will be able to move on and deal with other matters of significance. We are doing what God has called us to do right now, so let's just be patient and faithful."

In November, one of Fred's most significant roads came full circle as Stephen Olford preached in his pulpit at Cottage Hill. Dr. Olford was the man who first spoke the concept of the Lordship of Christ into his heart almost thirty years earlier, and now Fred was ministering on the same platform. "I believe," said Fred, "Dr. Stephen Olford is the greatest preacher I have ever heard. Week in and week out, I know of no one who preaches with the power of the Holy Spirit and great grasp of Scripture as he does. Without question, this man has had the greatest influence in my life of any preacher of the Gospel."

On Sunday, January 1, 1989, the countdown began to Dedication Day the next Sunday. But the week before the dedication would be a special one. The new worship center was finished, and one of the most important dedication events would happen over the next seven days.

On a table at the front of the new sanctuary, in front of the pulpit, sat a large Bible. During that first week of 1989, 314 individuals and family groups took thirty minute increments to read the Bible out loud, straight through, from cover to cover. So, for 157 consecutive hours leading up to Dedication Day, the Bible was being read aloud in the new auditorium, and the spiritual atmosphere was being prepared for the glory of God. After these individuals and families read for thirty minutes, they would record their names in the margin of the Bible, like a small stone of remembrance to mark their part in the story of God that was being written at Cottage Hill Baptist Church.

a Sermon

❈

The Battle for the Mind

THE BATTLE FOR THE MIND

by
Fred H. Wolfe

There's a titanic battle being fought. It's a battle in the mind. Paul talks about this battle in 2 Corinthians 10:3-5. "For though we walk after the flesh, we do not war after the flesh: (For the weapons of our warfare are not carnal, but mighty through God to the pulling down of strong holds;) Casting down imaginations, and every high thing that exalteth itself against the knowledge of God, and bringing into captivity every thought to the obedience of Christ."

Isaiah 55:6-8 speaks of this battle in the mind. "Seek ye the Lord while he may be found, call ye upon him while he is near: Let the wicked forsake his way, and the unrighteous man his thoughts: and let him return unto the Lord, and he will have mercy upon him; and to our God, for he will abundantly pardon. For my thoughts are not your thoughts, neither are your ways my ways, saith the Lord. For as the heavens are higher than the earth, so are my ways higher than your ways, and my thoughts than your thoughts."

The Christian life is not a playground. The Christian life is the battleground. As you read the New Testament, it is interesting to notice how Paul and other New Testament writers are always talking about the spiritual battle in the life of a Christian. Paul wrote to Timothy in 2 Timothy 2:3, "endure hardness, as a good soldier of Jesus Christ. No man that warreth entangleth himself with the affairs of this life; that he may please him who hath chosen him to be a soldier." Paul referred to Timothy as a good soldier of Jesus.

When Paul came to the end of his Christian life, what did he say? "I have fought a good fight. I have finished the course. I have kept the faith." Then, in Ephesians 6:10-11, Paul talked about the tremendous spiritual battle that children of God are engaged in, and he said, "Be strong in the Lord, and in the power of His might. Put on the whole armour of God, that ye may be able to stand against the wiles of the devil." Just a casual reading of the New Testament will convince you and me that we are engaged in an intense spiritual battle.

Not long ago I was counseling with a lady who was quite honest with me. She said, "You know, I'm not sure if I had known that the Christian life was going to be such a battle, I would have become a Christian. No one told me that once I entered the Kingdom of God I was going to be engaged in a warfare, a tremendous spiritual battle."

Now I'm convinced that the greatest battle for a child of God goes on within his mind. Not long ago, a book entitled *The Battle for the Mind* came across my desk. In every child of God that battle is going on in the mind. There is a con- stant spiritual battle in the area of our thought life. That is what Paul was referring to in 2 Corinthians 10 when he wrote, "casting down imaginations, and every high thing that exalteth itself against the knowledge of God, and bringing into captivity every thought to the obedience of Christ." Let's look at our thought life. If we are going to live a victorious Christian life, we must know how to deal with our thought patterns. One of the most sobering verses in all the Bible is found in Proverbs 23:7. "As he thinketh in his heart, so is he." What a person thinks is ultimately what a person does and what he becomes. What does the Bible say about our thought life? We as children of God can control our thoughts instead of letting our thoughts control us. Have you ever wondered why you think what you think? Have you ever wondered why some of the thoughts that flit into your mind seem to be so foreign to your own heart and spirit that God has given you? What about these unwanted thoughts that often pop into your mind? Our thoughts come generally from three areas.

First, from the world in which we live. What we see with our eyes, hear with our ears, smell with our sense of smell, and taste with our taste buds. From our five senses, thoughts enter our minds.

But the Bible also says something very alarming– that from our flesh, the unrenewed mind, thoughts enter our minds. Matthew 15:19 says, "For out of the heart proceed evil thoughts, murders, adulteries, and fornication." That is disturbing. Not only do our thoughts come from the world around us, but out of the heart, our flesh, our unrenewed mind.

The Bible also teaches that our thoughts also come from the devil or his demonic spirits. Ephesians 6:16 says, "Above all, taking the shield of faith, wherewith ye shall be able to quench all the fiery darts of the wicked [one]." There is a vivid picture of fiery darts (thoughts) being flicked into the mind of the child of God. Yes, from the world from the flesh and from the devil come thoughts that would gain control of our minds.

There is a difference between the thought process of an unsaved person and the thought process of a Christian, and you will never understand your thinking until you understand the difference that Jesus makes when he comes into your life.

Isaiah 55:7-9 describes the thought life of a person who is not a Christian, "Let the wicked forsake his way, and the unrighteous man his thoughts... For my thoughts are not your thoughts, neither are your ways my ways, saith the Lord. For as the heavens are higher than the earth, so are my ways higher than your ways, and my thoughts than your thoughts." One of the tragic things that happened when Adam and Eve sinned was that they began to think differently from the way God thought. Before Adam and Eve sinned in the Garden of Eden, their thoughts and God's thoughts were exactly one. However, when they sinned, their thoughts and God's thoughts were no longer the same. Shortly after they sinned, they began to be afraid. God came looking for Adam in the Garden of Eden, and God said, "Adam, where are you?" And Adam said, "God, I hid because I was afraid." I don't think Adam had fearful thoughts before that. We can see the change in his thinking process after he sinned. He began to be afraid. He began to think fearful thoughts, as well as being ashamed. Something drastic happened to the thought process of the human race when man sinned.

The thinking of a non-Christian is definitely different from the thinking of a child of God. The Bible says, "He that soweth to the flesh shall of the flesh reap corruption; but he that soweth to the Spirit shall of the Spirit reap life everlasting" (Gal. 6:8). A person who is not a Christian is sowing thoughts which are not of God in his mind. A non-Christian will receive the evil thoughts of the world, the flesh, and the devil. Their consciences may cry out against these evil thoughts, but often they receive them.

When a person becomes a Christian, God gives him a new heart and a new spirit. That's exactly what the book of Ezekiel says, "I will put within them a new heart and a new spirit." Second Corinthians 5:17 says, "Therefore if any man be in Christ, he is a new creature: old things are passed away; behold, all things are become new." A

Christian begins to think differently and respond to thoughts in a different manner. Before I became a Christian, there were thoughts that I would welcome–immoral thoughts, evil thoughts, garbage thoughts–and I would let those thoughts come into my mind, and my spirit would welcome them. But something happened when I became a Christian. Those same thoughts that used to find welcome in my spirit were disturbing. They were alarming, and I found that my spirit would cry out against them. I found a resistance in my spirit, after I became a Christian, to thoughts that I had welcomed before I became a child of God. One of the most encouraging comforts for a Christian is: Thoughts which come into your mind that you use to welcome, receive, and enjoy before you became a Christian, you no longer want. Your spirit says, "No!"

It used to disturb me after I became a Christian that thoughts I didn't want would enter my mind. Have you ever noticed how the craziest thoughts can dart into your mind? Thoughts you really don't want. Have you noticed how you can be in a spiritual meeting and all of a sudden, thoughts will flash in your mind, thoughts that are foreign to everything going on around you. You feel guilty because of those thoughts. You think. How can I be a Christian and have those thoughts in my mind? We must understand that the thoughts which come into our minds, in themselves are not a sin. I felt guilty because I had those thoughts, thoughts that I did not want, thoughts that were foreign to Jesus Christ. However, I soon learned that the thought itself is not a sin unless you accept the thought. You do not have to accept the thought. You do not have to receive it. Just because the thought arises does not mean it is a sin. You can refuse the thought. The thought itself is not a sin. It is what you do with the thought. You can refuse the thought. Think of your mind for a moment as an airport. Your mind is a landing field. There is an air traffic controller and that is your will. All kinds of airplanes come flying in and they signal, "We want permission to land on that field." And the person in the traffic control centers says, "You have permission to land," or he can also say, "You don't have permission to land." Thoughts want to land in your mind. Your will (air traffic controller) can grant them permission to land or not to land. It should bring you great confidence to know that the thought itself is not a sin. It is what you do with the thought that ultimately determines whether or not it is a sin. You can refuse the thoughts.

You might ask. "Why is it that I have these thoughts I don't want?" Let me give you three reasons why you have these thoughts.

One of the reasons Christians have unwelcome thoughts come into their minds is because Christians have an unrenewed mind. The Word of God says in Romans 12:1-2, "I beseech you therefore, brethren, by the mercies of God, that ye present your bodies a living sacrifice, holy, acceptable unto God, which is your reasonable service. And be not conformed to this world: but be ye transformed by the renewing of your mind, that you may prove what is that good, and acceptable, and perfect, will of God."

Before you became a Christian, a lot of things went into your mind. Think of all the things you read and saw before you became a child of God. Think of all the things that have been poured into your mind. Every thing that went into your mind before you were saved will not immediately disappear when you became a Christian. The child of God has to renew his mind.

How do we renew our minds? We renew our minds with the Word of God. All these thoughts that have come into our minds from the world, from the flesh, and from the devil before we were saved are still there.

We must begin to put this garbage out of our minds, and we have to put the Word of God into our minds. David said, "Thy word have I hid in mine heart." He was talking about his mind. "Thy word have I hid in mine heart, that I might not sin against thee."

A lot of people want to be instantly spiritual. "Push a button and make me instantly spiritual." That doesn't happen. It's a day-by-day growth in the Lord Jesus Christ. And lazy Christians who do not renew their minds with the Word of God are going to be Christians who grow slowly.

The reason you have some of your errant thoughts is that out of your subconscious mind thoughts emerged that have been poured into you before you became a child of God, and you must refuse those thoughts, and then renew your mind with the Word of God. One of the best ways to renew your mind is to read through the New Testament and find out everything the Bible says about you as a Christian. Believe what the Bible tells you about yourself in Christ. You renew your mind by refusing the thoughts from the old life and filling your mind with the Word of God– God's thoughts.

Another reason Christians have trouble with their thoughts is that those thoughts come from the world system around us. Have you noticed how the world system in which we live is trying to pour its thoughts into our minds? First John 2:15-16 declares: "Love not the world, neither the things that are in the world ... for all that is in the world, the lust of the flesh, and the lust of the eyes, and the pride of life, is not of the Father; but is of the world." Now when the Bible says, "Love not the world," it's not talking about God's created world; it's referring to the world system and its thought patterns headed by Satan himself. The world is always pushing its thoughts on us. You start driving to work and there are the billboards. They spend thousands of dollars to put those billboards up. Why? To put thoughts in your mind. Thoughts come through the media, television, radio, newspaper, you name it. The philosophy of this world system is to bombard constantly your mind with thoughts.

The world system is trying to fill your mind with thoughts that are not God's thoughts and ways that are not God's ways. You must filter them and refuse the thoughts the world tries to put into your mind, or you are going to be thinking thoughts that are not pleasing to God. The world system is constantly trying to fill the mind of the child of God with thoughts that are not God's thoughts. We must recognize and refuse these thoughts.

Thoughts also come into the Christian's mind from Satan. The fiery darts of the wicked are thoughts which are foreign to God and alien to the new nature that he has given us in Jesus Christ. Well, the big question is: How do you control your thoughts? How is this accomplished by the child of God?

First, we must guard what goes into our minds. You say, "Now, how can I guard what goes into my mind?" Use the Word of God to discern your thoughts. Hebrews 4:12 says, "The Word of God is quick, and powerful, and sharper than any two-edged sword, piercing even to the dividing asunder of the soul and spirit, and of the joints and marrow, and is a discerner of the thoughts and intents of the heart." The Word of God is a discerner of your thoughts and the intents of your heart. And the way you guard what goes into your mind is by allowing the Word of God to discern the thoughts you allow to go into your mind. No thought contrary to God's Word is to be accepted.

Also, allow the Word of God to guide your thoughts. Philippians 4:8 says, "Finally, brethren, whatsoever things are true, whatsoever things are honest, what soever things are just, whatsoever things are pure, whatsoever things are lovely, whatsoever things are of good report; if there be any virtue and if there be any praise, think on these things." The Word of God guides our thoughts. If it does not meet the test of this verse, we are not to think on it. Is it true, honest, pure, lovely, and the like? If the thought is contrary to this verse, do not accept it. Do not be controlled by your thoughts, but control your thoughts.

Also, you must learn how to refuse thoughts and how to receive thoughts. You can refuse thoughts that are contrary to the Word of God. How do you refuse those thoughts? You refuse the thoughts in the name of the Lord Jesus Christ.

You quote a Scripture the opposite of the evil thought. For example, if the thought comes into your mind to be immoral, you say, "I refuse that thought in the name of Jesus." Then quote a Scripture such as "Blessed are the pure in heart, for they shall see God." When a thought comes into your mind to be unkind to another person, you refuse that thought in the name of Jesus and quote a verse like, "Be ye kind one to another, tenderhearted, forgiving one another, even as God for Christ's sake has forgiven you."

If you do not learn how to refuse thoughts in the name of Jesus Christ, and then to confess God's thoughts, you are going to be defeated in your Christian life. How often do you have to refuse these thoughts? As long as they keep coming or until they stop. There was a period of time in my life about two years ago when I had a continuous thought popping into my mind. I battled that thought for six months. A lot of times, when I would be jogging, that thought would try to find lodging in my mind. I not only would refuse the thought in Jesus' name, but I would confess or pray the exact opposite from the thought that was planted in my mind. There was victory!

You refuse thoughts, but you can also learn to receive thoughts. Receive thoughts that are of God. Receive thoughts that are in agreement with God's Word. Receive thoughts that glorify Him.

Allow the Word of God to discern your thoughts and guide your thoughts. Refuse thoughts that are not of God and receive thoughts in agreement with God's Word. By the power of the Holy Spirit, control your thoughts. Do not let them control you. Your thought life can be pleasing to God. By the power of Jesus, win the battle in your mind.

CHAPTER 17

A BUILDING, A SNAKE, AND THE SBC

On Sunday, January 8, 1989, close to 4,000 people gathered in the new worship center, and all the people of Cottage Hill were able to worship together on their own property for the first time in fifteen years. During the previous twenty-eight months, God had provided, and the people had given, more than $8 million for the new building. Costs had increased somewhat during the construction phase, so that now only a balance of less than $800,000 remained. As more construction bills arrived, it became official in March that a total of about $1 million was still needed to pay off the project, but that was of small consequence to a church that had seen what very few churches had ever seen. The *Miracle in March* would be the last great push for finances for the building.

After March 5, Miracle Day, Fred wrote, "Sunday was truly a miracle! You gave $696,362 in cash for our building. There are $34,900 in pledges to be given over the next three weeks. This gives us a total Miracle Day Offering of $731, 262. Praise the Lord for this miracle!

"Our new building cost us $9,268,000. We have given $9,006,380. This means that only $260,000 is left to be paid on this building. We have not borrowed any money. All bills are paid and final bills will not be in until April 15. This means we have time to finish paying for the building. I will not be stressing the building from the pulpit. There will simply be a reminder in our Bulletin and the Handouts of what is needed to finish paying for the building. We need to move on to new ministries and emphases."

Cottage Hill's task over the last two years had not gone unnoticed by other pastors and churches in the city. In fact, it seemed to have emboldened other congregations to trust God for more than what they were already seeing, and some of those openly appreciated Fred's leadership. Toward the end of March, Fred received this letter from Dick Braswell, pastor of Life Church of Mobile:

"Dear Brother Fred:

As I prepared to receive our Tithes and Offerings this past Sunday morning, the Holy Spirit impressed me and the folks here at LIFE to seed this token offering into your Miracle Sunday effort to pay off the new Worship Center. In so doing, we stand in agreement with you and your people for total victory in raising the necessary funds to accomplish this goal.

Please accept this with all our love and best wishes.

Sincerely,
Dick Braswell, Pastor
Life Church of Mobile"

The early 1990s brought renewed vigor and vision to Fred and the people of Cottage Hill. The new Worship Center was making even more growth possible, and the church continued to expand in all of its areas of life. Everything seemed to be accelerating.

One of the areas of life in Mobile, Alabama that Fred had consistently taken a stand on for many years was the annual Mardi

Gras celebration that occurred for two weeks in mid winter. Fred, and by extension Cottage Hill, had become a bold voice decrying the revelry and drunkenness that marked the holiday. Because of that, he had drawn the ire of a number of Mardi Gras supporters in Mobile, and he never knew just how the repercussions might play out.

The Sunday before Mardi Gras, or Fat Tuesday, is known as Joe Cain Day, and it officially kicks off the last three days before Lent begins. In 1992, Joe Cain Day fell on March 1, the same day that David Ravenhill, Leonard's son, was at Cottage Hill as the guest preacher.

The morning worship service was progressing smoothly, and while two men sang a duet on the stage, Fred sat on the front row enjoying the music. As he watched and listened, though, he noticed that they both began shooting furtive looks to one of the side aisles, looking very uncomfortable. Fred shifted his gaze over in that direction, and there, coming down the aisle and stepping to the front, was a man with a dog and a snake.

But this wasn't just any man with any dog and any snake. The man was dressed much like the popular "Crocodile Hunter" of the day, with full Australian khakis, boots, and brimmed hat. Beside him stood a sleek German Shepherd, and draped around the man's neck was an 8-foot python.

Fred immediately jumped up to intercept him, and by the time he reached the man, a number of deacons had also surrounded the visitor. Fred walked up to him, careful to stay at what he considered a safe distance. "Sir," said Fred, "can I help you?"

"Yes," the man said, "I'm here to speak today."

"No," Fred said, "you're not. We already have a speaker today."

The snake writhed. "But," the man said, "you don't understand. God has sent me here to speak today."

Fred was having none of it. "No, I'm afraid you're the one who doesn't understand. You are not going to speak in this church today." He had no idea how this standoff was going to play out, but Fred was confident in his resolve. He could hear someone behind him speaking softly, with a quiet intensity.

Meanwhile someone had called the police, and in short order, a crusier arrived outside of the auditorium side door. Together, the deacons and the police officer escorted the man out and into the waiting car. But as Fred was watching him go, he noticed something was missing. He looked down, and there, muscling its way toward Fred's feet, was the python.

As God would have it, the officer just happened to have a ride-along guest that day— a professional animal wrangler, who came back inside and took custody of the snake. Afterwards, Fred would question the man who was talking under his breath behind him during the ordeal, Wayne Wood. "Wayne," he asked, "what were you saying back there?"

"Saying?!" asked Wayne. "Are you kidding? I was praying in tongues!"

"Well, for goodness sake!" said Fred. "If there was ever a time I needed to hear somebody praying in English, that was it!"

As the various ministries of Cottage Hill were gaining even more steam than before, Fred was still at work trying to help keep the Southern Baptist Convention on a conservative track. In 1993 and again in 1994, he was elected the Chairman of the Executive Committee, the most powerful committee in Southern Baptist Life. The Executive Committee essentially serves the Southern Baptist Convention as a denominational whole. It receives its authority and directives from the Convention, but it is not a Southern Baptist Convention entity, which means that it is also able to act as a watchdog of sorts, to protect the life and polity of the Southern Baptist Convention, from those without who may seek it harm, and from those within who may abuse their position.

So, some twenty years after Fred's arrival in Mobile, his loyalty and service to the cause of Biblical inerrancy and authority were being fashioned into a position where he could now do something about the denomination's direction. As Chairman of the Executive Committee, Fred and the other committee members took steps to ensure that the Conservative Resurgence that had taken hold in 1979 would continue unabated. One way to see to that was the firing of two editors of the Baptist Press because their reporting was clearly biased toward a theologically liberal viewpoint.

While serving in this position, Fred was approached in early 1994 by Dr. Adrian Rogers, who told Fred that he was the choice of the conservative movement to be the next president of the Southern Baptist Convention, the largest Protestant denomination in the world. There was in place at that time a certain "gentlemen's agreement" among the leaders of the denomination that whomever they chose, that candidate would run unopposed in order to minimize fracturing the fragile unity that existed in the denomination. Fred humbly accepted their decision and prepared to be nominated as the next president of the SBC.

In March of that year, that same group met with other popular and effective pastors in the Convention to let them know that Fred would be given the seat at the next Convention annual meeting in Orlando in June. On hearing the announcement, a few other influential pastors and leaders decided that, though they loved Fred, they wanted to nominate Dr. Jim Henry, pastor of First Baptist Church Orlando. The Annual Meeting was scheduled to be held in Orlando, and that caused some division among the conservatives.

These pastors moved ahead to nominate Jim Henry, though

they were asked not to do it. So, after Fred was nominated by Dr. Charles Stanley to be the denomination's next president, Dr. Jack Graham nominated Dr. Jim Henry, pastor of First Baptist Church, Orlando, to run against him.

Brother Fred would say later that when Jim Henry was nominated, that he should have graciously bowed out of the race and run again, unopposed, in New Orleans the following year. However, he felt confident that God had led him to run for the office, with no guarantees from the Lord that he would win. He sensed a mandate from God to be the one to continue to hold up the banner of total inerrancy, infallibility, and inspiration of Scripture.

Fred knew right away that he would be at a disadvantage with the Convention meetings being held that year in his opponent's very own city. It would be a small matter for thousands of Baptists in Orlando and other parts of Florida to attend the convention and vote. Each church could only have a total of ten messengers, or voting members. Then, when it became evident that a large number of Floridians had been brought in by vans from around the state, he knew it was all but lost.

Fred Wolfe lost the election for the presidency of the SBC in Orlando, but only by a slim margin. In one of the closest contests in years, Jim Henry was elected by a vote of 9,876 to 8,023. Even in Dr. Henry's backyard, Fred only lost by 1,800 votes out of the almost 18,000 that were cast.

Fred would serve as the Chairman of the Executive Committee again that year, but he would return to Mobile, disappointed and a little disillusioned, but ready to put this behind him and turn his focus fully back to his work and life as pastor of Cottage Hill Baptist Church.

About two years after moving into the new Worship Center, the people and pastor of Cottage Hill could finally catch their collective breath. The $9 million dollar marathon payoff had been grueling, but well worth the endurance. There was nothing like being in a brand new worship center and knowing that it was already paid for, while most churches struggled year after year to chip away at a 20+ year mortgage.

During that time, a group of people at Cottage Hill became aware that the old Greystone School building was up for sale. This, they reasoned, would be an excellent site for an expansion of Cottage Hill Baptist School. At the time, CHBS only went through sixth grade, but there had been interest for some time, and a growing sense of urgency, to expand into the higher grades, eventually taking students all the way through 12th grade. The Greystone building on Azalea Road was now available, and seemed a bargain at one million dollars.

Fred was interested in expanding the school, but he was absolutely not interested in borrowing the money to do it. Although the fatigue of the previous campaign was lifting, he didn't feel that it would be wise to ask people who just gave over $9 million so sacrificially to let him go borrow $1 million and end up back in debt. Being debt-free and staying that way had been the watchword of the major campaign just finished, and he was not going to be the one to ask them to step backward. However, just like in other decisions of his life, Fred gave room for the possibility that he could be the one who was wrong about this. So, he would put it to the Deacon Board and allow the Lord to lead him through them.

Fred presented the idea of borrowing $1 million to buy the old Greystone building, and the deacons considered it. They, too, were very interested in establishing a high school, but they were fairly evenly divided over borrowing the money for it. In the end, the proposal to borrow was turned away by a vote of 37 to 35. They, like Fred, were not willing to go right back into debt this quickly.

What surprised Fred, though, was the vehemence with which he was met from the small group of people who wanted so badly to buy that building. They not only felt that Fred was making a mistake, but they were angry, and the anger turned to bitterness. For years afterward, Fred would find himself opposed at every turn by this group of people, who had stopped following him, but would not leave.

Now that they were a couple of years removed from the joyful strain of building the new worship center, the people began to wonder what would be next. They asked the leadership what the vision was for the next building project on the campus. Fred's response, though, would become what he would consider one of the biggest leadership mistakes he would ever make.

Generally, there were three possibilities for the next project, but only one of them at a time could be pursued. One was a new Family Life Center where the gymnasium currently stood. The gym was really one basketball court and two goals, flanked on either end with average size meeting rooms both on the ground floor and directly above them. The gym had served the church well over the past 30 years as the site of Wednesday night suppers, various Sunday School department locations, and many, many youth fellowships.

Now, though, the new Worship Center included much more comfortable and updated spaces for all of those things except basketball. It was generally agreed on that the gym was past its expiration date, and a new Recreation/Family Life Center could meet the needs of hundreds of families and be a draw for people not yet familiar with Cottage Hill.

The second project for consideration was for a Christian Counseling Center that would be an extension of Cottage Hill's ministry and would operate on its campus. Counseling had been a backbone of the CHBC ministry model for many years, and the need for it never slowed down. It was hoped that a new Counseling Center would not only serve the people of Mobile more effectively, but it also might lessen the burden of the staff, who were continually doing that work.

The third possibility was still the expansion of the school into the upper grades. Even though the bid for the Greystone building had been denied, the desire to expand was still there, and it could still be a viable option in context of remaining debt free.

And so Fred, in an effort to hear the will of God through the people, did something that he realized later was a lose/lose situation. He put it to a vote.

Fred asked the people to decide what the church would undertake next, and when the people spoke, they were clearly divided three ways. It was essentially 33% for the Family Life Center, 33% for the Counseling Center, and 33% for the High School. Fred realized, too late, that no matter what he did, 66% of the people were not going to be happy about it. And it wasn't that Fred was overly concerned with making everyone happy. He learned decades ago that such a thing was not possible. What he did want to do, though, was to preserve the unique unity that had marked Cottage Hill Baptist Church all through the last building project, and he was grieved at the thought that the next project would be divisive from the outset.

The one thing that was clear was that nothing was clear. Fred decided that they would not move on any of these projects right away, but would do what they had always done in order to know which direction to take. They would pray. And they would wait.

CHAPTER 18

ANOTHER GOODBYE

On June 18, 1995, an Assembly of God church in Pensacola, Florida experienced an unusual move of God that became known as the Father's Day Outpouring, or the Brownsville Revival, after the name of the church, Brownsville Assembly of God. The church's pastor, John Kilpatrick, was as surprised as anybody at the things that were happening, but as Evangelist Steve Hill preached night after night, it was evident that hundreds of people were giving their hearts to Christ, and hundreds more Christians were being broken and revived.

Over the next months, the physical manifestations of the revival became a matter of controversy, and all the more so in the nearby Greater Mobile area as people from all kinds of churches traveled to Pensacola almost every night to participate in a genuine move of God. The controversy, especially in churches like Cottage Hill that allowed room for the activity of the Holy Spirit but had never seen anything like this, centered around the phenomena of shaking and "falling out" under the power of God.

Because Fred Wolfe had cultivated such a culture of spiritual hunger for so many years, a significant number of Cottage Hill members were attending the revival services faithfully, practically every night of the week, until the early hours of the morning, and were coming to church excited about what they were seeing. Others remained skeptical, wanting to be sure that the manifestations were really of God, and not of the flesh. Still others at Cottage Hill, a small group, had already decided that God or not, they didn't want that stuff catching on and happening at Cottage Hill. So Brother Fred went to check it out.

Fred already knew John Kilpatrick as a fellow large church pastor, and had a great respect for the man. After he attended one of the meetings, he was confident that it was a genuine move of God, and he would encourage people to come to it. In fact, over the next year, more than a dozen Cottage Hill members would be approved by Brownsville as members of their Prayer Team, a move that had to be accompanied by approval from Brother Fred, with him signing their applications and testifying to their spiritual and emotional trustworthiness.

Fred visited Brownsville when he could, and it was no secret that the pastor of Cottage Hill was embracing this revival. John Kilpatrick and Steve Hill openly honored his humility, and would describe how a "local pastor of a megachurch in Mobile" would come to the altar and stand with his hands held out, receiving from the Lord like anyone else. A year after the revival began, Fred was invited by Pastor John Kilpatrick to preach there on a Sunday morning. He gladly accepted.

"I want you to know," he told the packed house at Brownsville Assembly, "that I get calls, being a Southern Baptist and having pastored a Southern Baptist Church for 25 years, I tell you I'm getting calls from all over the country, and I'm wondering, 'What do these people want with me?' And you know what they're asking me? 'Brother Fred, what do you think about Brownsville?' And I say, 'I want to tell you something— God is moving at Brownsville.' And they say, 'Well, Brother Fred, what about all the phenomena?' And I said, 'Man, I ain't looking at the phenomena, I'm looking at the fruit.' Did you hear what I said? So many people, when they can't control something, they want to deny it. Let me give you one illustration of what I'm talking about.

"I told your pastor about this, I said, 'John, I don't understand all about signs and wonders, and phenomena, and falling under the power of God, I don't understand all about that. But to me, that's not the issue.' And we both agreed that the issue is changed lives. Jesus changes lives, and that's the bottom line! Perfect illustration: a group of our young people came over to one of the meetings, and afterwards, on a Wednesday night, about six or seven of our young people came down and said, 'Brother Fred, we've been over to Brownsville and we wanted to ask you some questions about it,' and I said, 'Well, ask me.' And they began to talk about falling out under the power of God, and so forth and so on, and I said, 'Well, you know, I don't understand all that, but I tell you one thing, people are getting saved, lives are getting changed. Why don't you tell me about yourself?' One of them said, 'Well, I went over there, and I was determined not to fall under the power of God.' And she said, 'But I did!' I said, 'Okay, let me ask you a question: how did it affect you?' And then she said it. She said, 'It's given me a greater hunger for God.' And I said, 'Hallelujah! That's good fruit!' Lord, give me 4,000 more with a greater hunger for God!"

1995 turned to 1996, and Cottage Hill had become a streamlined model of efficient ministry. Attendance was good, and giving was great. The tithes and offerings were exceeding the $5.5 million annual budget. Every area was humming along nicely, not just maintaining, but pushing and growing. Prayer Ministry, Youth, Music, Children, Singles, Senior Adults... these areas and more were flourishing under Fred's consistent leadership and loving gaze. And almost everyone was on board, with almost total unity. There was still that small group that was sore about the Greystone building, but there were no significant problems that threatened the life and the unity of Cottage Hill Baptist Church.

Fred had told himself years before, that if he were still at Cottage Hill after twenty-five years, he would take stock again and evaluate his future. After twenty-five years pastoring the same church, he knew, you are pretty much locked in until you retire or God retires you. As a pastor, your options begin to narrow.

And so, in the fall of 1996, with his 60th birthday approaching and his twenty-fifth anniversary coming up in a few months, Fred asked himself three questions: First, "Do I have a vision for the next ten years?" Second, "What about Anne and her health? Can she bear up under this much longer?" And third, "If I were not pastoring here, what would I do?"

It was probably the healthiest time to ask those questions. Fred wasn't being pushed out. He wasn't feeling driven away or hurried. He knew he could stay as long as he wanted.

"But is that what I want to do?" he asked. He began to realize that the answer to his first question might be the deciding factor. He did not, in fact, have vision for Cottage Hill for the next ten years. Everything they were doing was working, and it was all good. But did he really want to just coast into year after year doing the same things? What else might be waiting for him outside of these well-known walls?

And one day, sitting in his study, it came to him in a rush. He took a legal pad and a pen and in what seemed like a moment, he knew what would be next for him. It would be called "Barnabas Ministry: a Ministry of Encouragement," and it would involve giving out to pastors all over the country, everything that had been poured into him.

He wrote quickly. It would work like this: he would be invited to a particular church, and fly or drive into that city on Saturday, where he would have asked the host pastor to schedule some kind of meeting for Saturday night. It might be a full blown worship service, or maybe a prayer meeting, but if he was going to be in town, why not start ministering to the people right away?

On Sunday morning, Fred would preach in the host church, and again on Sunday evening. To Fred's thinking, though, the meat of the weekend would happen on Monday. The host pastor would have already sent out invitations to local pastors in his city, inviting them to a seminar on Monday morning that Fred would teach. There, he would cover three areas of interest to pastors: (1) the pastor's personal walk with God, (2) how to deal with discouragement, and (3) how to deal with division.

Fred sat back and looked at the ten or fifteen pages he had written in the legal pad. It was a good plan. There was just one more unanswered question: How would he actually make a living?

Fred had not taken for granted over the years, the benefits of a pastor's steady paycheck. The reality is that evangelists and other itinerant ministers tend to struggle with making a living on love offerings. He knew that many of the churches he would be going into would be smaller churches, and he was happy about that prospect. Very often, they were the ones who needed hope and encouragement as they toiled in relative obscurity. But if he did forty meetings a year and received a $500 love offering for each, that would only be $20,000 a year. Quite a drastic drop from what he had been making for the last two decades.

After thinking it over, Fred considered Cottage Hill's $5.5 million dollar budget. He decided that after his resignation, when he had laid out what he was going to do, he would ask the Finance Committee to appropriate $50,000 per year into the next three years' budgets. That would give him a good base to work from, and he was certain that they would approve the request. After all, he had given twenty-five wonderful years to the church. He was asking for less than 1% of the budget to assist him in a ministry of encouragement. Fred knew he had raised them right. He was confident they would do this for him.

And so, in the first week of December 1996, after almost twenty-five years at the helm, Fred sent a letter to the people of Cottage Hill Baptist Church to tell them that he was resigning as their pastor. It was a sad déjà vu for those who were there in November of 1979, and a bolt from the blue for everyone else. The shock was evident in the conversations of the people, but Fred took time the following Sunday morning, December 8th, to try and set the tone for what was coming. He began by talking about the various kinds of relationships that we have in our lives, and how none of us like change, and applied it to the special relationship between a pastor and his people. "Now, we all know," he said, "that concerning our relationship as pastor and people, we are in the middle of change. Change is taking place right now. You say, 'Well, Brother Fred, as we think about our relationship as a pastor and people, and in the midst of this change, what needs to happen?' Let me say, before I get into some things, the bottom line of what really needs to happen, hear me carefully. It is very important, in this time of change between our relationship as pastor and people, it is very important that God the Father be glorified. What is not important, is necessarily what I want or what you want. I want to tell you what's important-- that the Father in Heaven, who loves us, getsx glory in the midst of this change. We must be jealous of the glory of God in the midst of change. Not only must we be jealous for God's glory in the midst of change, but we must be jealous for the fact that the Son of God, Jesus, will be lifted high before the people of this city and this state, as the One who is sufficient in every area of our lives."

Christmas came, and Cottage Hill carried on with all of the normal activities, including the Mobile Christmas Spectacular. Meanwhile, the people began to pray about whom to nominate for the new Pastor Search Committee, and the names began to be turned in to the church office.

Fred had intended for his resignation to take effect the first of January, but that timeline was derailed by a physical complication. Early in January, he had arthroscopic surgery on his right knee. It was considered minor surgery, and it went well, as expected. Soon after, though, Fred found himself short of breath after having to run to catch a flight in an airport.

Somewhat alarmed, he visited his doctor to see if he might have pneumonia. After a thorough checkup, the doctor reported his findings. "No," he told Fred, "you don't have pneumonia. What you have is blood clots in your lungs. In fact, I'm not even letting you get up off that table." They immediately called for a gurney, admitted him to the hospital, and started him on blood thinners.

Fred was stunned. He had never had anything like that before, but there was, he knew, a history of blood clots in his family. His grandfather had died from a blood clot.

This unforeseen event changed the timeline of his leaving Cottage Hill, but only by a couple of weeks. His last sermon as pastor of Cottage Hill was preached on February 2, 1997. It was titled "Finish Well!" and it would be his good-bye to the people that he had loved for so long.

It was the unenviable task of Ed Keyes to design a worship portion of the service that would be Brother Fred's last as pastor. As always, though, the songs that were sung and the words that Ed spoke hit exactly the right note and bore the promise of healing at the end of the hurting. "Just keep your heart focused on Jesus right now," said Ed, "that's why we're here. So just keep your heart and your mind on Him, and what our desire is, is first of all to exalt Him in praise and then to move into His presence to worship Him. Keep that on your heart, and the choir is going to sing now one of the most glorious songs, 'I Will Glory in the Cross,' and nothing else but the cross of Jesus Christ."

The sense of hope and destiny continued to build as the whole congregation made the declaration together that, "My hope is built on nothing less than Jesus' blood and righteousness/ I dare not trust the sweetest frame, but wholly lean on Jesus' name/ On Christ the Solid Rock I stand, all other ground is sinking sand/ All other ground is sinking sand." Then all the emotion and the weight of the moment soared to its highest as Lee McDougald stepped to the microphone and the choir sang with him, declaring that, no matter what, "The Anchor Holds!"

The majestic worship gave Fred the confidence and boldness to forge ahead as he stepped into the pulpit for the last time as the pastor of Cottage Hill. "I know," he said, "that this is a time of mixed emotions, for me and for Anne, and for you. But we are doing what we ought to do, we are focusing our attention and our heart upon the head of the Church, who is Jesus. That's where our attention is. That's where our focus is. That's where we wanted it to be for twenty-five years, that's where we want it to be now, and that's where we want it to be in the future. Our eyes are upon Him, the Author and the Finisher of our faith."

And so, exactly twenty-five years after Fred Wolfe first stepped behind the heavy, white rock pulpit in a building with a leaky roof, he knelt for a final time beside a newer pulpit, in a newer building, and with a full and grateful heart, gave thanks to God for the privilege of having been the pastor of Cottage Hill Baptist Church.

PART IV

Chapter 19

A Ministry of Encouragement

After Fred had resigned, but before he had preached his final sermon, he had made the request to the Finance Committee to include support for him and the new Barnabas Ministry in the budget that would start on January 1, 1997. However, the reality was that after Fred resigned, his authority in these matters was over. He was no longer in a position to push for any budget item, much less something that would be for him. He would just have to trust the people.

At the appropriate business meeting, the proposal was made by the Finance Team just as he asked. Of course, Fred was not at this meeting, so the people were free to speak their minds. And the ones who did, were the same ones who were still bitter about having been denied the purchase of the old Greystone building months earlier. "No," they said, "we don't need to do that. Fred wouldn't want that. Let's just take up a love offering for him."

The Chairman of the Deacons who was leading the business meeting was caught completely off guard by the opposition. To him, the proposal made perfect sense and should have passed without dissent. This lack of unity was new to him, as it was to most people there. All that most of them had ever known was great unity among the people at Cottage Hill, especially in the area of finances. Having been thrown off balance by the discussion, he proposed that they table the matter, put it off and decide on it later.

But there was a certain woman in the room that night, a woman whose family had felt the grace of Fred Wolfe's ministry to them in their darkest times. She had not forgotten how much Fred had meant to all of them. She made her way down the aisle, to the microphone, and addressed the church members gathered there.

"Do you mean to tell me," she said, "that after this man has poured twenty-five years of his life into this church, that this is how we are going to treat him? It's a disgrace. Tell you what," she went on, "I will be here in the morning with a check for $150,000 to be designated for the support that he has asked for."

And she was good to her word. The next morning, she delivered the check. And, since it had already been proposed that the church receive a love offering for Brother Fred, they did that, too. God was once again faithful to provide for Fred's need, beyond what he had asked, even in the face of some who opposed him.

Immediately after his retirement from Cottage Hill, the requests for Barnabas Ministry appointments came rolling in. Fred welcomed the opportunity to travel on the weekends while still having more time to be at home with Anne during the week. He was excited about preaching in many different churches, but the main draw for him was the chance to minister deeply to pastors on a personal level.

Fred knew that he would only be preaching in a large church maybe once or twice a year now, if that, and the withdrawal from that was something to be considered. It is a source of a certain adrenaline rush to preach to thousands every week, besides knowing that the Word of God is going out to more people, and he knew that he would miss that. Most of the churches he would be going to now would be two- to three hundred people, some smaller, maybe some a little larger. But, in the final decision, that really didn't matter. What mattered was seeing Jesus change lives, and if he could speak into the hearts of pastors who speak into the hearts of hundreds, then, in the final calculation, his influence would be increased many times over.

Fred did not want to travel alone, both for the accountability, and because he just needed help. So, right away, he hired S.L. Williamson as his assistant, and together they began to take the Barnabas Ministry on the road.

For the next three years, Fred Wolfe invested himself heavily into the lives of churches and pastors all over the United States. Everywhere he went, he preached on the Lordship of Jesus Christ, being filled with the Spirit, prayer, and spiritual warfare. On Mondays, he spoke to pastors on the three major points that the Lord had given him before he left Cottage Hill— walking with God, discouragement, and division.

The Barnabas weekends were increasingly popular, and the ministry was in high demand. Fred's involvement in the Southern Baptist Convention and influence there for over twenty-five years was still bringing in a harvest.

In 2000, while still traveling regularly, Fred was asked to lead a Men's Retreat for Crossgates Baptist Church in Brandon, Mississippi, a suburb of Jackson. The retreat was well attended and well received, and afterwards, three brothers who owned the largest furniture store in town approached Fred with an offer.

"Brother Fred," they said, "you know how much we appreciate

your ministry, and have appreciated you over the years. The thing is, we have a young pastor at Crossgates, and he is a wonderful man and a very gifted preacher, but he needs a mentor. We have five or six men who are willing to pay you a little bit out of our own pockets each month if you will move to Jackson and be a spiritual father to our pastor. Again, we love him very much, and really believe in him, but he just needs someone who has been down this road before him to help him along the way. Will you come?"

Fred was intrigued by the idea. He could travel from anywhere, and now that he didn't have the responsibilities of a local church anymore and the Barnabas Ministry was running smoothly, he found that he had regained some emotional room. *It might be good to invest in this young man,* he thought. *I have definitely learned a few things.*

Fred prayed it through and talked it over with Anne, and they decided to say yes. They packed up and moved to Jackson, and began to attend Crossgates whenever Fred wasn't on the road. During the week, Fred would make himself available to spend time with the pastor.

Fred liked being at Crossgates very much. The young man was, indeed, a very gifted preacher, the people adored their pastor, and the church was dynamic and thriving. In fact, it reminded Fred so much of Cottage Hill in the early days that he could close his eyes and go back in time. He felt very much at home there.

It wasn't long, though, before Fred began to feel a little frustrated. He kept trying to get to know the pastor, but he was never able to get close to him. The young man didn't seem jealous or threatened, or anything like that, he just never let Fred into his life. Fred didn't personally need to be on the inside track, but since this was what he had moved to Jackson for, the polite but definite stiff-arming left him hanging on the fringes.

After about eight months of being at Crossgates as a member, and still traveling with Barnabas Ministry, Fred was on his way out the door to a meeting in Andalusia, Alabama when he received a phone call from one of the three furniture store brothers who had initially invited him to Brandon.

"Brother Fred," he said, "you need to be at the church tomorrow morning."

"I can't do that," said Fred, "you know I have this meeting in Andalusia tomorrow, I'm going there right now."

"No, you have to be at the church. We have a problem. Our pastor has gotten involved with a woman, and she is about to file a lawsuit against the church."

Fred recognized right away the seriousness of the situation. He arranged his schedule to allow him to be at the church and meet with the Deacon Board the next morning.

The evidence was presented to the deacons, and it was undeniable that the pastor was guilty. After the meeting, the deacons informed their pastor that he would not be going back into the pulpit. Due to the threatened lawsuit, they could not allow it. Once they knew about the accusation, if they let him preach again, they would make the church itself liable to prosecution.

The next morning, Brother Fred stepped into the pulpit of Crossgates Baptist Church as the Interim Pastor. The men who had brought him there were heartbroken and discouraged, and they asked him if he would come alongside their church and walk with them through this valley.

The people of Crossgates were so in love with the popular young pastor that they were in complete shock to hear that he was gone.

Fred had the hardest job of all, because he couldn't even tell them what had happened, due to the pending lawsuit. Nothing. He knew that they had a right to know, but no one could reveal anything until the lawsuit was settled, and who knew how long that might take? And so, Fred did what good fathers do. He loved them, tried to soothe their pain, and he told them that it was going to be alright. God was still in control, and He was with them even now.

Fred canceled his Barnabas Ministry appointments, stopped traveling, and just took care of that church for the next sixteen months. The first three months were like a long, drawn out funeral. The people were devastated and, for a while at least, confused. Over time, though, God healed the church, and they began to smile again, and the growth continued.

Eventually, Crossgates called a new pastor, and Fred, their "Pastor for a Season," resumed his travel. Soon, though, a church in Clinton, Mississippi asked Fred to be their "Pastor for a Season" as well, and he again put his road schedule on hold and served as the Interim at Morrison Heights Baptist Church for about a year.

When that time was finished, Fred and Anne moved to Fairhope, Alabama, across the bay from Mobile, from where he planned to continue to travel. While in Fairhope, though, a church called Faith Family Fellowship asked Fred to be their interim pastor, and so he had a good year with them as he and the people were blessed together. After a year, they called Joel Faircloth, and Fred turned again to the Barnabas Ministry.

In February 2007, Crossgates Baptist Church in Brandon, Mississippi once again found themselves without a pastor. The man they had called after Fred served them was a good man, and had a good ministry there, but he never quite felt at home. When another church in Oklahoma approached the pastor about coming there, he asked Fred what he should do. Fred advised him to take the call.

So, Brother Fred once again found himself Crossgates' "Pastor for a Season." He made the drive from Fairhope to Brandon every weekend to preach. It was almost like being back in seminary again, driving many miles for the privilege of pastoring on a weekend. Fred had been back there for about seven months, when, in August of 2007, Miss Ruby Rowe spoke something to him that changed the course of his life.

Ruby Rowe was a 90-year-old ball of Holy Spirit fire. She was well known in Charismatic circles, since she had been personally prayed for by the world famous Pentecostal preacher, Smith Wigglesworth, when she was a young woman. Through that, she had an experience with the Holy Spirit that had marked her and set her apart for the rest of her life. Miss Ruby was small of stature but bold as a lion. She had no one to impress, and nothing to lose by just obeying whatever God told her to do. She reminded Fred of Bertha Smith. He could tell she was a woman of prayer, and he trusted her immediately.

One night, while visiting Crossgates, Fred asked Miss Ruby if she would pray for him. Within moments, she spoke to him with a look in her eyes that said that she had heard from God. "Brother Fred," she said, "up 'til now, you have only touched the fringe. God is giving you a fresh anointing, and He is going to take your feet places where they have never been before."

Fred didn't know exactly what that meant, but he was struck by the power of it. He knew that he had just received a prophetic word spoken over him, and he also knew that whatever it meant, it was certainly going to happen.

CHAPTER 20

THE ACCEPTABLE YEAR OF THE LORD

It was just an ordinary early fall afternoon when Fred, in the den of his home in Fairhope, heard a word from God that was clearer and more powerful than anything before in his fifty years of ministry.

Since returning to the Greater Mobile area, Fred would occasionally run into people that he had pastored for so long at Cottage Hill. To his great disappointment, many of those people were not active in a church because they had felt disenfranchised for so long. Cottage Hill itself had undergone tumultuous leadership changes, and was hardly recognizable to so many of the people who had flourished there before. Fred took this personally. It was hard not to consider your life's major work as something of a failure if it couldn't stand the test of time.

On Tuesday, September 18, 2007, Fred was sitting in his den listening to some Christian music when the Holy Spirit spoke a strong word to him. It could not have been more powerful if it had been audible, which it almost seemed to be: *I want you to start a church for scattered sheep.*

The power of it pierced him through, and Fred started weeping.

But Lord, Fred responded, feeling a little like Moses on the backside of the wilderness, *I'm 70 years old, and I've never started a church before in my life!*

And the Lord repeated to him the words he had heard from Miss Ruby Rowe. *I'm going to take your feet places they have never been before.*

Fred gathered a small group of trusted friends to share with them what he had heard from God. There was an immediate consensus that this seemed like a real direction from the Lord. They pledged themselves to help however they could.

For the next three months, Fred had informal meetings, publicized only by word of mouth, to cast his vision for this new church. Fred had always been captivated by what Dudley Hall had called Jesus' job description in Luke 4:18: "The Spirit of the Lord is upon Me, Because He has anointed Me To preach the gospel to the poor; He has sent Me to heal the brokenhearted, To proclaim liberty to the captives And recovery of sight to the blind, To set at liberty those who are oppressed..."

Fred was eager to see Jesus do in the lives of these people what He said He came to do. And so, Luke 4:18 Fellowship was born.

Ed Keyes had stayed at Cottage Hill for a few years after Brother Fred's departure in 1997. His consistent leadership was a key factor in the church's continued strength and focus in the three and a half years it took for them to call a new pastor. Brother Ed, essentially, was the pastor of Cottage Hill Baptist Church during that time, even though other men carried the duties of preaching. The people all looked to Ed, and were comforted by his loving heart and soothing voice in uncertain days.

During the tenure of the new pastor, Ed felt that his time

at Cottage Hill was complete, and he accepted the call to be the Minister of Music at First Baptist Church of Opelika, Alabama. Ed and Jan made the move to Opelika and enjoyed a satisfying, fulfilling ministry there, downsized from Cottage Hill, but still in a vibrant, growing church.

By the Fall of 2007, Ed Keyes was living in Opelika, Alabama, where he had just retired from his position serving the First Baptist Church. It was there, one day, that Ed received a phone call from Fred that brought with it a certain déjà vu. Fred was starting a church in Mobile and he wondered if Ed would come serve with him.

This time, though, the man Ed was talking with was not just an acquaintance, but also his close friend of thirty-five years. Ed, though happy living in Opelika, knew what it would mean to serve alongside Fred Wolfe again, and he gladly accepted the offer.

On January 6, 2008, Luke 4:18 held its first official worship service in the Performing Arts Building of Davidson High School in Mobile. It was a group of spiritually tired, ragged people. Many of them had been left disillusioned by their post-Cottage Hill churches, and they were, as Fred has suspected, like sheep without a shepherd. About 450 gathered that first day, some out of curiosity, others like nomads to an oasis. In the weeks that followed, the attendance leveled out around 350.

Fred had decided that there were two things that they would not do for the first year. One, they would not advertise. For anyone to find out that Luke 4:18 Fellowship existed, it would have to be because someone told them about it and invited them. Of course, word that Fred Wolfe had returned to pastor in Mobile spread quickly through the city. That was big news indeed among the Christian community. Fred had no problem with word getting around, but the fact that it was word of mouth meant that the connections would be based on relationships, and that, he knew, was the healthiest way possible to plant a church.

The other thing that Luke 4:18 would not do for the first year would be to have a membership. No one was allowed to join the church for a year. Fred knew how other pastors saw this move. A number of pastors in town were skeptical of his motives, and some others were outright hostile toward him. Dozens of churches in Mobile had former Cottage Hill members from the "Fred Wolfe era," and many of those pastors just knew that as soon as those people heard that Fred and Ed were back together and back in Mobile, they would throw off their new church families and run back to the fold.

As it turned out, those fears were largely unfounded. A few may have done that, but most of them, due in large part to the spiritual maturity that they had gained in those years under Fred and Ed, stayed loyally committed to their new church homes. In fact, one of the first things Fred did was to send a letter to twenty pastor in Mobile, letting them know that if anyone came to Luke 4:18 from one of their churches, that Fred would actively discourage them from staying, and would do everything he could to get them to stay in their churches.

One year after the start, a constitution and bylaws were drafted, and Luke 4:18 Fellowship was officially established as a church. Within another year or two, it became evident that this church had vision and staying power. Even though Fred had no idea what to expect at first, the future was taking shape. Property was bought in West Mobile, on Sollie Road, and one more time, Fred Wolfe entered into a building program, not just for a new Worship Center, but for a whole new complex. This would not be another 3,500 seat gargantua, though. Fred had no intention, nor did he have the energy, to pastor another megachurch. He had done that, and done it well. No, the effectiveness of this church was going to be measured in knowing and minstering to the people who found them, not just growing a church because somebody had designated large numbers as the one true sign of church success. This fellowship would exist for the sake of relationships, and seeing Jesus touch lives on a very up close level, or it would not exist at all.

Before long, the people of Mobile could once again turn on their televisions on Sunday morning and hear Fred Wolfe preaching the Gospel. Luke 4:18 Fellowship continued to grow, gaining vision and seeking to find ways to connect more young families than were there at the beginning. Youth and Children's ministries were established and staffed, and Fred's reach and influence widened again.

One of the big differences between this journey and Fred's beginnings at Cottage Hill was that this time, he was thirty-five years older. The makeup of Luke 4:18 was getting younger, but Fred was still getting older. In January 2012, this fact hit home in a debilitating way.

Fred discovered at the beginning of that year that he had a heart problem. Doctors told him that he had a bad mitrovalve, and it wasn't going to get any better. They would need to do something about it.

Fred underwent surgery in January, and the bad mitrovalve was replaced with a pig valve, which would help him get off one of his medications. The surgery was a success, but he was told that it would take a year to recover. Eventually, Fred returned home, and after three months out of the pulpit, he returned to preaching at Luke 4:18 Fellowship.

Fred realized too late, though, that he made one mistake. He failed to emphasize to his doctors his family history of blood clots. In September, just months after heart surgery, he walked up the stairs of his home one morning and was completely out of breath. He sat down quickly, but his breath would not come back to him.

Fred called his doctor, who said he would see him in two weeks. He hung up the phone and called a friend who was also a doctor, and told him what was happening. "Come to my office this afternoon," he said, "and we'll run some tests."

When the test results came in, his friend gave him the good news/bad news speech. "The good news," he said, "is that you don't have any blood clots in your lungs. The bad news is that you do have fluid on your lungs."

"Fluid?" said Fred. "Why do I have fluid on my lungs?"

"Because," said the doctor, "your heart is not getting rid of it like it's supposed to, so it's collecting on your lungs. We need to go in and see what's happening with your heart.

A subsequent test revealed that the pig valve from his previous surgery was bad. Fred already couldn't breathe well, and now his emotional wind was knocked out of him. He was just now starting to recover from heart surgery and now they want to do it again? He could not wrap his mind around the possibility of being broken open again, with all the accompanying pain and recovery.

Fred had heard, though, of a new surgical procedure that he suggested to the doctor. "Listen," he said, "I've heard of this new da Vinci robotic surgery. Is that a possibility for me?"

The doctor replied that it was, and that it would be a good alternative to open-chest surgery again. With da Vinci robotic surgery, the surgeon uses a series of small incisions to manipulate tiny robots and magnified 3D high definition imagery that gives the surgeon much more dexterity and precision than is available through traditional methods.

The surgery was performed on October 4, just nine months after the first operation. But what should have been a four hour surgery turned into eight hours on the heart and lung machine for Fred. When the surgeon went in, he found that a blood clot had exploded onto the walls of the chamber of Fred's heart where the valve had been replaced. This required a precise and careful removal of every particle of blood from the wall of his heart. If even one was left, it could break loose and go straight to Fred's brain, killing him instantly.

Finally, after eight grueling hours, the heart was clear, and a mechanical valve was put in the place of the one that had failed.

Once again, the slow process of recovery began. This time, though, Fred entered a time of major depression that confused him for a while because he had never felt depression before. He had certainly walked through that dark valley with Anne for years, but she had been miraculously delivered from a deep, fifteen-year bout of it just two months before they planted Luke 4:18. Now he found himself in the dark, and it disturbed him deeply.

As he began to recover, though, the depression abated, but it left him with a deeper understanding and a new compassion for people who deal with both depression and chronic pain.

Fred was released from the hospital, but instead of getting closer to being out of the woods, he took another turn deeper into them. He could tell that not only was he not getting better, but he was getting worse, and fast.

One night, after calling Herb Fisher about a Missions Committee meeting, Herb asked him how he was doing. "Not good," said Fred. "I'm going down rapidly, Herb, I can feel it."

Herb quickly called one of two good friends who are respected cardiologists. One of them told Herb to have Fred in his office first thing in the morning.

In the doctor's office, the EKG quickly revealed that Fred had atrial flutter, an abnormal heart rhythm that can quickly lead to heart failure. One of the symptoms of severe atrial flutter is a sense of impending doom, and Fred definitely had that. The doctor was going to let Fred go home while they decided what to do, but Fred said, "Doctor, I ain't going home. I'm not leaving here until we get this thing fixed."

"Alright," the doctor said, "I'll find some reason to keep you." He did, and Fred was admitted to the hospital for the third time that year.

More tests revealed that Fred had too much scar tissue around his heart from the first surgery for his heart to perform normally, so, once again, with a procedure that was as minimally invasive as possible, the surgeons performed an ablation to destroy the offending scar tissue, and installed a pacemaker.

It was November of 2012, and finally, after two major heart surgeries, a third procedure that bordered on another surgery, and three more months out of the pulpit, Fred felt that he was finally about to turn the page on a very bad year, and that he was truly on a path to recovery.

Earlier in the year, in May of 2012, after four years in a high school auditorium, Luke 4:18 Fellowship broke ground and began building their permanent worship and education space on Sollie Road, just south and west of Cottage Hill Road. On October 13, 2013, forty-one years after Fred Wolfe crested that hill on Highway 90 in Spanish Fort and saw Mobile Bay for the first time, he once again found himself stepping behind a new pulpit in a new place.

But the 76-year old great grandfather that will open his Bible in this new pulpit each Sunday is not so far removed from the 34-year old man who laid open his Bible on the old pulpit week in and week out for twenty-five years just three and a half miles away. This pastor—just like that one—will continue to teach people to be filled with the Holy Spirit. He will keep kneeling beside the pulpit to pray in every single service. And, no matter what comes his way, this man—this pastor, this friend, this father in the city, this preacher of the timeless gospel of God—in every circumstance of life, he will always and forever proclaim one unchangeable, undeniable truth—Jesus Christ is Lord!

a Sermon

Healing for the Broken-Hearted

Healing for the Broken-Hearted

by
Fred H. Wolfe

Open your Bibles this morning to the book of Isaiah, find the 61st chapter. Also, we'll be using a part of the name of our church in the message today. Jesus came to preach the gospel to the poor, to heal the broken hearted, and so we're going to be speaking today on the ministry of Jesus to the broken hearted.

It was in August about 15 years ago, I had preached on Sunday morning here in Mobile and had left to fly to Nashville, Tennessee, to catch a plane to Fort Lauderdale. Some of our single adults were there ministering at a church there, and I was going to preach in that church on that Sunday night.

I remember having flown to Nashville, and I got on American Airlines flying to Fort Lauderdale. I was sitting in the seat right on the bulkhead of the plane and I was on the aisle seat and right beside me was a handsome 13-year-old boy. He caught my eye. He had on a baseball cap, had an open-collared shirt, and had a gold chain around his neck. He was a handsome lad but you know, to be honest, I didn't think a lot about this young man. I just planned to rest as we flew from Nashville to Fort Lauderdale. But about 15 minutes into the flight everything changed.

That 13-year-old boy began to cry, tears running down his cheeks. Man, it disturbed me. It troubled me. 13-year-old boys aren't supposed to be crying. It's supposed to be a happy time in their life. He didn't want me to see him crying. He brushed the tears out of his eyes and reached down under the seat and got out a Game Boy and began to try to get his mind to playing a little game, but every now and then he would cry.

Well, I didn't want to invade his space. I knew that he was hurting. Finally, I just made the decision to speak and I said, "Well, tell me, where are you headed?" and he said, "Well, I am going home to Fort Lauderdale. I spent the last six weeks in Savannah, Georgia with my daddy and my cousins. Now I'm going back to Fort Lauderdale to live with my mother and go to school." It hit me. He had a broken heart. He was crying because he didn't want to leave his daddy. I couldn't get him off my mind, just kept thinking about him, a 13 year old with a broken heart.

Well, the next day after I preached that night, I was flying back to Nashville and then back to Mobile. We had been in the air just a little while on that Monday morning, and seated across the aisle from me was an attractive 18-year-old girl. I'm going to tell you about her, she was sitting right beside me on the aisle. She caught my attention because – I don't know if it was bushy or curly, but she had different-looking hair, you understand what I'm saying? It was definitely an eye-catcher.

I didn't think anything about it though, but we'd been flying only a few minutes, maybe 30 minutes and I noticed that this young woman just dropped her head and, as ladies with long hair did, her hair just kind of fell over and covered her up. And she just stayed like that for about five minutes and then after that, she just threw her head back and you're not going to believe it, she was crying. And I was getting paranoid, I'm telling you right now. True story, so help me. I mean, it just absolutely shook me.

I struck up a conversation with her and she told me a sad story. She said, "I just graduated from Brentwood High School in June." This was August. "Just graduated from Brentwood High School in June," and said, "I moved to Boca Raton to go to college and play volleyball." She said, "You know, I dated the same boy for four years at Brentwood High School and I remember when I left the 1st of June, I told him I'd see him Labor Day. But I went out on an outing and when I got back in, there was a note on my door to call home, to call Nashville." And then she told me the sad story.

She said, "On Saturday night, my boyfriend and some of his friends had been to a Jimmy Buffett concert and they had been drinking." And she said, "They tell me that he leaned over to put a CD or a cassette in the cassette player and he swerved and hit a car, and was killed driving drunk."

Of and on, all the way to Nashville, she cried. It shook me. When she got off the plane, there were her friends waiting to hug her and to try to comfort her. But I tell you, about that time, God had my undivided attention. I said, "Lord, I want you to tell me, why did you let me sit beside that 13-year-old boy. I could've sat anywhere on this airplane." I said, "I want to know why you let me sit beside that 18-year-old girl whose heart was broken because her boyfriend had been killed. And I'm telling you, as clear as the still small voice of the Holy Spirit could speak to me, God said, "I wanted to remind you, that you're living in a world full of broken hearted people. And they're not only in the world, they're in the church." And you know, I want to tell you something. Everybody in this world, we either have a broken heart, we have experienced in the past a broken heart, or we will in the future know what it is to have a broken heart.

Well, needless to say, God had my attention. This was Monday. I began to cry out to God. "Let me ask you something Lord, what do I say to a 13-year-old boy who didn't want to leave his daddy? What do I say to an 18-year-old girl, whose boyfriend was killed driving drunk. You have a word for them. I know you do. You love them with a wonderful love."

And He turned me to Isaiah 61. I want you to look at it. I've read it many times. Many times. But I'm telling you, it leapt off the page at me and I saw it in a new and wonderful light. If I asked you this morning, "Why did Jesus come?" You would say exactly what I did. He came to die on the cross for our sins and shed His precious blood that through His sacrificial, substitutionary death, we could be forgiven and we could be saved. That's exactly right. But I'm telling you, that's not the only reason He came. Every blessing flows from the cross. But I want you to listen to Isaiah 61. This is the prophecy concerning Jesus. It is fulfilled in Luke 4:18. It says at Isaiah 61, "The Spirit of the Lord God is upon me." Isaiah says the Messiah is coming and the spirit of God is upon Him. Look at the next verse: "He has sent me". Now wait a minute—"He has sent me to heal the broken hearted. To proclaim liberty to the captives. The opening of the prison to those who are bound. To proclaim the acceptable year of our Lord. The day of vengeance of our God." And it's almost like He goes back to the broken hearted. Would you look at the next part of that verse? He says He's going to comfort all who mourned. He's going to console those who mourned in Zion. That's a picture of the church. He's going to console those who mourned in Zion. I love this. His going to give them beauty for ashes. The oil of joy for mourning. The garment of praise for the spirit of heaviness, that they may be called trees of righteousness. The planting of the Lord that He may be glorified. So all week I said, "Alright Lord, what's your word to the broken hearted? What is the ministry of Jesus to the broken hearted?" And I'm telling you three things from the word of God came into focus. I want to share of these three things with you right now. And the last thing I share with you is going to be a turning point in your life, because if you do exactly what God says, you can know the healing of a broken heart.

There were three things the Lord revealed to me. He showed me from the scripture:

1. That number one, that Jesus Christ understands and feels your broken heart. You've got to know that. You're not alone. There is someone who understands. There's someone who feels. There's someone who knows. Jesus understands and feels your broken heart.

2. The second thing is this, and it's a powerful thing. It gives me great hope this morning. That second thing is this, it's that Jesus is present today. He is present today, right here and right now, to heal the broken hearted. He has not changed Hallelujah! He understands and feels your broken heart. He is present today to heal your broken heart.

3. And then the third and last thing is; Jesus invites. He invites the broken hearted to come to him.

I never will forget the Sunday after God gave me this... I preached it hundreds of times all over this country. Let me tell you what I found.

There are many reasons people have a broken heart. Oh yeah, there are a lot of reasons. You know a lot of people have a broken heart, because of the death of a loved one. You know, I trust that we know the one that we loved has died, is saved and is going to be with the Lord. We know that. I trust that we know that they were ready to meet God. Maybe there were months where we could prepare ourselves, or maybe they left quickly, but I'm going to tell you something that I've found. Whether you are prepared for it or not, when someone you love dies, you are going to be separated from them for a while. I'm going to tell you what you have, man—you'll have a broken heart. It's a pain you can only know when you've walked through that valley when someone that you love is no longer with you and you won't have the joy of talking to them anymore on this earth.

You know some people have a broken heart because someone they love is seriously ill. You know what I find that people do? When someone that we love is sick and the doctors are doing all they can, and we're praying and crying out for God to heal them, yet the battle for their health going on, you know what you find yourself doing? You find yourself grieving. You find yourself living with a heaviness that just comes from just having a broken heart, because you can't fix it, and you're not able to just do something to get them out of that physical dilemma that they're facing.

A lot of people have a broken heart because of a wayward child. You know I've found out across this country that nobody can break your heart like your children. You see, they never get so old that they can't break your heart. And I've talked to parent after parent, in place after place, and they say "Brother Fred—" this one particular lady, I'll never forget this, she didn't even stop, she just patted me on the back as she walked out the church in Maryland, and she just went out the door and she said "Brother Fred, I raised my son to know and to love God, but he's away from God and he's living with a woman and he's not married to her. She said, he's breaking my heart." I'll tell you what, a lot of people have a broken heart because of a wayward child. A lot of people have a broken heart because of rejection. I tell you one thing and I'm gonna talk about this at length, but a lot of people have experienced rejection in their life and they're suffering. They've not yet been healed from that rejection. A lot of people have a broken heart because of a painful – and they're all painful – heart-breaking divorce. There are some people who are divorced who wanted to be, and there are some who are divorced who never wanted to be, but yet they seem to live with the hurt and the pain of a heart broken by divorce.

A lot of people are heartbroken because of their own personal failure. Listen, everybody in this room, we've written pages we wished we'd never written, we've written chapters we wished we'd never wrote, we've gone down roads we wish we'd never gone down, and we look back on them and say "My God! Why did I do that?" and we live with a broken heart A lot of people have a broken heart because of all that sin has done in their lives.

I could go on and on and on and on, but let's talk about the answer, okay? Because I'm telling you that Jesus Christ came to save you and to forgive you and to change you and to give you life abundant right now, but I'm telling you part of that is for him to heal your broken heart. Now see, let me tell you something that you can see clearly if you'll just listen to me. Because you really don't believe that God understands. You really don't believe that he knows and understands, but I'm going to give you one story that shows that he understands and cares, and that's the story of the death of Lazarus. You can read it later in the eleventh chapter of John, but I want you to listen carefully to the story. Jesus had eaten with Martha, Mary, and Lazarus in their house, and they were close friends. Jesus was in Jerusalem. Lazarus, Mary, and Martha lived in Bethany. The word got to Jesus in Jerusalem 'Lord the one you love is sick. Jesus, Lazarus is sick!' Well, you would think that Jesus would immediately make the two-mile trip to Bethany to Jerusalem to be with Lazarus, but he waited four days...four days! Evidently right after Jesus had got the news that Lazarus had died, four days later Jesus comes to Bethany, and he's got his disciples with him, and Martha, Lazarus's sister, hears that Jesus is almost there. And so she leaves the house where they were grieving – They'd already buried Lazarus. She left the house where she was grieving and ran out to meet Jesus and I want you to listen to her heart. I'm telling you, you can feel it, she said "Lord, if you'd been here, my brother wouldn't have died." It's almost like she said "Jesus where were you? I've seen you work miracles. Lord, if you'd of just been here, Lazarus would not have died." And Jesus said "Dear, but you don't understand." He said, "Your brother is going to rise again." She said, "I know we will in the resurrection." And you know what Jesus said? "You're talking to the Resurrection." Hallelujah! He said, "I am the resurrection!"

And so, Martha went back to the house where Mary was and said, "Mary, the master is here." So Mary got up and left. The people in the room, in the house where they were, that were crying with her, thought she was going out to the tomb to mourn. Anyway, Mary went out and she went to Jesus and guess what Mary said to Jesus? She didn't know what Martha said but you know what she said to Jesus? Mary looked and him and she said "Lord, if you had been here, my brother wouldn't have died." Man she had a broken heart but let me tell you what happened then. Jesus knew – now listen to me — He knew he was going to raise Lazarus from the dead. He had already told his disciples on the travel from Jerusalem to Bethany. He said, "Lazarus is asleep." They said, "That means he's getting better." He said, "No, Lazarus is dead." And he knew that, but I'm telling you, Jesus was knowing in just a short time, He was going to say "Lazarus come forth." and he was going to come back from the grave but you know He saw Martha's broken heart – Let me tell you what that says about Jesus. Now you get this, knowing that He was going to raise him from the dead. It says Jesus groaned. and was troubled in his spirit.

Now I'm going to ask you a question. Why did Jesus groan? The Bible says He groaned and He was troubled in his spirit, and then it says on down, about three or four verses later, in John 11. You know this verse. You know it and you can say what it is and the reason you know it is not because you're just a great bible scholar, because it's the shortest verse in the bible and everybody knows what the shortest verse in the Bible: "Jesus wept."

You know that verse never meant anything to me until I understood why he was weeping You know why He was weeping? Because Mary's heart was broken and Martha's heart was broken. Oh, He knew He was going to raise Lazarus from the dead but He was moved by the broken heart of Martha and Mary, and He saw their broken heart, and He felt their broken heart, and He entered into their broken heart, and the Son of God not only groaned, the Son of God wept. He wept! Let me tell you something, you think nobody understands? You think that nobody knows what you went through when you were growing up. You think nobody really knows and understands, maybe the rejection or the abuse that you've experienced. You say, "Well, nobody really knows how my wrong choices affected me." Let me tell you something, don't you believe that, the One who loves you the most, Jesus, knows you the best. And I'm telling you He understands, He feels, He weeps when you weep, He has groaned when He saw you in that place of your heart. The Bible says He can be touched by the feelings of our infirmities.

So you be encouraged this morning; you're not alone. Jesus Christ understands and feels your broken heart.

But you know there is something that excites me, as I thought about that 13 year old boy and that 18 year old girl and the hundreds and hundreds of people that I've talked to and you've talked to that experienced a broken heart. The second truth is this: Jesus is present today to heal the broken-hearted, that's the exciting news. Jesus Christ is present today to heal the broken-hearted; the name of this Fellowship is Luke 4:18, and you know what Luke 4:18 is? It's the fulfillment of Isaiah 61, and in Luke 4:18, Jesus went back to His hometown. He went back to the synagogue where He grew up, and they handed Jesus the book of Isaiah. Jesus opened it to Isaiah 61 and He began to read: "The Spirit of the Lord is upon me because He's anointed me to preach the gospel to the poor." This was Jesus in His hometown synagogue. He said, "Sent me to heal the broken-hearted" and He read Isaiah 61. Then He sat down and then He looked at the people in the synagogue and said, "Today, today, this scripture is fulfilled in your hearing. This is the acceptable year of the Lord. It is the year of Jubilee, when God sets people free." And I want you to know 2,000 years ago, Jesus started saving the lost, healing the broken-hearted, delivering the captives, giving sight to the blind, set at liberty those who are bound. 2,000 years ago, Jesus started healing broken hearts, and I've got good news for you—right where you are, Jesus Christ is still doing today what He did 2,000 years ago. He has not stopped. Glory to God. He is the same yesterday, today, and forever! The most powerful being in this world is the Son of the Living God. He has all the power in heaven and on earth, and you don't think He can change your life. You just don't know. Nobody can change your life like the Son of God can change your life.

So He's present today—Hallelujah!—to heal the broken-hearted. He can heal a heart broken by grief. He can heal a heart broken by guilt. He can heal a heart broken by rejection. He can heal a heart broken by abuse. You say, "Pastor, why did you choose those particular ones?" Because it covers it. I want you to listen to me. It covers it.

What's the difference between grief and guilt? Let's talk about that. I said He can heal the hearts broken by grief. He can heal a heart broken by guilt. The difference between grief and guilt is this: Grief is a clean wound. It is not a sin to grieve. No. Grief is a part, just as laughter is a part of life; grief is a part of life. You grieve over the death of a loved one. You grieve over someone that you love that is sick. You grieve over a wayward child. You grieve over a broken marriage. You grieve over a lot of things that just bring you grief, and you grieve over them.

But let me say something about grief. It's not a sin to grieve. You see, Jesus can heal the heart broken by grief with the Word of God, and by the Spirit of God, and by the presence of Jesus. As you cry out to him, I am telling you He can heal a heart broken by grief. The Word of God, and the Spirit of God, and the presence of Jesus, as you lift your grief to him, I am telling you with time in His presence, Jesus heals hearts broken by grief.

While grief is a clean wound, guilt is a dirty wound and it cannot be healed until it is cleansed. You see the reason we have guilt is because we're guilty. "All have sinned and come short of the glory of God." Hey. The only perfect one is the Lord Jesus. There is none righteous. No, not one. Every one of us, like sheep, have gone astray. All of us have gone astray but you need to understand that if we come to Jesus and we are guilty, "Lord, I have sinned against you. I made the wrong choices. I have sinned against Holy God and I am responsible for my sin. I cannot blame anybody else. I am responsible for my sin," but if you come to God with an acknowledgement of your sinfulness and brokenness over your sinfulness and a desire to be set free from your sinfulness, see you come with guilt. And you come to Jesus and you ask for cleansing. You ask for forgiveness.

Here's the awesome thing. You come to Jesus Christ with your guilt and you come in repentance and ask for forgiveness. Let me give you the good verse. "Though your sins be as scarlet, they shall be whiter than snow." If we confess our sins, God is faithful and just, to forgive us our sins.

You don't have to live with guilt. You don't have to live with shame. Let me tell you why. The blood of Jesus Christ has paid the price for your sin, and if you go to Jesus and confess your sin and ask His forgiveness, I've got good news for you. God not only will forgive you but He removes the guilt and He removes the shame. Hallelujah! And you're not guilty anymore.

The blood of Jesus Christ has not lost its power. The Devil lost when Jesus died on the cross. "The wages of sin is death, but the gift of God is eternal life through Jesus Christ our Lord."

Thank God for forgiveness! Where would we be without the forgiveness of a Holy God? We'd be forever lost, and forever separated. Jesus can heal a heart broken by guilt. He cleanses you. You say, "But I'm too bad." No you aren't; don't you believe that lie.

But the third thing is Jesus can heal a heart broken by rejection. You know this is probably, other than guilt, the major thing.

Can I tell you something about us now? You just got to understand this. God made us to love, and He made us to be loved. When God created us, He said, "It is not good for man to be alone," which means we are created to be a part of community, of people's lives.

And let me tell you something. We are created to love, but also there is the capacity to be loved. When someone who should love us, when someone who is important, who should love us, and reach out to us, and embrace us, and accept us, when that person, who is important to us, does not love us and embrace us, and accept us, it's called rejection. And I'm going to tell you something, it hurts bad, hurts bad.

Man, when somebody who really is important to you rejects you, sometimes it's not deliberate, sometimes they're just living out the rejection they experienced themselves. But it doesn't matter. You know what happens? When you're rejected and you don't deal with it, and you don't face it, and you push it down, you get angry. And you don't even know why you're angry, but the reason is this, rejection is the root! You never dealt with it, but anger is the fruit.

You say, "Well I'm going to get the fruit off the tree. I'm not going to be angry." You'll never get rid of it 'til you deal with the root, which is called "rejection."

A lot of people have a broken heart because of abuse. You know, verbal abuse, physical abuse. A few years ago, I had two people come to see me the same week. Both of them were ladies, probably in their forties. One of them came to me and she said, "Brother Fred, you know, I tried to kill myself." She said, "I just missed the main artery." And she said, "You know why?" I said, "Tell me." She said, "When I was seven and eight years of age, one of my relatives physically abused me. I never told a soul. I felt that it must be my fault." And here she was, forty years of age, she just up and said, "Until a few weeks ago, I never told a soul. I lived with the guilt, and the shame that it must have been my fault. And finally I could not live with it anymore, and I thought I'd just die."

Then the other lady came in, same story, except it was a grandfather or something. And she talked about how she had lived with it, it was hidden, she never said a word to anybody, and with the shame, she just said, "Finally I just could not take it."

You see, what we do, a lot of times it's so painful, we won't even let it come up. And she said, "I just can't take it anymore.'"

Praise God! They found out that Jesus Christ can heal a heart broken by abuse. Hallelujah!

And He can, you listen to me. He loves you, and He was there. Don't you think you were alone when you went through that! Don't you think that for a moment!

But, now here's the last thing, and the most important thing. Jesus invites the broken hearted to come to Him. Now, He invites you to come.

Now I'm going to give you a verse. Regardless of why your heart was broken, I want to give you a verse about how Jesus invites the brokenhearted to come to Him. It's in Matthew 11:28 and following, Jesus said, come unto me, "Come unto me, all you that labor and have a heavy-laden, and I will give you rest." Now listen, this is an invitation of the Son of God. "Come unto me, all you that labor, you burdened down, you heavy laden and I will give you rest. Take my yoke upon you, and learn of me; for I am gentle and lowly in heart, and you will find rest for your souls." Rest for your soul, your heart, your mind, your emotions. So Jesus invites us. We are not invited to a cold and lifeless religion. We are not invited to a condemning, pharisaical religion, we are invited to the living Son of God. And the Lord Jesus with open arm says, "Come unto Me." Jesus, I hear you. "Come unto Me, all you that are burdened down and broken down,

I will give you rest. You are going to find rest for your soul."

When we come to Jesus, we have to come in faith. You've got to believe He can heal you. You've got to believe that damaged soul, that broken heart can be healed. But the second thing you've got to do, you've got to come in obedience.

Now this is where you get set free, right here. This is where you make a choice and cross over into healing, or you don't make a choice and continue in your hurt. Jesus invites us to come to Him and we not only have to come in faith. We have to come in obedience, and the bottom-line is this: You know what we have to do, we have to forgive the person, or the persons, or the company, or the church, or the individual. We have to forgive the people who broke our hearts, and I'm going to tell you right now. When somebody or something or someone broke your heart. I'm going to tell you, it is not easy to forgive.

Now, can I ask you a question?

I mean, I know about forgiveness — God's forgiven me and He talks to me about forgiving others. He said, "You've got to do it, it ain't an option." But let me ask you a question: Why do we struggle with forgiveness? Why is it such a difficult thing. Why is it?

You say, "Brother Fred, I don't have any trouble at all with forgiving." You've got trouble with lying, that's what you've got!

Let me tell you why is it hard to forgive. And I will tell you how to forgive when I'm through.

You know why it is hard to forgive? Because the pain is real. Pain is real. You think physical pain is bad? What about emotional pain? I am telling you the reason is it so hard to forgive is because the pain is real. It's real. And you have to deal with it. It isn't easy to deal with it. You don't even want to face it, because it's too painful, but I am telling you, the reason you're struggling is because the pain is real, and that's why it is. Understand that. But there's another reason we struggle with forgiveness. It's not an emotion—it's a choice. Can I ask you a question? Who ever *felt* like forgiving? Somebody has broken your heart, and you say, "Well, we shouldn't be so sensitive." God made you sensitive, I hope and pray you're not hard. If you got the love of God in you and you love people, you are sensitive. But you see, forgiveness is not an emotion. It can become emotional when it's a reality in your life. Forgiveness is not an emotion, it's a choice. You have to go against your emotions, you have to go against your feelings, and this is what you do: "Lord, I don't feel like it, every emotion in me doesn't want to do it, but because you told me to, I choose, I deliberately choose to forgive him, I deliberately choose to forgive her, I deliberately choose to do that, and I know I don't feel like it and You know I don't feel like it, but I make a choice to forgive." Now let me tell you what happens to you when you go against your emotions and you make a choice, when you chose to forgive. Jesus begins to heal your emotions, He begins to restore your soul. You make that choice, He begins to heal your emotions and soon your emotions catch up with your choice and it's a reality. Here's the main reason, this is the main one that you struggle with forgiving. You think that forgiveness means approval. Oh! I've watched it in people, I would say to them, "Listen, I don't minimize your hurt!" I said, "Dear God, I don't know how you dealt with this," and I meant that, because they'd walked through some things I'd never walk through and I can feel their hurt. But I said, "I'm telling you something, by the grace and power of Jesus you can do what He said. You've got to forgive them."

They said, "Oh! What your saying is it didn't matter that he beat me, or abused me, or left me, or whatever. It doesn't matter, is it what you're saying is, Brother Fred? That it doesn't matter, you're telling me it's okay. You're telling me that it wasn't bad, it wasn't wrong?" Hey, wait a minute. Let me tell you something about that. Forgiveness does not mean approval. You know that. I want you to understand it is wrong. It's not right. It does matter. It's not okay. Did you get that? Forgiveness does not mean approval. You know why I know that? Because Jesus Christ forgave you and me of our sins and He never approved of one of them.

I'm telling you it was wrong. It's not right. It's not okay. It does matter. It was wicked. But you know our sins that were placed on Jesus were wicked. And God looked at us and said "I don't approve. But forgiveness doesn't mean approval. I forgive you even though I don't approve." Now until you understand that forgiveness doesn't mean approval, you're going to have trouble breaking out of that web that's holding you in bitterness and unforgiveness. I never will forget this and I only tell this story to let you know that some people struggle with some real things. Just like you do. I was preaching in Water Valley, Mississippi, it's south of Memphis. It was a Monday night. I preached on the healing of the broken-hearted, and I preached on forgiveness. And I had no clue who was there - you never know who's sitting in an audience. You just don't know. I got a letter from the Pastor two weeks ago that said, "Brother Fred, thank you so much for coming, and thank you for letting God lead you to preach on this thing of the healing of a broken heart and on forgiveness. Because we had a couple in our church — godly people who love God and who had been pillars in our church who'd just been so faithful," and he said, "you know they were just being gripped by bitterness, and gripped by unforgiveness. But let me tell you what happened. Two years ago. their son-in-law murdered their daughter. And he's in a Mississippi penitentiary for the rest of his life. But you know, Brother Fred when they understood that forgiveness did not mean approval, that what he did was wrong and will always be wrong, and he was justly paying for what he did—once they understood that forgiveness did not mean approval, they said they embraced the forgiveness of God, and they forgave him and Jesus set them free."

You see I don't know if I could do that, only by the grace of God could you do that. I promise you, with God's grace you can. Well let me tell you how you forgive, and we'll pray.

There are three pictures I want to leave with you. And this works, when you forgive a person, or a church, or an individual, or a group. When you forgive someone, you cancel the debt. They don't have to pay anymore. When you forgive a person, you cut the cord of unforgiveness. You release them and you let them go. When you forgive a person, you let them out of the cage of bitterness and unforgiveness and you release them. Now here are the pictures. These are Biblical pictures.

When you forgive a person, you cancel the debt. Now let me tell you how that works. We keep a record of our hurts. Did you know that? We forget a lot of things. We don't forget the hurts. "Hurt #1-- I'm writing that down!" "Hurt #2-- I'll remember that until I die." "Hurt #3-- I'll remind you of it until you die."

Have you ever noticed that? "Oh I've forgiven you, but I just don't want you to forget about it." Let me tell you what. There may be a lot of things written, but when you forgive a person, you cancel the debt. You wipe the slate clean. They don't have to pay anymore. They're forgiven. Did you know what it says in Colossians 2:13 and 14? The Bible says there were handwritings of ordinances—every sin I'd committed—against Fred Wolfe's name. Every sin you'd committed against your name. The Bible says, Jesus came and took away the handwriting of ordinances that was against us!

And He took our certificate of debt, that's what it was. He took our certificate of debt, and He cancelled it and He forgave us and He said, "You don't have to pay anymore," and thank God we don't! You know, you had a debt against you and Jesus came into your life and He wiped the slate clean. He cancelled the debt, glory to God, and you don't have to pay anymore. You've got to cancel the debt, they don't have to pay anymore. You've got to cut the cord. Unforgiveness is like a rope around your neck and it's around the neck of the person you haven't forgiven, and I'm telling you, you're tied to them with the cord of unforgiveness. You go 500 miles from home and you'll drag them all the way. They'll sleep in the bed right beside you because you're tied to them. When you forgive a person, you cut the cord, you cut the cord, you just release them. "Lord," you say, "I don't approve and it sure is painful and you've got to help me. I'm making a choice, I'm going against my feelings, but I choose to forgive them Lord, and I cut the cord. I'm just not going to drag him around anymore. I let him go."

Here's the last picture. Unforgiveness is like a cage. We get hurt, we get wounded, we get bitter, we get unforgiving, we get angry and we put that person in the cage of unforgiveness. Every now and then, we let him out, beat up on him, and put him back in the cage. Let me tell you a beautiful picture, when you forgive a person, you open the cage, you let him out, you pick up the cage and you throw it away. Cancel the debt, cut the cord, and let them out of the cage.

Now here's my question that I'm asking you:

You may be a Christian; you may not even be a Christian. Well, you've got to have God's forgiveness but you can take a step toward that, by forgiving others. You may have been a Christian for 1 year, for 5 years or for 50 years, but here's my question: Is there any person living or dead that you need to forgive? Now I don't know, but I want you to be honest in your heart, just be honest as you can now, with the Holy Spirit of God.

Is there any person living or dead that you need to forgive? Any company that fired you unjustly? A church that hurt you? A person? I'm asking you now, listen to me. Is there anyone, or anything or anybody that there's some bitterness, and some unforgiveness and some anger. I believe if there is anybody that you need to forgive, the Holy Spirit will bring them to your attention. I believe God will remind you. It may be painful to deal with it, but I believe God will bring them into focus and so now, you've got to deal with it.

You say, "But Brother Fred, the pain is real!" I know. But you're not ever going to get healed of that pain until you forgive them. You say, "But you don't understand! I don't feel like it. I mean it's the last thing I want to do." I know you don't feel like it, but you are going to have to go against your feelings and make a choice. But you say, "It was wrong and I don't approve." I am not asking you to approve, I'm asking you to obey Jesus and to forgive.

I want to tell you, Jesus wants to heal your broken heart, but you've got to forgive the person who broke your heart. And I want to ask you right now, will you forgive him? You say, "Brother Fred, I'm gonna make that choice. This is a word from God for me and I'm going to settle this issue and I'm going to walk with no unforgiveness in my heart as far as I know toward any man, any woman, anybody or anything. Today I will walk not only knowing God's forgiveness, but having forgiven any person God showed me."

Pray this in your heart to the Lord: "Father, please forgive me for my unforgiveness. Lord, You told me that I can't hold on to and harbor bitterness and unforgiveness because, since You've forgiven me, that I'm to be like my Savior and by His power I'm to forgive others. So please forgive me for my unforgiveness. Father in the name of Jesus, I forgive."

There are some of you that need to forgive yourself. You've already asked God to forgive you, but for some reason, you can't forgive yourself. I'm going to tell you something, you're not bigger than God. If God can forgive you, you can forgive yourself. The devil is condemning you. So maybe you need to let yourself out of the cage this morning.

"Father in the name of Jesus, I forgive. I cancel the debt. I cancel it, I wipe the slate clean. They don't have to pay anymore, they're forgiven. Father, in the name of Jesus, I forgive. I cut the cord. I release them. I let them go. They're no longer tied to me anymore with the cord of unforgiveness.

"By the power of Jesus, I let everyone who has hurt me out of the cage." Now just open the cage. Open it. Let them out. "And Father, I pick up the cage and I throw it away." Now just pick it up and throw it away. Then you say this to the Lord, "I forgive them forever. In Jesus' name, they are forgiven."

Listen, when you forgive a person, it does not mean you immediately forget. No. It takes time for God to heal you. But you settled it, I forgive them forever in Jesus name. The next time the hornet of memory flies, you can say hornet of memory, you can fly but can't sting me because I've pulled out the stinger of unforgiveness. Hornet of memory, you may fly but you can't sting me because the stinger of unforgiveness is gone in Jesus name. I forgive you forever. I forgive them forever in Jesus name.

Now, I want to pray for you:

Right now, I ask You, Son of God, to heal those who just prayed and forgave. I ask You to heal them, to restore them, and let the healing of their broken heart begin. Let there be new peace, a new joy and a new assurance. Do it, Jesus, and I want to thank You for the freedom that comes, Lord Jesus, when You forgive us. In Jesus name, Amen!

ENDNOTES

1. Bertha Smith, How the Spirit Filled My Life (Broadman Press, Nashville, TN, 1973)

2. "The New Rebel Cry: Jesus Is Coming!" *Time,* 21 June 1971: 61. Print.

You have a story.
We want to publish it.

Everyone has as a story to tell. It might be about something you know how to do, or what has happened in your life, or it may be a thrilling, or romantic, or intriguing, or heart-warming, or suspenseful story, starring a cast of characters that have been swimming around in your imagination.

And at Wyatt House Publishing, we can get your story onto the pages of a book just like the one you are holding in your hand. With professional interior design and a custom, professionally designed cover built just for you from the start, you can finally see your dream of being an author become reality. Then, you will see your book listed with retailers all over the world as people are able to buy your book from wherever they are and have it delivered to their home or their e-reader.

So what are you waiting for? This is your time.

visit us at

www.wyattpublishing.com

for details on how to get started becoming a
published author right away.

CPSIA information can be obtained at www.ICGtesting.com
Printed in the USA
LVOW12*0451181013

357296LV00002B/5/P